Thomas Hodgkin

Thomas Hodgkin
Wandering scholar

Michael Wolfers

To Tony Pearson
with gratitude for
a long friendship
and the affection of
the author

[signature]

31/3/07

MERLIN PRESS

First published 2007 by The Merlin Press Ltd.
96 Monnow Street
Monmouth
NP25 3EQ
Wales

www.merlinpress.co.uk

ISBN 9780850365818 paperback
ISBN 9780850365801 hardback

British Library Cataloguing in Publication Data
is available from the British Library

Printed in Great Britain by Cromwell Press, Trowbridge, Wiltshire

Contents

Foreword

My first meeting with Thomas Hodgkin came at his home in Oxford on 14 May 1966. My last meeting came on 7 January 1982 in Sudan where Thomas had gone to escape the English winter. Thomas's health was frail and I feared he might die before I had the chance to see him again. On 25 March 1982, I heard of his death in Greece where he had paused for a further vacation on the return journey to Britain.

During the years of research and writing of this biography, I have had help from members of the Hodgkin, Gaster, Davin and Crowfoot families and of friends – too numerous to name individually, with the following notable exceptions. The Trustees of the Barry Amiel and Norman Melburn Trust generously funded the early research years on an application with crucial letters of support from Thomas's friend Basil Davidson as the doyen of Africanist scholars in Britain and from Thomas's daughter Elizabeth (Liz in this book) for the family. I am further indebted to the Trustees for a contribution to publication of this work. Liz as literary executor ensured unfettered access to Thomas's published and unpublished papers. The latter – letters, diaries, lecture notes, jottings – were largely unsorted, and at the time of writing remained in family hands – to be directed to the Oxford University libraries system.

The principal source, therefore, is the correspondence and where interviews were made for corroboration the contemporaneous written evidence was preferred over later recollection. I have followed a rigorous chronology in this narrative where all events can be firmly dated. Selections of Thomas's correspondence from the Palestine and early Africa years are published in *Thomas Hodgkin: Letters from Palestine 1932-36*, London, Quartet, 1986, edited by his brother E.C. Hodgkin, and *Thomas Hodgkin: Letters from Africa 1947-56*, London, Haan Associates, 2000, edited by Elizabeth Hodgkin and Michael Wolfers.

Thomas was married to Dorothy Crowfoot Hodgkin (Dossie in this book), a towering scientific genius and one of the most distinguished British women of the twentieth century. Long after Thomas and I had an understanding that I would one day write his life, I was walking with him in the Warwickshire village of Ilmington to which he had retired from Oxford. I broached the idea of a joint biography and I mentioned Robert Browning and Elizabeth Barrett. Thomas responded with enthusiasm. I soon allowed this conversation to trail away. I had been thinking of Thomas and Dossie. I realised that Thomas was talking of the first great love he had for Maire Lynd (BJ in this book) several years before his courtship and marriage. After Thomas's death, BJ gave me a long memoir on her love for Thomas.

I am deeply indebted to Sarah Benton for reading draft chapters and giving valuable advice. My thanks go to the many archivists and librarians who assisted my exploration of the background, especially in: Balliol College Archives and Library; Bodleian Library; British Library; Bruce Castle Museum; Dartmouth College Archives, New Hampshire; Friends House Library; Library of Congress; London Library; London School of Economics Library; Northwestern University Archives; Oxford Union Society Library; Oxford University Archives; Post Office Archives; Public Record Office; Rewley House Library; Rhodes House Library; School of Oriental and African Studies Library; Tate Gallery Archives; University College London Library; and Wellcome Institute for the History of Medicine.

Michael Wolfers

Prologue

Dorothy Forster Smith, a sheltered 22-year-old, felt shy and apprehensive as she drew up to Barmoor Castle in Northumberland late in the afternoon of Tuesday, 4 August 1908. She was responding to an invitation from Violet Hodgkin, an older family friend more of her parents' generation than her own. Dorothy could still recall from 12 years earlier an alarming experience of going from her family's holiday home in Bamburgh village to lunch alone with Violet in the splendid Keep of Bamburgh Castle that the Hodgkins then inhabited. They had sat at each end of what seemed yards of table and were waited on by a butler or footman.

Dorothy's immediate family was once more on holiday at Bamburgh, some sixteen miles from Barmoor. She went on the train from Belford to Beal and was met by a groom driving a smart dogcart. They took the Lowick road into Barmoor Castle's long drive, to find the Hodgkin family at tea on the lawn although the day was cold for August. She knew little of this battlemented country-house's history: that a defensive border tower had been built near Lowick and the Kyloe Crags some eight centuries earlier after the Norman Conquest. In the late eighteenth century, that tower had become the property of a branch of the Sitwell family, whose architect, John Patterson, transformed it into a commodious country mansion. Dorothy saw only the splendid results: the pillared doorway leading to a large circular hall, lit by a glass roof two storeys above, and a main tower of four storeys.

Barmoor Castle since January 1899 had been the rented home of the Quaker Thomas Hodgkin, DCL, semi-retired banker turned historian and antiquarian, and of his wife, Lucy Anna Fox. The Sitwell family remained nearby in the dower house on the estate, but the younger Sitwells tended to be at their London house. The Hodgkins in the castle had space to house or entertain their six surviving children (one son, John Alfred Hodgkin, had died in infancy in 1872). They had previously lodged in the even more impressive Bamburgh Castle on its basalt outcrop overlooking the North Sea with inspiring views of Holy Island and the Cheviot Hills.

Their new home was inland and high above sea level: Holy Island and the Cheviot Hills could still be seen within a short walk through the fine trees and spreading lawns around the house. Visitors were almost invariably taken to a spot at the edge of the grounds where from what was known as the sunset seat they could see the Cheviots slumbering in the sunshine. Hodgkin had celebrated his move to Barmoor Castle by inviting a bookbinder from London to help select from his library a thousand volumes for rebinding – a modest proportion of his collection. The exercise was a mark of Hodgkin's business success and scholarly passion.

In the mid-seventeenth century, the Hodgkin ancestors belonged to the Cotswolds yeomanry. They were among the early adherents to the doctrine preached by George Fox and the Society of Friends of Truth, or Quakers (originally a pejorative later accepted as a proud ascription). A John Hodgkin, born in Shipston-on-Stour in 1766 as the son of a shopkeeper and wool-stapler, moved south to Pentonville in London to earn a living as a writing master and private tutor and by 1815 was settled in Tottenham. He had a large house and garden in Bruce Grove. The Grove was virtually a Quaker enclave whose mansions included the London winter home of Luke Howard, a manufacturing chemist best remembered for devising the classification and naming of cloud formations such as nimbus and cumulus. The writing master's eldest surviving son was the medical doctor Thomas Hodgkin who died in 1866 and is remembered for describing the disease of the lymph nodes still known as Hodgkin's disease.

The next son, the conveyancing barrister John Hodgkin, married as the first of his three wives a daughter of Luke Howard. Their child Thomas was born at 14 Bruce Grove on 29 July 1831. The boy – known as tumbling Tommy in childhood – was a prize student whose progress was marred by ill health. He intended to follow his father's profession and in late 1852 entered the chambers in New Square, Lincoln's Inn, of Joseph Bevan Braithwaite. Early in 1853, the legal studies ended when Thomas had an epileptic seizure in Braithwaite's chambers. He was carried back to his stepmother's care in Tottenham. To recuperate he went on a walking tour of the continent with an old school friend, Alfred Waterhouse, newly qualified as an architect and keen to make a leisurely study of the architecture of France, Germany and Italy.

Thomas returned to Tottenham and attempted to study topics other than law – including biblical Hebrew – but decided that for his health's sake his future life must be in the country. One option was the life of a country banker if he could gain banking experience. Cousins of the Leatham family who were intermarried with the Howards had a bank at Wakefield and Pontefract, the latter within three miles of the Howards' country home at Ackworth. Thomas was allowed to study banking at Pontefract in the summers of 1854 and 1855 and to spend his spare time with Luke Howard's circle of family and friends.

The Leatham bank offered no prospect of partnership. Thomas moved on in February 1856 to a small and newish branch bank at Whitehaven in Cumberland owned by the Head family and with a quasi-promise of being one day admitted into the firm. Whitehaven was flourishing with fishing, shipbuilding, coal and iron mining and enjoyed an industrial importance that has now vanished. Thomas remarked how all day long carts moved slowly through the streets bringing the rich, slimy red ore to be shipped from one of the piers. Thomas and his sisters, Mariabella and Elizabeth, lived over the bank but his clerk's pay covered only a third of the household expenses. He learned much of the craft of banking but saw no prospect of advancement in the Cumberland bank.

In the autumn of 1857 he visited Falmouth, centre for a branch of the well-known Quaker family of the Foxes. He spent some time with Alfred Fox at Glendurgan where the household included six sons and six daughters. He saw his sister Elizabeth's friend, little Lucy the fifth daughter, growing into woman-hood and began to dream of marriage. By mid-1858 he had decided to move on from Whitehaven to enhance his prospects.

He heard of an opening in Newcastle-on-Tyne where a new private bank was looking for young men with capital to take it over (for Thomas, this meant a loan from his barrister father, John). Thomas was keen but wanted partners with local knowledge. The eventual partnership including John William Pease of Darlington began business in St Nicholas Square, Newcastle, on 14 March 1859. The barrister Edward Fry, Thomas's closest friend from student days at University College, London, and Mariabella Hodgkin were married on 6 April. Thomas was lodging at Royton and sharing with his sister Elizabeth. Early in 1860 she left to marry Alfred Waterhouse, Thomas's school friend and the architect companion on the recuperative continental tour. Later in 1860, Helen Fox of the Glendurgan household and Pease were married. Thomas Hodgkin and Lucy Fox were married on 7 August 1861 in the Friends Meeting House at Falmouth. The banking partners became brothers-in-law.

The banking venture was hugely successful. By 1866, Thomas was able to build a mansion designed by Waterhouse at Benwell, then two miles to the west of Newcastle (but now absorbed into the city's sprawl). John and Helen Pease's grand house, Pendower, was at Benwell and nearby Thomas and Lucy's Benwelldene home. On 19 March 1869 the Hodgkins' first child Violet was born; (followed by John Alfred in 1871 who died in infancy next year); followed by Edward on 20 September 1872; Elizabeth (Lily) on 22 November 1873; Ellen (Nelly) on 16 May 1875; Robert (Robin), the future father of the subject of this biography, on 24 April 1877; and George on 22 August 1880.

Thomas pursued historical scholarship and writing alongside professional banking. He had twin passions in the histories of Italy and Northumberland. In 1879, Violet aged ten helped spot a howler in the proofs of the first volume of *Italy and Her Invaders* for the Clarendon Press in Oxford. She assisted on the full work, a labour of 26 years running to eight main volumes, some with several parts. In 1883, Thomas made one of his many visits to Rome and his first to Bamburgh. On 30 June 1886, he was to his immense pride invited to Oxford to receive the honorary degree of Doctor of Civil Law. Lucy Hodgkin and Violet Hodgkin travelled up from Exeter to meet Thomas travelling from Newcastle. They stayed in Bradmore Road, Oxford, with the historian Professor Henry Pelham and his wife in what Violet found a cool, shady house.

On 21 October 1893, Dr Hodgkin completed the formal sale of Benwelldene as a blind asylum. He was about to be without a home for himself, wife and young family plus a library of some five thousand books. During a train journey on 23 October, he had a chance meeting with a trustee for the Durham Bishop Crewe estates. Dr Hodgkin made an offer on 3 November to rent the Keep of Bamburgh Castle for five years. This offer was accepted on 6 November, and then came an offer from the Newcastle armaments manufacturer and industrialist William Armstrong to buy the castle outright. A compromise was reached that for a month in each year of the tenancy the Hodgkins would exchange with the Armstrong house in Jesmond Dene.

By 30 May 1894, the Hodgkins were installed for their five-year stay at the Keep in the castle courtyard of Bamburgh Castle. The eldest son, Edward named for his paternal uncle by marriage, Edward Fry, went to Trinity College, Cambridge. He took a first in 1894 and on 10 June 1895 joined the family bank, becoming a partner in December 1898 and announcing his engagement to Catharine Wilson. Dr Hodgkin had been spending more time on his writing and withdrawing from routine work for the bank so that by 1899 he was effectively retired, except for attention to the private ledger.

The second daughter, Lily, married on 30 August 1900 a Trinity College, Cambridge contemporary of Edward's, Herbert Gresford Jones, who was then a Church of England vicar in Liverpool. Their son, Michael, was born on 21 October 1901. The third Hodgkin daughter, Nelly, was educated at home but went on to Somerville College, Oxford. On 8 July 1902, she and Robert Carr (Carr B) Bosanquet married. He was also a Cambridge Trinity friend of Edward's and the elder son of the neighbouring Bosanquet family of Rock Hall who included Carr B's uncle Bernard Bosanquet, one of the British idealist philosophers who followed Hegel. Carr B was director of the British School of Archaeology in Athens where he and Nelly set up home. In 1905, Carr B succeeded to the family estate. He returned to Britain to take a newly established chair of classical archaeology in the University of Liverpool.

The second surviving son, Robin went to Seabank preparatory school at Alnmouth in 1887 and to Repton School in Derbyshire in September 1891. He spent only two terms there and suffered from what the family termed a delicate chest. A doctor advised that he go to a school farther south. Robin transferred to Leighton Park School in Reading in 1892. This was a new Quaker school financed out of the closure of another Quaker school attended by the family in Bruce Grove, Tottenham. He spent four years there along with other cousins of the Hodgkin clan and latterly with the companionship of his younger brother George. George followed his brother Edward to Cambridge when he went up to Trinity College in 1898 and despite a severe attack of influenza took a first in the natural science tripos. His eyesight was found to be weakened, and as the condition worsened he embarked in 1901 on a long journey that a doctor prescribed – to Greece, Egypt and Palestine. George travelled in 1902 to New Zealand on a scientific project and became increasingly involved in Quakerism. In pursuit of open-air employment, he spent three years in Sunderland studying civil engineering. When the training was completed, he was appointed assistant inspector of piers and harbours in the Isle of Man.

The family of Dorothy Smith, the future mother of the subject of this biography, had strong links with Northumberland on her mother's side. Mary Florence Baird was born on 3 December 1855 in Newcastle-on-Tyne as the first of seven daughters of a minor Northumbrian landowner and unsuccessful barrister John Forster. The Forsters were a widespread Northumbrian clan but John Forster descended from a line that was living in Bamburgh village in the mid-eighteenth century. He had taken the name Baird on succeeding to property at Bowmont, and in 1854 Baird had married Emily Jane Brinton, from a prosperous Kidderminster family of carpet-makers.

John Baird changed homes frequently and found the lure of foreign travel irresistible. As Baird travelled for the sake of his health and opportunities for painting watercolours, Mary and her sisters were trooped around the continent and had a patchy formal education. In the early 1860s, Baird would also take the family to Bamburgh and rent the Wynding House from Miss Thomassin Darling. In summer and autumn, the Baird children enjoyed the sands of Bamburgh (as Mary's descendants continued to do a century and a half later in an unbroken tradition into the fifth generation). Baird had no gainful employment but a large family and an extravagant life style. Throughout life Mary retained from her childhood an anxiety, a haunting fear from her father's casual remark that the money would not last.

By comparison with the Bairds, Dorothy's father, Arthur Lionel Smith (AL as he was usually known) came from genuinely straitened circumstances. AL's father, William Henry Smith was a civil engineer and one of 22 children, 19 of whom survived to maturity. He was of English stock but born and raised in Ireland. W.H. Smith worked on Marc Isambard Brunel's innovative and perilous project of cutting a tunnel under the Thames in London. He was married in 1843 to Alice Elizabeth Strutt from an Essex family proficient in the arts. She was brought up in Italy where her father, the painter, etcher and portraitist Jacob George Strutt, had settled but continued to send an occasional landscape to the Royal Academy.

The engineer and the artist's daughter set up home in the Holborn district of London and had five children. The first was a boy, William. The second son, Arthur Lionel who was to become a pioneer of adult education, was born on 4 December 1850. Another son, Reginald, died as an infant in a cholera epidemic. W.H. Smith died too, at the early age of 37, leaving Alice a widow with four surviving children. A family friend arranged a presentation for Christ's Hospital for AL, aged six (preferring him to William, precisely because he was so young). William went away to sea and Alice Smith with two small daughters, Mary and Miriam, went to Rome where her brother, in their father's footsteps, was making a reputation as a painter. Alice Smith remarried in 1859, an American, Freeman Silke. They moved to Chicago with her daughters and were later to have two more daughters of their own, Alcmena and Lucy.

AL was left to fend for himself in the harsh environment of some eight hundred boys at Christ's Hospital in London, where food was scanty and playing fields non-existent. On a paved playground, a form of hockey was one of the favourite games and a basis for AL's lifelong enthusiasm for the game (along with ice-skating). He lived entirely at the school for six years, suffering three bouts of rheumatic fever, but he read voraciously and distinguished himself academically. In November 1868, he was awarded an exhibition to Balliol College, Oxford, and came into residence in October 1869. In June 1871, he took a first in classical moderations, designed by the university authorities as a severe and exacting examination in Latin and Greek. The success came in time for his first reunion with his mother since his early childhood.

Freeman Silke, in poor health, travelled from Chicago to Rome and died of consumption. The twice-widowed Alice Silke had as the young Alice Strutt been friendly with Emily Brinton's eldest sister Martha Eliza Brinton. Martha had gone on in 1845 to make a successful marriage to a Halifax carpet manufacturer and philanthropist, Frank Crossley. His carpet firm was the largest in the world in his day, employing more than 5,000 workers and collecting royalties from other manufacturers for a patented and innovative loom. Crossley was a Yorkshire MP from 1852 until his death in 1872 and had been created a baronet in 1863. It was arranged for AL Smith to hold a reunion with his mother, Alice Silke, and to meet his two half-sisters at the home of Lady Crossley. Mrs Silke and her daughters soon returned to Chicago.

After their departure, Lady Crossley kept a hugely benevolent eye on AL. She provided him with a home in the vacations at Somerleyton, a magnificent country estate in Suffolk. She even provided modest employment for AL in coaching her only child. He was an Eton pupil, Savile Brinton Crossley, and at 14 only a few years younger than his new mentor. Balliol followed this lead by finding more pupils for AL. Lord Lymington became the first of an array of lordlings and princelings that helped AL make ends meet. Lady Crossley continued to subsidise AL at Balliol and he went on from his first in Greats in 1873 to a year in the history school and a second in 1874. He was elected to an open fellowship at Oxford's Trinity College, tenable for seven years but ceasing on marriage. By November 1876, he had moved on to London lodgings in South Kensington as he read for the bar.

Savile Crossley was Mary Baird's first cousin and she made occasional summer visits to Somerleyton (since her aunt Lady Crossley saw in Mary a potential spouse for Savile). Mary had met AL and gone sailing in Savile's yacht with her cousin and his tutor or on coach drives through the Suffolk countryside. They met again in Oxford when Lady Crossley was invited to an Oxford commemoration, in those days spread over several days of dancing and entertainment. In the autumn of 1877, Mary Baird and AL Smith became engaged.

The Master of Balliol, Benjamin Jowett, a legendary holder of that appointment, arranged for AL to be offered a tutorship in modern history at Balliol for 1879 when the Trinity fellowship lapsed on marriage. The engaged couple chose a future home in the new residential area growing up in North Oxford. The address was 7 Crick Road. They called it Somerley in recognition of the Crossley house where they had met.

They were married on 25 June 1879 at Teddington where the Bairds had settled. Mary's relatives were numerous but AL had in addition to friends only his maternal uncle, Charles Strutt. He was known as the Solitary Relative for astonishingly turning up from Australia on the wedding day. The Smiths spent their honeymoon on and about the River Thames, essentially in a tiny outrigger skiff with overnight stops at riverside inns. AL rowed and his wife Mary steered. They went on to Canterbury (AL typically examining) and visited other friends before settling in the new Oxford house and Balliol about 1 October 1879.

In the summer of 1880, Mrs AL, as she was known in a style of the time, was well into pregnancy when Jowett proposed that AL take the young Lord Weymouth to the continent to be coached for Balliol entrance. AL explained that a child was due in August, but was urged to go abroad anyway. Their son Lionel was born in Baden Baden in Germany on 19 August 1880 after Mrs AL endured a prolonged and dangerous labour. By chance, the vicar who had officiated at their wedding was in Baden Baden and on hand to baptise the child.

The next six children were daughters born less dramatically in the Crick Road house: Gertrude on 1 March 1882; Mary on 12 June 1884; Dorothy on 1 March 1886; Miriam on 14 February 1888; Margaret on 10 May 1890, Rosalind on 20 September 1892.

Jowett continued to plant potential Balliol entrants on the Smiths despite their cramped accommodation. He planned and offered a larger official tutor's residence that was being built on a plot of land known as the Master's Field. The new house was close to completion in 1893 when Mrs AL, with memories of Bamburgh holidays from her childhood, had the idea of taking the family there. AL was attracted by the archaeological and historical interest of Northumberland. The Smith family took the long journey to Bamburgh in August 1893 returning at the end of September for the final move to the new house, the King's Mound. Their delight in the new surroundings was marred when on the day of the move they received news of Jowett's death – on 1 October 1893.

Lady Crossley had died on 21 August 1891 leaving her niece Mary a significant legacy from the Crossley fortune. This was to be put to good use as part-payment towards the purchase and enlargement of a permanent holiday home in Bamburgh. St Aidan's on the village street just at the foot of Bamburgh Castle was a relatively small but, as it proved, very elastic house. St Aidan's had to find space for the family, a handful of servants and several students. A cunning but incautious builder constructed two additional tiny bedrooms in the gables of St Aidan's. These became known as the matchboxes more for their scant size than the real fire risk they represented. The house could be let in the early summer before it was needed by the Smiths.

The Smith family was continuing to expand. A seventh daughter Barbara was born on 24 February 1896 three and a half years after Rosalind. A ninth Smith child and second son, Hubert, was born in Oxford on 12 August 1899. This, however, was Bamburgh time and the baby when two weeks old was whisked off to be baptised in Bamburgh Church. He was the last child in a sequence sometimes categorised as seven sister roses with a brother thorn at each end, although the beautiful daughters were known in less courtly undergraduate circles as the Smithereens.

By the summer of 1894, the Hodgkin and Smith families from their disparate origins had converged on Bamburgh. The families met, but almost literally as in the Victorian hymn – with the rich man in his castle and the poor man at his gate. The encounter was consolidated in 1895 when Robin Hodgkin joined the procession of young men being coached by AL for Balliol entrance and lodged with the Smiths in their Oxford home, by now the King's Mound.

Robin was successful and came into residence in Balliol in 1896. His closest Balliol friend was Richard Douglas (Dick) Denman, tutored by AL Smith. Robin and Dick went on to share Oxford lodgings and Dick was a frequent visitor to the Hodgkin household. They made an adventurous journey to Russia, working their passage in a cargo steamer to St Petersburg and travelling roughly and economically down the Volga to the Black Sea. Another Balliol contemporary was the music prodigy, Donald Tovey, who had gone up to Balliol in 1894 as the first holder of the Lewis Nettleship memorial scholarship in music and graduated in 1898.

On the male side at least, the Victorian network of philoprogenitive families and rippling circles of school and university friends was encapsulated in the Balliol hockey club. Hockey was introduced to Balliol by AL Smith in the early 1890s, by tradition as an import from the sands of Bamburgh although the Christ's Hospital experience would also have played a part. For the season of 1897-98, the eleven-man team captained by Robin Hodgkin included AL Smith and Dick Denman. Another player as halfback was Francis Urquhart, who after Smith coaching for entrance to Balliol had won an exhibition in modern history and come into residence in October 1890. He shone with a sleekness that by 1892 won him the nickname Sligger.

The Hodgkin household and Robin were much affected by the outbreak of the Boer war in 1899. Robin graduated in that year taking a first in history, and joined Queen's College, Oxford, as a history lecturer (being elected a fellow in 1904). He also volunteered for service with the Northumberland Fusiliers. This was contrary to the Discipline of the Society of Friends and brought severance from the Quakers. Dr Hodgkin showed understanding of his son in the comment that the proposition against using physical force for the maintenance of right ought to be accepted by unwarped conviction and not forced by external authority.

In 1903, Dick Denman brought his fiancée to stay at Barmoor with Dr Hodgkin and his family. She was Helen Christian Sutherland, born 24 February 1881, as the daughter of Thomas Sutherland, who had famously worked his way up from a junior clerkship with the Peninsular and Oriental Steamship Navigation Company to become its chairman in 1881. Sutherland had married Alice Macnaught, daughter of a clergyman and granddaughter of a wealthy Liverpool physician. Helen was educated at a boarding school in Barnet and at the Convent of the Assumption in Paris. She was small in physique and shy in character and had not enjoyed the role of society girl her mother expected of her. Dick introduced Helen to the Smith family at the King's Mound. Helen and Dick were married on 11 February 1904, with Dick's Oxford contemporary the writer John Buchan as best man. The Denmans set up house in London in Swan

Walk, Chelsea, and Dick, who had political ambitions, became private secretary to a Cabinet minister, the Postmaster General, Lord Buxton.

The older Smith children were beginning to scatter from the King's Mound. Lionel had a brilliant all-round record at Rugby School and Balliol. His sporting talent (including being capped for England in hockey against Wales on 7 March 1903) meant that he slipped to a second in Greats (where a first had been expected). He went on to a reading party at Sligger's chalet in Switzerland to prepare for a new school and returned to Oxford to a first in history in 1904. This success was sealed with election in November 1904 to a fellowship at All Souls along with Frederick Barrington-Ward. Another friend of Lionel's, the Balliol science don Harold Hartley, was wooing Gertrude Smith. Gertrude and Harold were married on 23 June 1906. Mary (known as Molly) had gone to Cambridge in 1902 on a history scholarship at Girton College.

Dorothy entered Oxford High School in 1893 and spent 11 years there, emerging in 1904. She had spent two years in the sixth form and was awarded an exhibition to Holloway College. She decided not to take it up in favour of an earlier ambition for nursing training (although this may have been out of deference to constraints on the Smith family finances). She spent a year as a daughter-at-home being too young to go away for the training she had chosen. In October 1905 at the age of 19, she became a probationer at the Great Ormond Street Children's Hospital. The hospital experience was tough and unpalatable and in April 1906 she gave notice to quit and went back home to Oxford.

Late in 1906, Dick Denman wrote to AL asking if one of his daughters could come and help for some weeks with the preparation of a concert series Donald Tovey and he were planning for Chelsea Town Hall. Gertrude was married, Molly at Cambridge, so Dorothy, next in line and unemployed, was designated. She was a one-finger typist, with little experience of managing money and no musical knowledge. She felt unfitted but stayed with Helen and Dick in Chelsea, and helped in selling concert tickets, dealing with programmes and printers and Town Hall staff for Tovey's series of chamber music concerts held in February and March 1907. The Denman marriage was not succeeding. However, an unsuccessful pass from Dick to the innocent Dorothy Smith had the effect only of binding Dorothy and Helen Denman into what became a lifelong friendship.

Meanwhile AL's financial situation was partly eased with the award in 1906 of a Jowett fellowship under a scheme devised by a Balliol undergraduate contemporary (Jim Hozier become Lord Newlands) to improve the emoluments of Balliol dons. A condition of the endowment was that AL be one of the two initial beneficiaries. More money meant less pressure on AL's time. He used the slice of freedom to help the Workers' Educational Association (WEA), founded in 1903 by Albert Mansbridge to support the higher education of working men.

AL was nominated in 1907 to the joint committee of WEA and Oxford representatives to examine how this could be implemented in Oxford.

In the AL Smith dynasty a new generation was beginning as the first grandchild came with the birth of Gertrude and Harold Hartley's daughter, Diana, on 18 January 1908. The baby when aged five months was among the family group at the wedding on 6 June 1908 of Molly to Frederick Barrington-Ward, who was using his All Souls fellowship as a springboard to a career as a barrister. The bridegroom was the eldest of nine children and the bride the third of nine children so a strong contingent from both families could form a procession across the Master's Field. Dorothy and her spinster sisters were bridesmaids. By the end of July, it was time for them to travel to Bamburgh for the now established summer holiday, and for Dorothy to take up Violet Hodgkin's unexpected invitation.

On Dorothy Smith's first afternoon at Barmoor in August 1908 the tea party she encountered comprised Dr Hodgkin, two daughters, one son and a family friend. Dr Hodgkin had just turned 77. Violet, the eldest child, was unmarried, but mindful of a painful broken engagement. This was to another of her brother Edward's Trinity College contemporaries, Malcolm Corrie Powell, whose subsequent marriage to Olive Hannay on 11 May 1904 had begun to fail within weeks. Lily was already married to one future bishop and young mother to another. Robin was a bachelor at 31. The houseguest was a friend of Violet's, Paula Schuster, who would provide hospitality in London for Hodgkin visits. George, as yet unmarried, was away at his work on the Isle of Man. Between tea and dinner Robin took Dorothy for a spin in his small car to look for cream cheeses in the Wooler shops (without success) and to enjoy views of the Cheviots under the rain clouds. Violet was a reluctant third in the expedition. She had been unable to persuade other members of the party to go and she felt that being in the small car's tonneau joggled her appendix. Horse-drawn carriages were still the principal means of local outings, and the railway for most journeys.

Dorothy was conscious of the luxury and spaciousness of Barmoor as she climbed to the main rooms on the first floor by a long but easy staircase. The staircase had a prominent brass bar along the top of the banisters to make sliding down them impossible; the staircase curled up through four storeys of the castle and this was a house with many child visitors. On the first floor were Dr Hodgkin's study or library, then the oval saloon with no exterior walls and lit by a glass roof, then a drawing room opening out of it with conventional windows and ceiling.

The staircase carried on up to bedrooms and closets. Only a best visitor's room and the top floor nursery had bathrooms attached, and most bedrooms were served by hipbaths and huge cans of hot water. A quiet dinner was followed by Dr Hodgkin reading aloud from Robert Southey's narrative poem 'Thalaba the Destroyer'. Dorothy could retire to bed by ten in a room where a lamp had already been lit by one of the servants.

On Wednesday morning, 5 August, with unsummery raging wind, Dorothy had a clearer picture of the prosperous establishment when family, guests and servants assembled for daily prayers before breakfast. A long file of staff came in and took up places by the chairs set in the oval saloon. The door was opened by Thomas Littlefair, who served as butler for 30 years, and the procession was headed by the cook, Mrs Drury, who served the family for a similar term. They were followed by two lady's maids, then two or three housemaids, and young kitchen and scullery maids, and at least two footmen – and then the outdoor staff, including coachman and gardener.

After prayers and breakfast, Dorothy went to read in the garden. Violet took breakfast in bed in her round room in the centre tower over Barmoor's outer hall and had instructed Dorothy to come up and see her. Violet had been suffering since her youth from increasing deafness, but was also a hypochondriac and could be most selfishly demanding. Dorothy, who was apparently unaware of hidden reasons for her invitation to Barmoor, funked the encounter. After lunch Robin took Dorothy in the car to Berwick where they succeeded this time in buying cream cheeses. Robin, troubled by the car's sparking plug and rear lamp, was reluctant to talk much while driving. They returned through a wind that was sufficient to break the Hodgkin family habit of having as many meals as possible out of doors. They took tea indoors. After dinner Dr Hodgkin completed the 'Thalaba' reading, at a hard gallop according to Violet's diary.

On Thursday morning, 6 August, Dr Hodgkin left on an early train to London. Violet received a warning of a mumps scare at the Cots, the former coastguard cottages at Budle Bay taken by the Hodgkins for modest seaside rests. The warning came from Margaret Edina Duckworth married in 1889 to the barrister Henry Newbolt, recently retired to become a gentleman of letters and a well-liked poet. The Newbolts had become regular summer visitors. Violet was driven over there to investigate. Also at the cottages was Robert Bridges, retired from medicine in favour of literature and on the way to becoming poet laureate. Violet had been a bridesmaid at the marriage in 1884 of Bridges to a Hodgkin cousin, Monica, the daughter of Alfred Waterhouse and Elizabeth. Robin and Dorothy went on to Bamburgh where Dorothy had a few minutes with her own family.

She returned to Barmoor where the sun blazed out in the early afternoon. Violet, wanting to be alone, sent them off after lunch in the carriage for a picnic. On return Dorothy and Violet chatted about Helen and Dick Denman.

Dorothy mentioned that she was intending to leave next day. Violet speedily passed this news on to Robin.

They dined outside on the lawn, Violet seated between Lily and Paula, Robin and Dorothy making up the table. After dinner all five were going to see the sunset. Violet and Paula slipped away to another part of the garden. Lily went into the house, soon to be joined by Violet and Paula for what seemed a long wait.

Robin invited Dorothy to go through the patch of woodland beyond the Barmoor rose beds to the sunset seat at the edge of the wood. There Robin asked Dorothy to marry him, to her astonishment and consternation. She was unaware that Violet's invitation was at Robin's request and part of a plot patched up by Robin in Oxford a month earlier. Robin at Violet's instigation – after Wednesday's hard gallop through Southey – had talked to Dr Hodgkin about the intended marriage. Dorothy responded to the proposal with ambiguous floods of tears.

They returned to the house and Robin sent Violet a note 'Do go to Dorothy'. Violet went to Dorothy's room, found her in great distress and tried to calm and comfort her. She then went to Robin's room and found him less consolable so gave him veronal to help him sleep. All three spent a troubled night.

On Friday morning, 7 August, Violet was awake by 6.30 in the morning and soon despatching Robin to drive in his car to Bamburgh to seek the belated consent of Dorothy's parents for the engagement. Robin made a halt at Wooler for breakfast, then drove towards Bamburgh, pausing an hour on the moor to ponder the scene and his future. He called on the Smith house, and then lunched at the cottages with the Newbolt family. He made a second call at St Aidan's to complete his task of securing Smith parental approval for the marriage proposal. Meanwhile Violet determined that Dorothy was to be given a deliberately dull day to quiet her nerves. She was set to picking lavender and making sachets. Robin returned at teatime to a more relaxed household.

On Saturday morning, 8 August, Paula returned to London, and Robin drove Dorothy over to Bamburgh to see her mother, and her immediately older and younger sisters. He left Dorothy with the Smiths and went to lunch with the Newbolts at the cottages. In the evening Robin drove her back to Barmoor to see his mother who was returning that day from a family visit. Robin's car would not start when it was time to meet Lucy Hodgkin's train, so she was met by a brougham and a bicycle. Dorothy was charmed by Mrs Hodgkin who treated her as if it was all settled that she would be a daughter-in-law. Dorothy told Robin she was afraid of being alone with him.

On Sunday morning, 9 August, Dorothy accompanied Robin and his mother to church. In the afternoon Robin and Dorothy sat talking in the heather on the moors and Dorothy hesitantly agreed to a trial engagement. Before she returned to the shelter of the Smith family she permitted one kiss.

Chapter 1
Charmed circles: Dragon, Winchester and Balliol: 1908-1932

An acquaintanceship of more than a decade between the young historian Robin Hodgkin, now teaching at Queen's College, Oxford, and Dorothy, one of the many daughters of his Balliol mentor AL Smith, flowered swiftly into romance in the Northumbria countryside. Once an engagement was agreed in early August 1908 and approved by both families Robin was swift to action. Dorothy was hoping for leisurely preparation for a spring wedding. Robin urged that they be married before Christmas. With four of the Hodgkins about to embark on a visit to Quaker communities in New Zealand and Australia, an early wedding was set for 15 December.

By the first week of September, Robin had dashed to Oxford to find a house. Dorothy was chary of suburban North Oxford's neo-Gothic. She was content with Robin's acquisition of Mendip House on Headington Hill, then almost rural and a good bicycle ride from the university's spires and domes below. The house had dining and drawing rooms, five bedrooms and a study-library. It stood in an acre of grounds, with lawns, shrubbery and kitchen garden – so Knight the gardener was taken on with the purchase.

The engaged couple made day trips to London to choose good furniture. Dorothy startled bystanders by appearing in a Kensington store window to try out a large and comfortable sofa that became the first purchase for Mendip House. Wedding gifts too helped furnish the new home – a Balliol fellow, Jimmy Palmer, departing England on 29 October to become Bishop of Bombay, contributed six Chippendale chairs. A fellow of Queen's, Albert Augustus David, conducted the service in St Cross Church, Holywell, with the assistance of the bridegroom's cleric brother-in-law Herbert Gresford Jones. The bridesmaids were Dorothy's four younger sisters and the Hodgkin family's friend Celia Newbolt. The pages were Robin's nephew, Charles Bosanquet, and the last of the Smith children, Hubert, substituting for another of Robin's nephews, Michael, as there was illness in the Gresford Jones house.

The initial honeymoon destination was the same for Dorothy as for her sisters. This was Rose Cottage at South Stoke, Oxfordshire, the riverside country home of her widower maternal uncle, Sir Edward Cook, a former newspaper editor now engaged with Alexander Wedderburn on the 38-volume library edition of John Ruskin's *Works.* Sir Edward warned that a December sojourn would be less attractive than a visit in June. The honeymoon was continued to Mentone on the French Riviera, but transmuted abruptly when Dorothy found she had measles. Mrs AL's help was speedily invoked and she arrived to nurse Dorothy.

Dorothy Hodgkin became pregnant in the summer of 1909. The Kensington sofa had found a place at Mendip House in Robin's study-library at the head of the back stairs. Dorothy would lie there in the evenings and make long robes and flannels for the unborn child. On Low Sunday, 3 April 1910, the baby was born at 3.45 in the afternoon: a boy weighing in at 6¼ pounds and initially with a mop of rich red hair. The baby at birth had already ten aunts and ten uncles (fifteen by blood) and his advent was the signal for a procession of family visitors. Missing was the paternal grandfather, the patriarchal AL Smith. He was a reluctant traveller but had agreed to take the springtime Hilary term as a sabbatical to deliver a lecture series at New York's Columbia University. AL sailed back to Liverpool in early May and on 17 May the baby was introduced. A christening at Queen's College followed on 6 June performed by the veteran Provost, Dr J.R. Magrath. The child, named Thomas Lionel after the two grandfathers, cried under a liberal splashing of cold water. Helen Denman, the daughter of the prosperous shipper Sir Thomas Sutherland and an intimate friend of Violet and Dorothy, was a godmother. A godfather was another Balliol don, the classics tutor J.A. Smith (a close family friend but unrelated), who brought a silver christening mug.

In the custom of the time, the children of well-to-do families were essentially left in the care of the nurse or nanny. Tommy's nurse was on holiday for ten days in March 1911 for part of which Robin was also away. Dorothy was delighted to spend a whole week at the King's Mound in sole charge of her son. The end of Oxford's summer term signalled a round of holiday visits. They took a night train to Northumberland in time for Dr Hodgkin's eightieth-birthday celebrations at Barmoor on 29 July. On 7 August came magnificent celebrations at Barmoor for the golden wedding of Lucy Hodgkin and Dr Hodgkin.

The family was dispersed at Christmas. Tommy with his nanny went to the Smith family gathering at the King's Mound. Robin went to his father at Barmoor, where Christmas was celebrated in the accepted style of patrician paternalism. A hundred children gathered at a Christmas tree in the village clubhouse. Dr Hodgkin called out the name of each child and handed out a gift cut from the tree by one of his sons. Dr Hodgkin wrote on Christmas day to his sister, Lady Fry, that his physical strength was failing. The lease on Barmoor Castle was ending. He was growing tired of the darkness and cold of northern winters and looking for sunnier surroundings. He was drawn to the Falmouth of Lucy's Fox family origins. He and his wife and eldest daughter Violet took Treworgan, a house standing on the coast about four miles west of Falmouth, for a trial month. Dr Hodgkin warmed to the sunshine of Treworgan and could even manage the steep path through pine trees to the seashore and sandy bay. On Sunday 2 March, Dr Hodgkin read at morning family prayers then called for a carriage to attend Quaker meeting. Lucy was in the carriage but before Dr Hodgkin could join her, he collapsed and died.

Tommy in a homemade white satin suit was a page for the wedding on 29 July 1913 of his maternal aunt Margaret to a Balliol graduate John Gordon Jameson, a son of Lord Ardwall. In August, Tommy was taking an interest in writing, largely self-taught, and could write most of the alphabet. In the household there had been much talk of another child expected. A cot was ready and Tommy began to look into it each morning. Mendip House was the setting for the birth on 25 August 1913 of the Hodgkins' second child, a boy later christened Edward Christian (Teddy). Tommy only occasionally rued the presence of the new baby as a rival for his mother's attention.

The assassination of the heir to the Austrian throne occurred at Sarajevo on 28 June 1914. The Hodgkins carried on preparations for a summer visit to Lucy Hodgkin at Falmouth. Treworgan in July brought happy long afternoons on the beach for two small boys, their mother and grandmother. The mood changed when Britain declared war on Germany on 4 August. Lucy and Dorothy were staying with the children and the nanny at the Polullian Hotel. Tommy was old enough to be troubled about the war and wanted to know why God had let it come. He tried to follow the war news. The national anxiety was distressful for Robin in a specific way, as his convictions differed from those of his actively Quaker mother and sister and his younger brother, George, who was adamantly against the war. Robin spent the last part of the long vacation at an embarkation camp in the New Forest.

His severance from the Quakers had stemmed from his volunteer membership of the Northumberland Fusiliers at the time of the Boer War. He applied to rejoin his old battalion. He was accepted and posted in December to battalion headquarters at Alnwick. At his medical, he was classed as unfit for foreign service: he was to serve on the home front. Dorothy adjusted to the new conditions of wartime and tried to keep the family as close together as circumstances would permit.

On 20 September 1915, Tommy had his first experience of school as he entered the kindergarten class of a new school opened at White Lodge, Headington. His nanny reported that he had taken well to the other schoolchildren. After a few days, Dorothy found Tommy crying in bed at night, and he confessed to unhappiness at school. He was soon caught up in the excitement of new words and new agility in simple arithmetic, and some rote learning that appealed to him.

Tommy's transition to school and minor independence was timely as on 8 October Dorothy and Robin's third child, a daughter, was born. Tommy showed himself fond of the new arrival but remained less engrossed than Teddy who was closer in age. Robin came home from 9 to 11 October to see his daughter and again for the child's christening on 14 November as Elizabeth (Betty), at a ceremony performed by his colleague, Canon B.H. Streeter. Dorothy had a special tenderness in her feeling for a daughter.

Dorothy continued to visit her intimate friend, Helen Sutherland, in Chelsea (Helen's marriage to Dick Denman had been annulled in 1913 and she had reverted to using her maiden name). By late January 1916, Tommy was at a different local school – Headington School for Girls where in his first term report he scored four excellents. Robin on service in Kent had been exploring ways of bringing the family together again. He found lodgings at Herne Bay and by the beginning of May they were settling in to a new setting. Dorothy tried to give Tommy lessons at home but these were irregularly interspersed between many family outings. Tommy was content to read to himself and was showing a fondness for poetry, generally out of *The Oxford Book of English Verse*. He made friends with half a dozen children of the neighbourhood and began regular kindergarten schooling at the Alexandra School, a tiny establishment about a hundred yards from home for this handful of children.

In Oxford, the Master of Balliol, J.L. Strachan-Davidson, died in the summer of 1916 and AL Smith was elected to succeed him. The promotion meant an awkward move from the cheerful and familiar King's Mound to the comparatively dreary Master's Lodgings in college. In the Easter vacation of 1917, the family was back in Oxford, on a visit to the Smith parents in their new Balliol setting. Tommy enjoyed exploring this new domain, especially the cellars.

The family left Herne Bay for Tadworth in August and then to London, as Robin's military service took him to the War Office. In October Tommy went to the Norland Place School in Holland Park Avenue, a full-sized establishment of some 250 pupils and taking boys up to the age of 12. The move to London brought him closer to the Barrington-Wards and their daughter Sylvia. The Hodgkin family settled in at 65 Bedford Gardens, Campden Hill, W8. Tommy continued to read voraciously, would borrow books from Sylvia, and from the neighbouring Fletcher family, the physiologist and medical administrator Walter Morley Fletcher, married to Mary Frances Cropper, whose son Charles was a few months younger than Teddy and a pupil at Norland Place. Tommy spent his first term in Class IIIA, a young form for his age but this had been his parents' request to ease the transition. He did well and was promoted at the end of the first term to a higher form, where he was among the youngest. Dorothy noted that Tommy was always entering into long conversations with people on buses or trams or in shops. She and Robin would hear him speaking most friendly farewells with complete strangers after about half an hour's ride.

Dorothy took her children on 23 September to a new home in London at 79 Ladbroke Road, and Tommy returned to his Norland Place School. He was in a new form and began Latin and hockey. On 11 November 1918 an armistice was signed and signalled that Britain would be returning to peacetime norms. Robin was waiting for his War Office appointment to end. Tommy said good-bye to the Norland Place School. In the New Year of 1919, the family made their way back to Oxford and in mid-January Tommy joined the Lynam family's Oxford Preparatory School in Bardwell Road. Robin was soon demobilised and could rejoin the family in Oxford where the university's workload was becoming heavier than in the years before the war. Queen's, along with other colleges, was taking in more undergraduates than before and a larger proportion was reading for the history school.

Robin took a long lease on a house at 20 Bradmore Road, formerly the home of his father's friend Dr Henry Pelham. The house was in the neo-Gothic style of suburban North Oxford that Dorothy had succeeded in avoiding on marriage. The consolation was that the house inside was roomy and comfortable and stood only five minutes' walk from the Parks, the river, and schools for the children. The house provided several reception rooms, half a dozen main bedrooms including the younger children's nursery, and four more servants' bedrooms, although one of these was given over to Tommy. Cook reigned over a dark semi-basement kitchen.

Tommy was placed in Miss Bagguley's class IIIa, and was about one and a half years below the average age of the 14 boys in his form. He made a good beginning and came top in French and second in English in the first fortnight. He was also adept at Latin. Teachers soon dubbed him the most promising boy in the form. The end of the First World War was celebrated with a peace day on 12 July. By the end of the school year in July Tommy had moved up another form and came out top. From the prize-giving he brought away prizes for his Latin and for Divinity. The Latin prize was a slim volume of *Songs of the Blue Dragon*, poems in celebration of boats owned and skippered by the school's headmaster, C.C. (Skipper) Lynam. The boating ethos was so strong that soon the Oxford Preparatory School became known as the Dragon School. Robin was thinking about Tommy's secondary education and put Tommy's name down for 1923 with Arthur G. Bather, housemaster of Winchester College's Sunnyside House. In February 1920 Robin heard from Bather that Sunnyside was being handed over to a Malcolm Robertson, who would do his best to fulfil Bather's commitments.

For the summer holidays of 1921 from late July to mid-September the Hodgkins took the Crewe Lodgings, a part of Bamburgh Castle. During the summer, golf suddenly became the rage interspersed with evening episodes of dancing, singing, parlour games and charades. More elaborate than the games was a theatrical performance of a melodrama, 'The Parson's Vengeance', largely composed by Tommy and performed by young members of the house party. More formal opportunities for acting came at the Dragon School where Tommy had been elected a prefect. By beginning of term in January 1922 he had reached the top form and the top set for mathematics and English. He was cast as Lucentio in the Dragon School's production of 'The Taming of the Shrew' and had to woo Bianca, played by Lesbia Cochrane. Tommy's best school friend, Pat Cotter, played Hortensio. Tommy was equipped with careful notes on when to kiss Bianca's hand or hair. The real incentive came from the schoolmaster Skipper Lynam who, somewhat to Tommy's indignation, stood in the wings holding up the shilling pieces he had promised for good lovemaking. In Tommy's lovemaking, 'elfin detachment' was observed by a reviewer in the school magazine *The Draconian*.

Robin was disturbed in mid-August to hear from Malcolm Robertson, the new housemaster of Winchester's Sunnyside, that Tommy was not high enough on the applications list for 1923 to have any likelihood of a place. Robertson assumed that Tommy would be likely to win a scholarship to College. Robin was not so sure, was most unwilling to put pressure on Tommy and was keen to have the option of a place in Robertson's house, which he thought he had secured in his earlier correspondence with Bather.

On 20 September the Dragon School reassembled. Tommy, now head of the dayboys, was doing well at most subjects. Helen Sutherland's mother, Lady Sutherland, had died in July 1920 and left her substantial wealth to her daughter. Her father, Sir Thomas Sutherland, had died on 1 January 1922 and left his fortune to charity. Helen was reshaping her life. She was moving from the modest house in Vale Avenue to a grander setting and had bought the lease of the house at 4 Lowndes Square. For the New Year of 1923 spent with Helen the Hodgkins were almost bombarded with treats: in the theatre 'Private Secretary' and 'Hansel and Gretel', and the circus at Olympia.

Tommy shared in the intensive preparation and rehearsal for the Dragon School production on 20 January 1923 of 'Twelfth Night', with Tommy in a striking tow wig as Sir Andrew Aguecheek and Pat Cotter as Sir Toby Belch. Hodgkin's excellent elocution was noted in the reviews. Tommy was also noted, in *The Draconian* of April 1923, for the contribution he had made to a speech competition with a precocious attack on the Arabella B. Buckley history text-book favoured by the school. He complained that the book was dull and over-loaded with facts: 'My wish is that all the copies of her venomous history book should be burned in a huge bonfire on the School field.' Tommy's teachers were both amused and impressed and after this rhetorical intervention the school experimented with other sources for the teaching of history.

The sixth formers were preparing for the vital round of public school entrance examinations. The Dragon School put three candidates in for Winchester. Robin and Dorothy drove to Winchester in their car and took a teacher G.C. (Cheese) Vassall, Tommy and the two other Dragon schoolboys. A telegram on 9 June brought the result: 'Hodgkin is eleventh on roll. Exhibitioner'. Dorothy was disappointed that he had not been awarded a scholarship for College at Winchester. Tommy's Winchester exhibition was honorary but the headmas-ter, Dr Montague John Rendall, could offer a place in one of three houses in which Robin was interested. Robin decided that Tommy should not go in for the Rugby scholarship examination; he could be an exhibitioner at Winchester rather than try to be a scholar at Rugby. Tommy should go to Major Robertson's Sunnyside where Tommy's Hodgkin cousin, Charles Bosanquet, had been. For the holiday months of August and September the Hodgkins in a family syndi-cate rented the fine set of rooms known as the Captain's Lodging in Bamburgh Castle. Tommy's bachelor housemaster-to-be, Major Robertson, and his host-ess sister Sheila, spent two nights with the Hodgkins at Bamburgh to deepen the acquaintanceship.

Dorothy travelled down with Tommy to Winchester. He wore a bowler hat and carried an umbrella, both swiftly discarded forever. Dorothy had tea with the Robertsons at Sunnyside and came away by the six o'clock train, with a deep hurt at leaving her son. Her parting gift to Tommy was the second edition of *Winchester College Notions* by Three Beetleites. The book published in 1910, the year of Tommy's birth, was a guide to the arcane language and customs of Wykehamists.

Tommy arrived as one of three new boys in Sunnyside in Short Half – the autumn term of 1923 – along with Charles Hollins and Richard Wood. Tommy wrote home in his first days at Winchester: 'I'm not homesick all the time.' He was initially homesick for most of the time. He wrote home each day and some-times twice in a day. A tone was set in a letter of 23 September within a few days of Tommy's arrival: 'I'm afraid that until a little time ago I thought I could get on for a short time without you and all the family. I've made a huge mistake, will you forgive me?'

Under the Winchester system, a new boy was for the first two weeks a pro-tégé known as a Tégé (with anglicised pronunciation Teejay) of a more senior member of the school. Tommy was under the protection of Charles Arthur Evelyn Shuckburgh, whose family was living in Hampstead's South Park Hill. The protector was replaced by a socius – contemporary – chosen each term as a regular walking companion.

Winchester boys were allowed holidays, called leave out days, based on the red-letter Saints' days that did not fall within the first ten days of term or on a Sunday. By Tommy's third leave out day on 30 November, he seemed to Dorothy to have overcome his sadness at being away at school. A school report showed him in second place in a form of 26 and first in a Greek set of 20. His housemaster, Robertson, now known in the Hodgkin circle by his Winchester nickname of the Bobber, wrote to Dorothy and Robin: 'This report is a nice Xmas card for you both, and I should like to congratulate you on the way Tommy has settled down in the house, and really enjoyed his work and play and new friendships, I think.'

In the second term, the focus of Tommy's letters home shifted to stamps for his collection and consignments of sweets and cakes (cargo in Winchester notions). He was writing a play in his spare time and extending his school friendships. He returned to Oxford on 2 April on the eve of his fourteenth birthday. In Balliol Sligger was carrying much of the burden of running the college during an illness of AL Smith who died in the early hours of 12 April. The body was laid in a flower bedecked Balliol chapel for a communion service early on 15 April followed by a funeral service in the university church of St Mary's. Tommy walked beside Dorothy in the funeral procession to the burial plot in Holywell churchyard.

Another mourner was a former classics tutor at Balliol, A.D. (Sandie) Lindsay, now a professor at Glasgow University, who had been sounded out whether he would be willing to return to Balliol as Master. He was a Socialist, a member of the Independent Labour Party (ILP), and by the standards of the time something of an unconventional choice. He was the candidate of the junior fellows. Sligger declined to be a candidate and was closely involved in the smooth succession. Lindsay saw himself in the AL Smith tradition of extending Oxford University scholarship to wider audiences and was opposed to élitism.

Tommy returned to Winchester at the end of April. He was collecting birds' eggs for his brother Teddy. This pursuit and church architecture provided a purpose to long bicycle rides into the countryside. His usual companions were Evelyn Shuckburgh, Randall Swingler, and Uvedale Lambert who were also keen on eggs and churches, plus Charles Hollins who was less enthusiastic. Hollins had chosen Tommy as socius under the Winchester system of pairing, because Richard Wood was already matched and Hodgkin was the only other new boy in the house. The fortuitous relationship persisted.

Dorothy and Robin, with Helen, had again booked the Captain's Lodging in Bamburgh Castle for the summer holiday. As the Smith and Hodgkin grandchildren were growing in number and age they were separating into clusters. Tommy was building a close friendship with Diana and Lucy Bosanquet. He was also encouraged to invite Wykehamist friends. David Orr and his family were spending the summer nearby. Teddy and Betty Hodgkin constituted an inseparable foursome with their cousins Mary and Andy Jameson.

Tommy took the train south on 19 September to Winchester for the start of his second year. Charles Hollins remained Tommy's socius but with Uvedale Lambert in quarantine Tommy was temporarily socius with Randall Swingler whom he invited home for a leave out day. The affection and admiration for Randall deepened in the second year to real friendship akin to devotion. Tommy's letters home became less frequent and dogged. He and Randall engaged in a schoolboy prank of writing hoax letters under pen names to the *Daily Graphic*. Two letters were accepted: he wrote as a regular camper out to ask for a cure for midge bites, and as an ardent ornithologist to ask for the identification of a strange bird's egg he professed to have found. The correspondence drew several replies, including a presumably hoax riposte that the egg belonged probably to the Great Auk.

Tommy returned to Oxford on 3 April, his fifteenth birthday, for the Easter holidays. He carried back the prize for being first in his form and a special prize for mathematics. Tommy's housemaster was looking for leadership qualities in him and in an end of term report suggested that he should join the Natural History Society and organise a party of supporters in Sunnyside. Tommy and Randall decided to enter for the English verse prize on the theme 'When the morning stars sang together', taken from the book of Job.

Tommy was resisting the Bobber's encouragement to join the Natural History Society. He was highly cooperative in Sheila Robertson's project for low comedy to be performed at the beginning of July to the Rudmore mothers arriving in charabancs from the Winchester mission in Southampton. Tommy's costume included a crepe hair moustache, mauve tie, saffron socks and brown boots. The Bobber noted in a house report that Tommy and Randall Swingler did a lot to sharpen each other's wits. Meanwhile Tommy had been working on his English verse entry and produced some eighty lines of alternately rhyming couplets of marked religiosity. The competition was open to the whole school and he did not win. Robin and Dorothy were told informally that he came in third.

Tommy returned to Winchester on 18 September for his third year with greater confidence. He was eligible for membership of the school debating society and made a maiden speech on 21 October. He was attending Church of England confirmation classes following his mother's religious background rather than his father's Quaker upbringing and was confirmed on 28 November in Winchester College Chapel by the Bishop of Winchester.

Tommy, returning to school on 20 January 1926, was disappointed that Randall Swingler had not won a promotion to join him in the same form. On Wednesdays Tommy paraded with the Officers' Training Corps 'to build up the British Empire' as he commented wryly in a letter to Dorothy. At the same time he skipped a debate of 27 January on the proposition that one Briton was worth two foreigners. He described this as 'a completely pointless and untrue assertion'. On 2 March, Dorothy's fortieth birthday, Teddy, Betty and the housemaids (Annie Bull and her sister Ethel Bull) were thrilled when a Mr Amiss brought round a wireless for the Hodgkins to try. He left it on loan while they thought about buying one. The borrowed wireless set was shown to Tommy on 6 March when he came home for a leave out day and took his fancy. Mr Amiss came on 20 March and installed the Hodgkins' own first wireless. Dorothy was uncertain of its value but confident that the servants would appreciate it.

At Winchester Tommy was trying to balance the demands of seven cantos of Spenser, mathematics, the Lewis Carroll *Alice* books, romantic verse composition, Shakespeare readings, a junior steeplechase and classics. By late March the Bobber, Sheila Robertson and the house matron thought he was overworked. He was fed on chocolate biscuits and made to sleep on a Saturday afternoon. Robin and Dorothy drove to Winchester for Tommy's end of term on 31 March. They learned from Sheila Robertson that Tommy after missing a repeat of the mathematics prize had won the Gillespie prize for English literature.

In the summer term Randall was now in the same form as Tommy. They began scheming together. They were to write a poetry anthology, have it printed by the school bookseller in an edition of 100, present five copies to each of their respective families, and sell the rest to prominent people for a guinea a time. They expected to gain at least £30 apiece. They would write all the poems under assumed names. Tommy began with a sonnet on the feelings of a jilted man.

Dorothy was dividing her attention between Tommy's letters from Winchester and Britain's General Strike, which began on 3 May. Dorothy followed the changes on the recently installed wireless set, especially when the newspapers could not appear. Tommy was sent to the sanatorium for what he called a non-existent disease – the tinea cruris fungal infection that had occurred in Sunnyside in the previous term. The Bobber called daily to read extracts from the *British Gazette* about the industrial situation.

Dorothy and Gertrude Hartley went to Oxford Town Hall and enrolled as cars with drivers to be called on if needed against the strikers. She told Robin who was annoyed that he had not been consulted. However, Robin on 9 May went off to Hull to take strike-breaking undergraduates to help unload ships at the docks and spent the night away. On 11 May Dorothy heard the unexpected news on the one o'clock broadcast that the General Strike would end that day.

Her thankfulness at the end of the strike was clouded by a letter from Tommy disclosing a dreadful depression he did not know how to fight or bear. She was writing to the Bobber when another parent Mollie Hunt telephoned offering a lift as she and her husband were driving to Winchester for the Ascension Day holiday next day, 13 May. Dorothy accepted joyfully and sent Tommy a telegram to announce her arrival. She reached Sunnyside about noon and took Tommy to lunch, where he began to open up about his depression and misery and fear. To Dorothy he seemed bewildered and frightened and on the brink of tears though able still to joke and talk of mundane things. Tommy was not able to tell Dorothy all his feelings, but essentially it was a compound of over-work and adolescent despair mixed with fears about insanity or suicide (the latter had occurred of another Wykehamist of his year, F.M.L. Tottenham who had died on 2 April early in the Easter vacation). Tommy was spending time weeping alone in the chapel. He was in thrall to the romantic idea of love with an idealised female and held an innocent loving affection for Randall, who combined athletic and academic brilliance.

Tommy's depression recurred in milder form at the end of June, but did not prevent him sitting the School Certificate examinations of the Oxford and Cambridge Schools Examination Board, or coming fourth out of 21 in the end of term placing so that he was assured of promotion to the senior form known as Sixth Book. Meanwhile he had acquired a passport of his own on 16 July and was ready in August to join his family for a summer in France, spent in a rented villa at Etretat in Normandy. The Etretat experience brought confirmation that a summer at Bamburgh was what all members of the family preferred.

At the end of the family vacation Tommy sailed on 17 September to Southampton. He went straight on to Winchester for the start of his fourth year. He wrote home to Dorothy in triumph on 19 September to say that he had passed School Certificate with credits in every subject. This opened the way for university entrance to Oxford or Cambridge. His seniority in Winchester now gave him a variety of privileges: he could keep a hat on indoors, follow a special route through senior door, leave buttons undone to read papers, and sit on a table. The Bobber wrote to Robin on 22 September to confirm Tommy's safe settling. He confirmed with regret that he did not see any prospect for an ordinary vacancy in Sunnyside for Teddy, whose admission would be contingent on his doing well in the scholarship examination and winning a nomination from the headmaster. Robin pressed the point but the Bobber was firm as he had three or four younger brothers unplaced for the following year. Robin was arranging to send Teddy to Eton rather than risk waiting for the June 1927 round of

Winchester scholarship examinations. Teddy was accepted for Eton and went there on 28 April for the Summer Half of 1927. Tommy, who had regretted that Teddy was not to come to Winchester, took on the role of wise counsellor. He wrote from Winchester on 30 April: 'I don't suppose you are quite acclimatised yet, but after about a week or a fortnight you will probably find that term is in its way as jolly as the holidays, at any rate that is my experience.' Teddy was to look out for hearty chaps who could be invited to Bamburgh.

Dorothy was at home, for the first time since mid-1913 with only one child, her daughter Betty who was in the Dragon School sixth form. Dorothy kept company with Betty at her homework or pastimes in the nursery, and was juggling her diary to sustain regular visits to Tommy and Teddy at their respective schools, and visits to Helen in London. Robin was seeking from the Oxford authorities a sabbatical year from October to work in London and on sources in Germany and Denmark for a history of Anglo-Saxon England whose preparation had already occupied many vacations.

Charles Hollins and Tommy were chosen for training in the next school year as potential assistant scout masters after they left school. The School Scout Troop was a new initiative under a Wykehamist don, John Pinsent, and was intended to lay foundations of social usefulness. Tommy saw that it would relieve him of many OTC chores but found it difficult to imagine himself running about in khaki shorts making weird animal noises and roasting buns. Tommy writing to his mother on 24 July reported an encounter with a tramp:

> He was the most Shakespearean Welshman I have ever known, and had wonderful fair hair and a lovely accent. He came to the door and asked for a pair of boots (his toes were showing though his present ones), so I searched in changing room and found an old pair – of Shuckburgh's, I believe, he hasn't discovered it yet though – and gave them him – quite à la Robin Hood. He was frightfully grateful and didn't ask for money, but it struck me when he'd gone I ought to have given him some, so I dashed after him and asked him where he was going. He said he was walking from Monmouthshire to Plymouth to get a job whateffer (a rather round about route!), so I gave him sixpence – I feel that I ought to have given him half-a-crown which was the only alternative, but I remembered the collection today – he then said that he hadn't broken his fast today, and he certainly looked horribly thin; he added that times were hard, with which I fervently agreed …

While Tommy was in camp, Robin, Dorothy, Teddy and Betty drove north in stages to reach the Captain's Lodging in Bamburgh Castle on 30 July, where

Helen again joined the family party. Robin on 31 July wrote to consult a family friend and fellow of Balliol, Cyril Bailey, on the strategy to bring Tommy to Oxford. Bailey advised Robin on 3 August to put Tommy's name down at once with the Master or with Roy Ridley who had taken over admissions from Bailey.

Betty at Bamburgh was complaining of slight pain on 5 September, and returned to bed after breakfast – with just an ordinary tummy-ache. She remained in her bedroom high up in the Castle on the following days, receiving visits from the other members of the holiday party. The Hodgkin family was concerned at Betty's continued pain and agreed with the village doctor on 7 September to call for a second medical opinion. A surgeon arriving from Newcastle at 11 that night diagnosed appendicitis. Betty was to go to Newcastle for an operation next day. Helen's Rolls Royce was waiting at the door when Betty was brought down. Robin sat in front of the car next to Mills the chauffeur and Dorothy squeezed in the back next to a bed of cushions on which Betty lay under a rug.

They reached Newcastle in the early hours and Betty was taken to a room to await a noon operation. She died on 8 September under the anaesthetic. Robin Hodgkin and Nelly Bosanquet made a garden of love-in-the-mist (from the Bosanquet estate at Rock), roses and lilies round Betty's hospital bed where a vigil was kept for a night and a day. The family sent a telegram on 9 September to Lady Elliott in Oxford breaking the news and asking if her daughter, Betty's friend Anne Elliott, could stay on as this helped Teddy. Tommy turned to his panacea of poetry and sketched the beginning of a poem:

There shall be laughter on the hills
Lying deep amid the friendly heather
And all adown the melancholy shore
The wind is hushed – the wind shall sweep no more ...

Robin brought Betty's body back to Bamburgh where she lay in the Castle surrounded by fresh flowers and mourners until the burial. The grave in the Bamburgh churchyard was lined by her young cousins with heather from the moors. Dorothy recorded the funeral date of 11 September as a 'wild and stormy day, with a huge wind that seemed to make even the castle shake, and huge waves thundering on the rocks'. Dorothy withdrew into her grief. Robin sought solace in his historical research. Teddy went sadly back to Eton.

Amid the family crisis Tommy's return for his crucial fifth year at Winchester was delayed for three weeks by an attack of paratyphoid B. Randall wrote from Sunnyside on 1 October to tell Tommy that he had been made librarian of the debating society in his absence. Within a few days Tommy was able to return to Winchester.

Robin and Dorothy went through the Bradmore Road house on 5 and 6 October clearing it to be let during Robin's sabbatical. Dorothy found the hardest task of all was to tidy away Betty's toys and clothes. Robin and Dorothy were going to stay with Helen at 4 Lowndes Square. Robin went ahead early on 7 October to warn Helen of the arrival of 11 boxes of Hodgkin luggage. Dorothy stayed on in Oxford while a house agent came to take an inventory of the furniture to be used by tenants. Dorothy joined Robin in London on 8 October, a date that would have been Betty's twelfth birthday. Cookie (May Fox from Seahouses) was staying on in the Bradmore Road house and Annie Bull too remained in Oxford.

Tommy adapted to his grander status at Winchester. He was, as the Bobber had promised, a prefect along with five others of Tommy's circle: Randall Swingler, Evelyn Shuckburgh, Uvedale Lambert, Charles Hollins and Richard Wood. He had a gallery seat in chapel and was responsible for monitoring the attendance of a row of nine schoolboys, but had the privilege of entering the gallery after the chapel bells had stopped.

Tommy reported new school glories on 23 October. After nearly four years of Sunday readings of Shakespeare in Sunnyside, Tommy was invited to join the school's established Shakespeare Reading and Orpheus Glee United Societies (SROGUS). He was also in the Essay Society where six scholarship holders from College and six non-scholarship commoners could discuss problems of the day. Canon Streeter, a fellow of Queen's like Robin, visited Winchester and discoursed on the problem of pain. Tommy followed this up with a long discussion on the subject with the assistant master and Balliol classicist James Cullen that made him late for lunch.

Tommy was learning about scouting and by the end of October had passed his Tenderfoot test. In Oxford Annie Bull was engaged to be married. Dorothy, Gertrude Hartley and their mother Mrs AL began the search for a house and persuaded Annie to agree on a cottage at the foot of Cumnor Hill, with Robin contributing to the rent. The banns were called for a December wedding. Dorothy went with Helen Sutherland on 9 November to see modern art in London and did not care for the many pictures by Roger Fry (Robin's first cousin, and a prominent Bloomsbury Group member as painter, art historian and critic). She enjoyed the next day spent with Annie Bull in London in a hunt for a wedding dress.

The Bobber was taking a hand in Tommy's future. He gave him particulars of a Balliol War Memorial Scholarship for English literature that would be examined on 13 December. Tommy thought the odds were against winning the scholarship at this attempt but saw it as a trial run for the January round of examinations. He noted that Evelyn Shuckburgh was going away next term on the public school Africa tour for which the required dress was a double-breasted blue suit with brass buttons and yachting cap and commented to his father on 13 November that he would rather stay at school than 'go to Africa on a glorified Sunday School treat'. Robin and Dorothy were inclined to leave the literature scholarship decision to school guidance. Tommy consulted the headmaster of Winchester, the Rev. Dr Alwyn Williams, who immediately supported his entering for the Balliol examination and wrote to the Master of Balliol asking Balliol to overlook a day's lateness in Tommy's application.

The Bobber was concerned about signs of strain that Tommy showed and encouraged him to be careful with early nights and adequate sleep. Dorothy wrote to Tommy on 2 December asking if he had told the Bobber 'no Hodgkin can stand going to bed late, and no Smith can stand getting up early'. Robin and Dorothy had been the previous day to Oxford to Annie Bull's wedding in icy cold weather. Since Cyril Humphries, the bridegroom, was a shop assistant the ceremony had to be on the statutory early closing day, a Thursday in Oxford.

Tommy, preparing for the Oxford examination, was still showing mild symptoms of being an invalid. He was said to be suffering from the rather indeterminate complaint of a cold on the liver. Dorothy was puzzled why this should make Tommy want to sleep so much. Tommy travelled to Oxford on 12 December to his aunt, Gertrude Hartley, for the literature examination for Balliol, and on 16 December to Winchester for the final week of term. The result was due about 19 December. Tommy sat by the fire in the house prefects' room. The weather was so cold that the water in the washing basins froze overnight. When the Balliol results came through Tommy, in what had been perceived as a trial run, came out fourth in the scholarship examination. Harold Hartley gave Dorothy an insider's view from the Balliol fellows. Tommy was regarded as promising, his work 'bright and lively but not solid enough yet'. His average mark in classics was beta and Cyril Bailey said he did some good things, but made a good many mistakes. Although Tommy's entrance to Oxford was assured he was aware of some disappointment in his parents, especially Dorothy, that he had not gained a scholarship. He set himself demanding tasks for his final terms at Winchester.

He was reading for the English Literature Prize offered by Winchester. He decided also to mount a tongue-in-cheek campaign as the Labour candidate in a mock election to be held by the school debating society on 14 March. He formed a committee and founded an ad hoc Winchester College Labour League with badges of red string that some supporters were persuaded to wear in buttonholes. Tommy and friends went to the Winchester shops and bought two yards of red material from which they made one immense red flag and many small ones. They found the words of the 'Red Flag' to sing on election day. Tommy wrote for advice to Ramsay Macdonald, a Labour Prime Minister and leader of the Labour Party – apparently without reply.

Tommy described his election speech to Robin as a mixture of Burke and Pericles and Rupert Brooke and confessed almost on the eve of the mock election: 'I must say that however good Socialism is as a theory in practice it seems awfully weak.' He enjoyed the debating society meeting when he and his supporters sang the 'Red Flag' and made a great deal of disturbance. The result was a win for the Tory candidate with 90 votes; 52 for Tommy for Labour; 13 for the Liberal; ten for the Independent and three for the Communist. Tommy understood that the previous highest score for a Labour candidate was 21.

Tommy's end of term report showed that he had fallen just short of first rank in classics and English. He was second in senior division but a long way ahead of the other pupils, most of whom were scholars in College. He returned to Winchester at the end of April to seek new challenges. He embarked on a thesis on the classical Greek novel that entailed a succession of appeals to Dorothy for obscure texts from the Oxford libraries and bookshops. He decided to enter for a poetry prize as well. On 31 May came publication of the life of AL Smith by Mary Smith, published by John Murray with the modest description 'A biography and some reminiscences by his wife'. Within a week of the AL Smith publication Dorothy's own project of a memorial life of Betty was complete. This was a collection of reminiscences and images privately printed by Basil Blackwell in Oxford. Dorothy began distribution to family, contributors and special friends. Tommy completed his thesis on the Greek novel and took his final examinations at school. The headmaster's valediction commended 'a quick and able brain, plenty of taste and real liveliness of mind', albeit tempered by a tendency to be erratic and to resort to guesswork. As in the previous term Tommy had just missed the highest rank. His thesis on the Greek novel did not win and he had an honourable mention in the Latin speech prize.

Tommy spent August and September with his family at Bamburgh and returned to Oxford on 9 October ready to unpack his possessions for Bradmore Road and to begin his Oxford University career as a Balliol undergraduate. For Tommy Hodgkin (or Thomas as he gradually became known) the move from Winchester to Balliol in October 1928 was a simple transition from one charmed circle to another much the same. His maternal grandfather AL Smith, who had died as Master of Balliol only four and a half years earlier, was fondly remembered. When Thomas walked through the Balliol gate as an undergraduate for the first time he came with numerous Balliol connections plus an introductory network of old Wykehamist friends (some at New College founded, like Winchester, by William of Wykeham). The Hodgkin and Smith family ties spilled into the Oxford University setting.

David Orr, by now in his second year at Balliol was part of Thomas's Winchester, Northumberland and Scotland world. A Wykehamist of an earlier cohort, Bickham Sweet-Escott, was in his second year at Balliol and soon became a new friend of Thomas. Another second year Balliol undergraduate, George Kirkpatrick White, son of the Regius Professor of Divinity in Dublin and educated at Marlborough, became a close friend and confidant.

In the Balliol first year, Lionel Hale, from Charterhouse became a friend, along with his third year older brother James (Jim) Hale, a classical scholar who had befriended a contemporary, Alec Peterson, an exhibitioner from Radley. Another clever Balliol third year man who became a friend of Thomas was Felix Markham, a scholar from Eton. A Balliol freshman from Charterhouse, Richard Usborne, was a friend of Lionel Hale. Charles Hollins was a Balliol contemporary. Randall Swingler was at New College with another close Wykehamist of Thomas's circle, Geoffrey Cross. Evelyn Shuckburgh went up to King's College, Cambridge, but was to be found at the London dances that Thomas attended occasionally.

Thomas's Balliol tutor for classical moderations was Cyril Bailey, a family friend who spent summer vacations in Embleton close to Bamburgh. Helen Sutherland became an adoptive Northumbrian when she gave up her London house in Lowndes Square and leased Rock Hall from the Bosanquets (they lived in Rock Moor, another house on their extensive estate). To retain a foothold in London, Helen took a large flat on the eighth floor in the new Grosvenor House in Mayfair.

Thomas glided easily into the Oxford undergraduate world and appeared to his contemporaries as clever and stylish. He gravitated quickly towards the Oxford University Dramatic Society (OUDS) of which Lionel Hale was becoming a prominent and talented member. Thomas wore at first a commoner's gown after taking his entrance examination at the age of 17 on a trial run. He worked and played hard in his first term and in December 1928 at his own choice sat again for the college's War Memorial Scholarship. He was in Edinburgh visiting the Jameson family when news came that he had this time won a scholarship at Balliol, to his parents' delight and to his own relief. He wrote to them on 18 December: 'Chiefly I am glad because it has pleased you both, and also because it was about time I did something to justify my parentage.' He would in future wear a scholar's gown, as did many of his Oxford friends.

He was reading the classical Greek text of Demosthenes in the vacation and conjuring up an Easter holiday visit to the classical sites of modern Greece with one or more of those Oxford friends. Geoffrey Cross had proposed a journey with Thomas and was collecting practical information on possible routes and the cheapest fares and combinations of train and boat. Thomas was collecting new candidates for the venture, and unilaterally invited Balliol's George White and Bickham Sweet-Escott. Geoffrey would have preferred either a party of two or a third person both knew and liked. Geoffrey wrote to Thomas on 7 January 1929 accepting the plan with good grace: a group of four would be less easy prey to brigands.

When George White was clear of classical moderations and Oxford term had ended Thomas, armed with visas for Greece and Albania, set off with his friends, though the four had become five with the addition of Alec Peterson. They crossed to France (third class) at night on 17 March by Newhaven and Dieppe and arrived in Paris early on 18 March. They carried on that night by train through Switzerland to Italy where they could take the boat from Brindisi to the Athens harbour Piraeus. Thomas thought it quite a feat to have gone from Oxford to Athens entirely third class – good experience of discomfort.

They travelled in Greece mostly in pairs and returned to Athens on 17 April. Geoffrey Cross and George White were travelling back to England in time for the start of Oxford term, Thomas and Bickham had an extension from Balliol and planned a three-day walk in Macedonia. Thomas was hoping for an adventurous return by way of Albania, but told his parents to expect him back in Oxford by 28 April. Bickham and Thomas took the train on 18 April to the northern terminus at Kalambaka. They prepared for an expedition by buying food for their walk: eight large slabs of chocolate and three strings of figs each, and bread plus brandy in case of accidents. On the second day of walking, Thomas developed a fever and Bickham coaxed him to Metsovo and medical advice that fortunately came free from a philanthropic foundation. They were running short of money and time. They put aside thoughts of Albania and made slow progress by mule, bus, and foot to a ferry from Preveza to Corfu, and then by the boat to Brindisi and then making the long train journey to reach Oxford on 2 May.

For August and most of September the Hodgkins had taken the Captain's Lodging at Bamburgh. Lionel Hale joined them on 2 August. Thomas was preparing for moderations. Bickham, concerned with ancient history for Greats in the following year, arrived in mid-August. The style was for the undergraduates to work all morning, to enjoy moorland walks or games on the sandhills in the afternoon, and to work again at least from tea to dinner. By late September, the Bamburgh party was breaking up. Robin and Dorothy drove back to Oxford leaving Thomas as Helen's guest in the new luxury of Rock Hall, before he went on to a few days of lone study at Heather Cottages – with a stock of ginger snaps and raspberry jam. Helen was also entertaining John Buchan and his family. Thomas discussed career prospects with Buchan and wrote teasingly to Teddy on 26 September: 'Will you come to a colony with me to govern Sudan or something?'

Thomas returned to Oxford and into a new set of rooms in Balliol. He had the additional confidence of being a second year man enjoying a wider acquaintanceship than many of his contemporaries with members of women's colleges. Contacts between women and men students were mediated through a set of petty restrictions intended essentially to constrain them by the strictest propriety. Women were often in bed-sitters and could not receive men visitors in a room with a bed. They did their entertaining in college common rooms. Men in colleges would have sets of rooms including a sitting room which two women together would be permitted to visit. It was considered innocent and acceptable for a woman and man to go for open air walks together, and Thomas was fond of such country walks. Helen Sutherland had encouraged him to meet Nicolete Binyon, the youngest daughter of her friends the historian Cicely Powell and poet and historian Laurence Binyon on the staff of the British Museum. She invited Nicolete to Rock Hall in the summer of 1929 before Nicolete went up to Lady Margaret Hall (LMH). Visits to the Bosanquet cousins in Somerville and from them to Thomas's rooms brought the easy manners of Bamburgh into Balliol.

Nicolete came to LMH from St Paul's Girls School where she had a group of girls a year junior to her whom she would take to museums and art galleries. Several of her Paulina school friends came up to Oxford with her or followed on, and several were at Somerville with the Bosanquets. Thomas's Wykehamist and Balliol circle became interlinked with the Paulina circle and rippled out to the sisters and cousins of these young women friends. A Somerville fresher and Paulina with whom Thomas became friendly in October was Sheila Lynd, whose writer parents, essayist Robert and poet Sylvia Lynd, favoured an Irish spelling of her name as Sigle. The Lynds were living at 5 Keats Grove in Hampstead, then regarded as rather remote from fashionable London. Robert Lynd was an Ulsterman by his birth in Belfast on 20 April 1879 but he identified with the Irish nationalist cause. He had found his way to London by 1901 and become a freelance journalist. In 1904, he met Sylvia Dryhurst at a meeting near Oxford Street of the Gaelic League. They were also Hampstead neighbours. Robert was in lodgings at 9 Gayton Road. Sylvia was living at 11 Downshire Hill with her parents: Roy Dryhurst, administrative secretary of the British Museum, and his Dubliner wife, Nannie Florence Robinson. For four years the Dryhursts opposed a marriage.

Robert took regular employment in 1908 as an assistant to the literary editor of the Quaker and Liberal *Daily News*. On the strength of this new status and Sylvia's early ventures as a literary reviewer, opposition to their wedding ended.

They married at the Hampstead register office on 21 April 1909, and moved soon after to a house at 14 Downshire Hill, close to the Dryhurst home. Sheila (Sigle), their first child, was born on 28 February 1910, and at home was nicknamed 'Baby' by Sylvia. Their second child, another daughter Moira (or Maire in the preferred Irish form) was born on 2 March 1912. With Sigle only two and still known as 'Baby', Sylvia nicknamed the second daughter 'Baby Junior', and that became abbreviated to 'BJ'.

Robert Lynd became literary editor of the *Daily News* in 1913 and from that year had an additional following for his regular essays in the *New Statesman*, latterly under the pen-name YY (conjectured by some to stand for 'too wise'). The Lynd family left London during the First World War and came back to Hampstead in 1924 to 5 Keats Grove, previously occupied by older Dryhurst relatives. The Binyons and Lynds shared British Museum and literary connections and were friends. Nicolete Binyon, whose home in the 1920s was in the British Museum, was friends with Sigle and Maire Lynd at St Paul's.

Thomas held a tea party in Balliol on 16 October for his Somerville cousins and invited Sigle Lynd and several of his Balliol friends. They in turn were a pool of potential dancing partners for the Somerville hops each term. Thomas writing to his grandmother Lucy Hodgkin in November noted: 'It is being a jolly term on the whole and the presence of the Bosanquets at Somerville does add a lot to happiness. With home and them term is prevented from becoming too termy.'

Nicolete early in December tentatively asked Thomas if he would join her for a dance in London on 19 December and Thomas accepted. She described the event at 59 Finchley Road, NW8, as the 'Lynds' dance'. The dance was not grand but fitted a comfortably upper-middle-class ambience. Thomas, thought to be a little enamoured of Sigle, danced also with her younger sister, BJ, and drew on his spring visit to Greece to talk of the differences of pronunciation between ancient and modern Greek. Thomas confided to George White that the notion of a proposal to Sigle had crossed his mind. Thomas in full bachelorhood went to Northumberland to visit Helen Sutherland. George White, pleased that Thomas had not made any marriage proposal, wrote on 29 December that charming, beautiful, attractive and altogether delightful as Sigle was, he hoped he might be allowed to say that she was not as beautiful as her sister. Sigle's twentieth birthday on 28 February was marked with a birthday ode from Thomas. She was keeping a guinea pig dubbed 'Hodgkin', living loose about her Somerville room, eating twice his volume in lettuce a day and showing a taste for the icing sugar on sponge cake.

Thomas joined other candidates in classical moderations and was expected by his tutors and friends to do well. It would be a culmination of his years of training at Winchester and the gateway to studies of Greek and Latin philosophy and history in the original tongues for Greats. The moderations results came out at the Examination Schools in Oxford on 14 April and were published in *The Times* of 15 April. Thomas, for whom a first was expected, took a second. He received letters of commiseration and condolence rather than congratulation, including from Lionel Hale (whose third was even less befitting a Balliol Scholar) and Sigle Lynd (who had failed the physics part of her own preliminary examination in Natural Science and would have to take it again.).

In the Trinity term after moderations Thomas pursued travel plans for the summer and refused invitations to commemoration balls in Oxford in June and to the Eton and Harrow ball in London in July. Sigle was trying to make up a party for one of the Oxford commems. Thomas in turning down Sigle's invitation to Christ Church encouraged her to invite Peter Howard as a substitute. Peter Dunsmore Howard was a famously handsome Oxford figure, a physically imposing sportsman with an aesthetic side to his character. He had been at Mill Hill School and came up as an exhibitioner to Wadham College in October 1928. He became a Rugby Blue in the Oxford team that beat Cambridge on 10 December 1929. The sporting prowess was particularly significant to Peter and to his schoolmaster father, Ebenezer Howard, for Peter had been born in Maidenhead on 20 December 1908 with a seriously defective left leg whose corrective treatment lasted through his childhood. He exhibited a strong drive to overcome physical handicap and this made him in some eyes unusually, albeit understandably, self-centred. After Howard accepted the Christ Church invitation, Sigle commented to Thomas: 'He is gloriously handsome and Rugby Internationals certainly add a certain cachet … But I'm afraid he lacks your pretty wit – and sure he lacks your brio in the polka.'

Thomas's preoccupation was to make the Albania adventure that had proved impracticable on the expedition to Greece at Easter 1929. He wanted another try with Bickham Sweet-Escott. Bickham had taken his finals in Greats that summer term but was not due for a viva until late July. Bickham had agreed with his cousin Doris Bulstrode that she should come as well, though Thomas's plan for a fourth person had fallen through. Three-month visas for Albania and Yugoslavia were stamped into Thomas's passport on 17 June.

All this while Sigle was drawing closer to the Hodgkin family circle. She invited Thomas's mother to tea in Somerville and Dorothy formally confirmed Thomas's informal invitation to Sigle to come to Bamburgh during the Hodgkins' summer stay. Sigle wrote on 18 June that she was spending much of the summer in France and she could accept only for the last half of September if Sylvia Lynd (Mammy) had not made other plans for her.

Thomas left Oxford to join Bickham and Doris, and on 20 June retraced the 1929 route to Italy. This time they were heading for Bari to take a boat to the Albanian port of Durazzo (as the starting point for a three-day walk across Albania and into Yugoslavia). They paused in Florence and Rome. They were not a well-matched trio. Thomas found Bickham charming as usual but was not sure whether to be angered or amused at Doris who was seeing Italy for the first time. She cried out in Florence for a little Sports Morris. She was lost in Rome's Coliseum and had to be rescued by Italian soldiers.

In Oxford Peter Howard took Thomas's offered place at the Christ Church commem on 23 June. Sigle and BJ were among some six hundred revellers. Howard danced much of the evening with BJ, to her delight at such attention from a Rugby International (capped early that year for England against Wales). Sigle warned BJ of Peter Howard's reputation as a frightful flirt. BJ, in her last days as a Paulina, wrote to her close school friend, Diana Hubback, that it was fun and that she was not going to allow her heart to be broken again yet awhile.

Thomas with Bickham and Doris crossed the Adriatic from Bari on 24 June and landed at Durazzo. The British consul reassured the visitors that Albania was the safest country for Englishmen there was. An Albanian whom they met on the boat from Bari had earlier warned of troublesome dogs. Bickham, Doris and Thomas, following the route of an old Roman road close to the river Skumbi, began their walk towards Lake Ochrida. The walking through Albania's hot sand was exhausting. Bickham secured a mule and muleteer to carry their bags and rucksacks to the frontier with Yugoslavia. Thomas was more prone to thirst than Bickham and much more afflicted than Bickham or Doris by terrible bites, especially from bed bugs at Elbasan – they caused great, itchy pink lumps over him.

The three travellers slept out on 27 June, breakfasted on coffee and black cherries and arrived at the frontier posts of Albania and Yugoslavia on 28 June. They submitted their passports to the various controls and formalities. As they waited, a small dog suddenly ran up behind Thomas and bit him on the calf. Doris bandaged Thomas's bloody wound. This troublesome dog was on the Serbian side. The Yugoslav officials were apologetic that such a thing should have happened and they shot the dog (Thomas declined their kind offer to let him shoot the beast).

A great scramble followed to secure treatment for Thomas against possible rabies. Thomas was more perturbed by the bugs in the Yugoslav town of Struga, more varied and numerous than those of Elbasan. The doctor in Struga had no Pasteur vaccine; they must go to Salonika. Salonika had no vaccine; they must go to Athens. In Athens Thomas was advised to take the train to Paris where there were specialists in handling the rabies vaccine. The train journey would take nearly three days. Thomas seized the opportunity to return, less from fear of the dog bite than from discomfort at the bed bugs and secretly from doubts about Bickham's cousin (courtesy prevented him disclosing the latter anxiety). Bickham and Doris continued their journey through the Levant as intended and Thomas took the train through Yugoslavia and Switzerland and into France on 5 July – and to Victoria next day.

Commiseration on the news of Thomas and the dog bite flowed in rather as it had after his second in moderations. Sigle's letter of 22 July invited him to lunch at Keats Grove on 28 July if he were taking an afternoon train from London (Thomas was to join up at Peterborough with the Hodgkin family migration to Northumberland). Thomas went up to London and to 5 Keats Grove to take up Sigle's invitation to lunch. He was welcomed by Sylvia Lynd, and shortly afterwards BJ arrived home. Sigle was absent and no explanation was offered. After lunch BJ and Thomas went to Selfridges to buy mackintoshes. Thomas chose a duplicate for an orange-brown coat that Dorothy had given him. He wanted to conceal from her that this was lost. BJ chose a white Mac, almost an umpire's coat. They called them the sun and the moon in the beginnings of a shared private language. Thomas missed his train.

Sigle returned late that evening and was indignant to discover that her sister and mother had each assumed that the other had explained her own absence. She wrote to Thomas that she did not generally ask people to lunch and then go away. She had been delayed in Bexhill for repairs to a damaged car. BJ had returned by train on the previous night because of school and could be in time to receive Thomas. Sigle and her sister were going off to France within a couple of days to spend the summer mainly at La Croix in the Var. Sigle had also felt obliged to turn down Dorothy's invitation to Bamburgh for September as Sylvia had made other plans and arranged special coaching for another attempt at the physics prelim.

Thomas responded with a suggestion that Sigle come to Bamburgh in the spring or summer of the next year and that BJ join this year's party for a week in September. BJ sent a willing but diffident acceptance on 9 August, with the reminder: 'I'm not at all a good understudy for Sigle, being quite different from her, and unable to talk a lot and make jokes and, above all, act.' Thomas expanded the original one-week invitation to suggest that BJ stay longer, for a fortnight – 'as long as you possibly can'. BJ spent the first week of September at Valmondois close to Paris. She could give only vague indications to Thomas of her arrival at Bamburgh. Her parents were anxious about her making a long train journey alone and would take her by car and drop her on their way to Scotland. She should be expected on the night of 11 or 12 September.

The uncertainty was partly because the Lynds in an unfamiliar car would be driving slowly with an overnight stop at Peterborough (and BJ did not disclose that Robert Lynd, with a passion for sport, would ensure that the family took in the St Leger at Doncaster on the way). BJ arrived at Bamburgh late on the afternoon of 10 September, a day earlier than expected. The younger members of the family circle were playing hide-and-seek in the treetops. Mary Jameson, a spirited 16-year-old to BJ's demure 18, had just fallen out of a tree and was looking mildly shaken. As a room was prepared, another guest, a recent Balliol graduate Brian MacKenna, took BJ aside for a short walk to tell her about the family and why Thomas's mother wore black – still in mourning for Betty's death three years earlier in the operation for appendicitis.

BJ's room was high up beside the entrance to the Tower. She joined a beguiling regime. Family prayers in the morning were followed by individual study (BJ was reading Homer), a communal lunch in the dining room, then more study or a neighbourhood expedition before tea. There might be some exercise before dinner and the meal would be followed by readings aloud or literary games. Permutations of these pursuits filled the days and in the evenings BJ would gaze at glorious sunsets. She found Bamburgh a place of extraordinary happiness and delight.

Thomas was greatly drawn to her, as George White suspected. George wrote from Dublin on 16 September teasing Thomas about the law permitting someone to marry a deceased wife's sister: 'It is running things a bit fine to marry her before your wife is deceased or even before she is your wife.' Geoffrey Cross was among the Bamburgh guests. Alec Peterson, in London job hunting, met Sigle, cramming for physics and a little envious of BJ in Bamburgh.

The literary evenings continued at Bamburgh. On 21 September, the last night of BJ's and Mary's stay, each was to choose a poem to read. BJ was handed an anthology of modern verse. She could not immediately see something she wanted. She pretended to read but in fact recited lines from James Elroy Flecker's 'Stillness' ending 'And only know I should drown if you laid not your hand on me'. Thomas perceived she was reciting rather than reading. He was enchanted. They agreed to meet in the Tower to look at the night stars. BJ went up several times, but Thomas failed to appear. Then Dorothy came and asked if BJ needed help with her packing. BJ retreated to her room and gazed out of the window, and did not know that Thomas was gazing at her and shy of tapping on her window or at her door. Thomas confided in a letter to George that he had intended that night to propose marriage to BJ. George in response categorised Sigle 'as the perfect wife for you, BJ good but not so good'. Sigle, he argued, belonged to a 'lively, bouncing, energetic, humorous and witty side' of Thomas, and BJ to the 'sensibility-romance' side.

Sigle went to Oxford to retake her physics prelim, was ploughed again and she packed for a definitive departure from the university. She informed Lucy Bosanquet and Thomas that but for missing them she would not mind two hoots about abandoning Oxford for good. She would go to Paris almost at once to learn more of the French language and to waltz on skates until Christmas.

Lionel returning to Balliol a few days before term (and to take up the editorship of *Isis*) reported a possible hitch over the lodgings he was preparing to take with Thomas and with George White. The fourth sharer, Peter Howard, had apparently fallen out with his father and might not be coming up at all in the new term. Lionel wondered whether they would have his reflected glory at 33 Beaumont Street. The lodgings conveniently close to Balliol were spacious and despite Lionel's foreboding Peter Howard did return to Oxford, to the tiny staff of *Isis* and a place in the digs. The large airy rooms included two sitting rooms and two or three bedrooms to spare.

BJ had also come into lodgings in Oxford. She joined the university as a home student and on arrival boarded at 11 Rawlinson Road in North Oxford. In loco parentis to her were Oxford's Wykeham Professor of Logic, H.H. Joachim, and his wife Elisabeth. The professor was a former Balliol man with a son at Balliol a year junior to Thomas. BJ found the 62-year-old professor charming, but completely shut off behind his spectacles and his quiet, educated voice. Mrs Joachim was kind but had a disconcerting facial twitch. BJ reported these details in a letter of acceptance to Thomas's invitation for a walk on the first Saturday of term. She hoped for a long walk but had to find time to meet an aunt and uncle who were visiting their young son as a new entrant to the Dragon School.

Thomas and BJ made frequent walks, mostly by Ferry Hinksey up to the wood on Boar's Hill or to Cumnor. As Peter Howard was in digs with Thomas, BJ could scarcely avoid meeting him again. The three shared an unsuccessful lunch on 21 October. BJ thought Howard's appearance still adorable, but confided in a letter to Diana Hubback: 'My sadness at the discovery that I'm no longer in love with Peter made me silent.'

Mrs Joachim gave BJ a motherly warning that Thomas was the kind of young man who must always have a girl to worship. He and BJ were meeting and writing each day, although some other pursuits were maintained: for BJ the Bach Choir rehearsals; for Thomas a presentation to the Balliol Society and his continuing interest in undergraduate theatre. The OUDS chose Thomas's 'Which Side Woodness' as one of their one act plays alongside Lionel Hale's 'Old Friends' and other submissions by Balliol men. BJ agonised over her emotions: on 26 October all the clouds had silver edges; on 27 October she thought her behaviour cold because of the beastliness of the day.

During a Saturday afternoon walk up Cumnor Hill on 1 November the doubts seemed resolved. Thomas and BJ had reached the top and were gazing out at the sunset, with BJ seated and Thomas leaning against a cedar tree. Thomas said: 'I love you so much and I can't bear to think of my life without you. Will you marry me?' BJ was bewildered and shy and inconsequentially replied that she had heard that morning of the death on 30 October of her grandmother, Nannie Dryhurst. Then she accepted a secret engagement to Thomas, without a kiss to seal the pact. At tea together next day, in the Beaumont Street digs, Thomas asked if he might kiss BJ and she chastely offered him her cheek.

Thomas wrote to Sigle in Paris with news of the attachment to BJ. Sigle responded on 11 November with pleasure, qualified by the blackest of curses on them both if they became openly engaged, especially as an open engagement of young people who could not marry for years would upset both sets of parents. BJ was keen to break the news to her parents; Sigle remained adamant that she should not: 'You're more likely to see Tommy in the vac. if you don't tell them than if you do.' The secret of BJ's engagement to Thomas was broken to the Lynd parents – coming as less of a shock to Sylvia Lynd than Sigle had expected – and to the Hodgkin parents. Dorothy Hodgkin was reacting with caution, and wrote on 2 December to Sylvia Lynd suggesting that opposition, or even interference, would be a mistake at present, although some demands or prohibitions as to behaviour were advisable and necessary. She hoped nothing would be regarded as settled for at least a year.

The end of term on 6 December brought a partial separation although the almost daily exchange continued of love letters, filling all crannies of the page and often spilling over to the backs of envelopes. Thomas and BJ were together for a theatre visit in London on 8 December. They were apart on 9 December when Dorothy Hodgkin and Teddy joined Thomas at Twickenham for the Varsity rugby match – tickets given by Peter Howard, who was one of the Oxford team's forwards in the drawn game. Thomas bought violets in the hope of finding BJ who was somewhere else at the ground – and was teased by a boy offering to sell him a cushion for his flowers. They met again in London the following weekend, and on 14 December Thomas and BJ had lunch with Bickham Sweet-Escott. Thomas reported to his mother the pleasurable lunch with BJ followed by a dinner party and dance – 'returning to Hampstead at twelve for the fag end of an offensively literary party – Priestley and Humbert Wolfe playing charade games worse than we but with more applause'.

In the New Year of 1931 the Hodgkin family circle was taking to BJ, despite Lynd misgivings. Thomas's paternal grandmother persuaded Sylvia Lynd to permit BJ a visit to Treworgan in the coming Easter vacation. Thomas travelled with BJ to Cornwall on 20 March. At the additional family inspection – by Lucy

Hodgkin of Treworgan, and Violet with her husband, John Holdsworth, from nearby Bareppa House – BJ more than passed muster. Thomas described to his mother how Violet paraded each of the young couple on an arm, with 'Uncle John and Granny holding on too'. Violet further signalled approval by presenting an inscribed copy of her book *Quaker Saints* to BJ. Late on 2 April Thomas poured out in a letter to BJ their shared feeling for love and poetry, and as he wrote heard the striking of midnight that ushered in his twenty-first birthday – 3 April 1931. Thomas came in to family money that would he thought give him an income of £300 a year – 'surely enough for us to be married on', Thomas wrote to BJ.

Dorothy and Robin with Thomas and Teddy began a family holiday at the Bell Inn, at Brook near Lyndhurst to go riding in the New Forest, and within a few days BJ arrived, though feeling a little constrained. She almost welcomed the drama of a terrific forest fire on 14 April that spread before the wind for over a mile, and lasted for two hours of sunset. The entire group helped by beating out the flames and they ended with black smudges on red faces.

On Sunday 24 May BJ went to tea with Gilbert Murray, Regius Professor of Greek at Oxford and translator of classical Greek drama, who gave her azaleas out of his garden, and in the evening she joined an expedition to the Rose Revived Inn, near Witney. Two carloads included Thomas, Sigle Lynd, Diana Bosanquet and Lucy Bosanquet, Mary Fisher – daughter of the Warden of New College H.A.L. Fisher, who had a distinguished career in politics, and his wife Lettice Ilbert – George White, Peter Howard and a sporting friend of Peter's, John Williams. They went punting before supper, with Peter punting well and Thomas clumsily so that his punt floated broadside downstream. BJ found the supper a meal of rather forced gaiety. Peter Howard's attentiveness to her during the weekend was stirring the past.

Thomas and BJ were to meet on 26 May – the Tuesday of the Eights Week rowing events – as part of a busy day, which BJ wanted to divide between the river – and possibly cricket in the Parks – and her lagging academic work. After lunch she went to her first appointment, to meet an undergraduate Oliver Woods on the New College barge. She was due next on the Magdalen College barge with her moral tutor, Dorothy Lane Poole, from the Oxford Society of Home Students. Thomas was asked (in a note on the envelope to her letter of that morning) to come to the Magdalen barge at half-past five, so that they should then go on to Balliol's barge.

When Thomas and BJ did eventually go to the Balliol barge Peter Howard was standing at the stern. He took BJ's hand; she felt an electric shock, and against her will found herself falling in love again with Peter. In her uncertainty she thought that Peter was making her love him (perhaps so that Robert

Lynd would give him a job on the *Daily News*; perhaps as an exercise in sheer power).

A flurry of ambiguous messages and meetings ensued until the weekend when BJ wrote her farewell to the engagement: 'Thomas I'm very sorry, but I do believe that I can't love you any more and our engagement must end. You know that I can't tell you this to your face because I'm too fond of you and so much hate to see you miserable.' She asked that they not meet for some time, and hoped the autumn might make them friends as they had been at the very beginning. She added: 'All this term I have really been in doubt – with only splendid intervals of perfect happiness.' She also wrote to her family in Hampstead with news of her change of heart.

For Thomas the disclosure came with the force of bereavement. Condolences and encouragement came from the close friends to whom Thomas turned for comfort and from BJ's relatives. Thomas's grief persisted and, in reply to a consoling letter from Nicolete Binyon, he wrote on 13 June: 'It is more strange and unbearable than anything to lose the centre of your life and yet feel it still there, if only you could reach it. But I believe that what began in such glory and has had such a lovely course for seven months must somehow have a lovely ending too – I don't know how or what sort – But I have faith that loveliness will come of it.' He wanted his friends to comfort BJ in any way they could.

Thomas wanted also to comfort BJ. They met briefly, but unsatisfactorily, in the closing days of full term. Thomas wrote to BJ on 20 June that there had been far too much for them to pass easily into friendship. He suggested that after a year they might be far enough from the 'horribleness' to be able to begin a true friendship: 'And if there seems no happiness possible then we'll wait apart till there is. But I am sure that in the end there will be some sort of loveliness for us.'

It was the season of dancing: Thomas quit the city for London and to embark on a month's walking in Europe with Geoffrey Cross as his travelling companion. BJ was in Oxford: at the Hertford College commem on 22 June and dancing with New College scholar Goronwy Rees who was unsuccessfully wooing her, then at the Balliol floor polisher on 23 June in a party with Peter Howard and John Williams. The evening began badly with a dinner when Peter showed jealousy to BJ over Douglas Jay – a fellow of All Souls, economic journalist and her father confessor of the time – and later refused to dance with her, so that John Williams had to escort her throughout the evening.

BJ attended the Oxford and Cambridge cricket match in London, but principally was absorbed with Peter Howard. They lunched in Soho and in a taxi on the way back Peter proposed to BJ and she accepted what they agreed should be a fairly casual engagement. On 8 July the night of Oxford's victory against

Cambridge they attended the Vincent's Club ball at the May Fair Hotel. Peter Howard kissed a shy, silent, inexperienced BJ for the first time, and teased her that Thomas had not taught her to kiss better.

In the wake of that casual engagement, BJ wrote to Howard three times; his communications to BJ were one note, one telephone call and one telegram. Peter made an assignation to meet her on 14 July outside the Regal Cinema at Marble Arch. BJ stood there alone for half an hour and Peter did not show up. Howard, unable to persuade his family to pay his Oxford debts, had left the university and was collecting jobs that would allow him to clear the backlog. The Howard family wanted Peter to read for the bar. In the short term he was alerted by Lord David Cecil to the need of a young baronet, Sir John Dyer, for cramming for the Oxford entrance examinations. On offer: £5 a week and all expenses to take the candidate, in poor health, to Switzerland for six months of coaching.

Howard as tutor, his pupil and the pupil's grandmother and sister, settled into the Kulm Hotel, St Moritz. Peter entered for the summer tennis tournament, as did some of the tennis champions in France. They could practise on the hard courts beside the hotel. Peter Howard on the hotel balcony teaching the young Dyer looked down and saw a girl playing tennis on the hard court below. He fell in love with her and three days after they met, he proposed to her: three seconds later she had refused him. She was Doris (Doe) Metaxa, French born of Greek parentage and at the age of 22 a junior tennis champion of France. The brief loving notes Peter Howard sent from Switzerland to BJ dried up to nothing.

Thomas in the company of Geoffrey Cross sought distraction in a tour of Italian cities until Geoffrey returned to England on 16 July 1931. Thomas, with guidebook and compass and a volume of Hume, went on to Padua – for the Giottos – to Florence – for the Botticellis – and then to spend a week at a Sligger reading party at the Chalet des Melezes, Saint Gervais – a tradition Sligger had inaugurated four decades earlier but now coming to a close, since he was in poor health. Dorothy and Robin in Oxford tried to sneak a look at Thomas's prospective new lodgings at 15 Oriel Street, to be shared with Geoffrey Cross, but failed to gain admittance as the landlord, A.I. Earl, was out. George White breezed into Oxford to take his degree on 15 October prior to leaving at what he called the screech of dawn on 17 October to take up a school teaching post at Trinity College, Kandy, in Ceylon. Thomas took up boxing – boasting of a jab to the heart to perplex his opponents, and taking hard knocks. He played soccer in mistake for rugger on 27 October, finding soccer a game where a player who was not good was abandoned by fellow players. He abandoned soccer and on 10 November returned to hockey, playing in the Balliol first team.

Thomas had a new Balliol confidant, a second-year Jewish undergraduate Derek Kahn who had come up from Rugby as a classical scholar and through a Paulina cousin Phyllis Kahn had come into touch with Nicolete Binyon, and with BJ. She was living in her second year with the Fishers in the Warden's Lodgings at New College, but she and Thomas were not meeting. Thomas was in the early stages of job-hunting and wavering between colonial service and archaeology. He was inclined to the latter with thoughts of going to Palestine or some part of the Near East where he could build on his embryonic interest in the Arabic language and explore crusader castles for a research project he had in mind. He was quizzed by his tutor, Duncan Macgregor, about the relative merits of a short-term spell on a Palestine archaeological dig and a permanent appointment in another field of employment.

Macgregor wrote on 23 March that if Thomas were thinking seriously of Palestine he should write to the archaeologist and classical scholar John Myres during the vacation, and could find out about prospects in Cyprus from James Cullen. Thomas duly wrote to Myres in April about going to Palestine or some part of the Near East. (Myres, a Wykehamist and now the Wykeham Professor of Ancient History, was a friend of the recently retired director of education in Sudan, John Crowfoot, who in 1927 had become director of the British School of Archaeology in Jerusalem. Cullen was director of education in Cyprus and Thomas had known him as a master at Winchester.) Thomas collected testimonials to support his job hunt. Cyril Bailey, from his temporary stay at the University of California, supplied one for a possible appointment in the colonial service. A former Balliol classics tutor, J.A. Smith (the godfather who had provided Thomas's silver christening mug in 1910), now a fellow of Magdalen, agreed on 26 May to be another referee for Thomas's application to the Colonial Office.

When Thomas's finals began on 2 June, he wore subfusc (the dark formal attire required for Oxford examinations) but characteristically with borrowed plumes, including boots, gown and tie from a young classics tutor from Balliol Colin Hardie. The boots and gown were to be returned, but for the tie Colin urged that he 'keep it for keeps and wear it for visits to Excellencies or Herren Sanitatsrate, instead of your book-strap or old braces or even bootlaces...'

Thomas was aware that in June 1931 he had written to BJ that after a year of absence from each other they might be far enough from the 'horribleness' to be able to begin a true friendship. With the year almost up he wrote to BJ at the Warden's Lodgings in New College to invite her for a walk as short as she liked when his schools would be over and before he went away from Oxford. They walked briefly among buttercups, and later Thomas gave her some of the poems of Gerard Manley Hopkins.

Thomas had a job interview for the BBC then went from Oxford to join his brother Teddy as travelling companion for strenuous walking and climbing in Thomas's familiar haunts – Germany, Austria and Yugoslavia in particular – in the weeks before Thomas was due to take his viva. The Colonial Office wrote offering Thomas an interview for 22 June and Dorothy replied that Thomas would be abroad and would want to attend at a later date.

Thomas and Teddy travelled through Bosnia in a fourth-class railway carriage and by 26 June were in Ragusa. In Venice, they joined up with Hugh Elliott, a childhood friend of Teddy's, and soon went on to stay with Derek Kahn at La Casina, Sori, a villa near Genoa. Copious dinners at La Casina were followed by discussion and poetry. Although the news might have gone unnoticed at La Casina, Peter Howard and the tennis star Doe Metaxa announced their engagement on 9 July, a year and a day after Howard's casual engagement to BJ (and after discreet inquiries about Howard's character to Mill Hill School by the prospective mother-in-law, Mrs Metaxa, had proved satisfactory).

Thomas returned to Oxford for his viva on 21 July, and in the brooding time before the results attended a Colonial Office interview in London. He thought it went badly and he was rather baffled by his interlocutor. The interviewer seemed certain that there would be no possibility for a Near East post that year or even the next: 'The only things he offered were 20 African vacancies and a possible Hong-Kong one among 500 applicants.' The interviewer disclosed close knowledge of Thomas's family. Thomas wrote from Helen Sutherland's Rock Hall to his mother to ask who the interviewer was. He did not know that Ralph Dolignon Furse, since 1931 the Colonial Service's director of recruitment, had married Celia Newbolt, a daughter of the poet Henry Newbolt, in 1914. Newbolt had been on one of his regular holidays close to Barmoor at the time of Robin's swift courtship of Dorothy in August 1908 – and Furse had been there. Celia Furse before her marriage had been a bridesmaid at the Hodgkin wedding.

The examination results for Greats were posted in the Examination Schools in Oxford on 30 July. The news flashed through Thomas's Oxford and family network that Thomas was among the firsts. The newspaper publication of the list on 1 August provoked a broad stream of congratulations, including from BJ and from the Archbishop of York William Temple, who as a Rugby pupil had shared a study with Thomas's maternal uncle Lionel Smith. BJ hoped she would see Thomas before he went to Palestine as he intended. Thomas from the Captain's Lodging at Bamburgh wrote to BJ that the Palestine project seemed uncertain: 'The Colonial Office thinks that Tropical Africa is the healthiest and jolliest place for young men. But it doubts if I am worthy of it.' Thomas in the wake of the Colonial Office interview with Furse was called for further interview and was offered one of the African vacancies – in the Gold Coast administration at £450 a year. Thomas's friends and Balliol mentors were almost universally opposed. Cyril Bailey and Colin Hardie thought he would be throwing himself away. Sligger on 11 September wrote from Lynton: 'I hear you are preparing to go off to the Gold Coast. Why, Oh Why? Have you really taken serious advice on the subject? Heaven forbid that I should not respect your judgment in so important a matter, but I cannot help feeling that you could find better things to do.' Thomas consulted Alec Peterson and Alec sent him Saki's 1912 cautionary novel *The Unbearable Bassington* about Comus Bassington, the boy who went away to the oubliette of West Africa and never came back.

Thomas decided to turn down the Gold Coast job, even before Sligger's letter had been sent, and he wrote to Furse accordingly. Furse was understanding. Thomas explained his thinking in a letter of 13 September from the Captain's Lodging in Bamburgh Castle to Sligger:

> It was beautiful of you to write to dissuade me from Africa. I am dissuaded. Three days ago I wrote to them a humble letter giving it up. … I had really slipped into it rather than chosen it – meaning to go to Palestine as you know – but when they fixed me with their honest blue eyes, and said how magnificent Africa was I was led away by them and agreed. I had to make up my mind in a minute whether to stand for Africa or no – so like an ass I said I would … I am certain that it would be impossible to give up friends and sociabilities unless one could continue learning, and forming relationships in that way – and one couldn't do that in The Gold Coast – a country with no past and no history – and no present either – only perhaps a promising future – and that at a Kindergarten level. So now I shall try to find Archaeological work for the time being – if they will have me as a learner – at Ithaca and then Jericho: that would take me where I want to be – and it will at any rate be an interesting beginning.

Thomas was tenuously writing a novel, studying for the All Souls fellowship examination in October 1932 and probing for openings in archaeology. Liverpool University's Professor John Garstang, a former director of the British School of Archaeology in Jerusalem, was leading an archaeological expedition in Jericho over several years and Thomas offered himself as a volunteer for the next season. Thomas entered for the All Souls fellowship examination and the John Locke Scholarship in Mental Philosophy. He was not chosen for All Souls, and it seemed a near miss (although the three who were chosen – the Wykehamists Richard Wilberforce and Patrick Reilly and Isaiah Berlin from St Paul's – were strong competition). Thomas's Balliol friend, Denis Rickett, already an All Souls fellow of three years' standing, wrote on 3 November that Thomas was 'very seriously considered for election and that everybody agreed in hoping that you would stand again next year'.

BJ was still a student and living with the Fishers. Thomas and BJ went for a country walk as he prepared to leave England amid a flurry of farewell activities. The OUDS was presenting a three-night run of one-act plays including Thomas's comic satire 'Old Boys' Dinner'. Among his dinner guests at the OUDS for the opening night of 17 November was the New College don, Christopher Cox, who had agreed to write to Magdalen in support of Thomas's research plans and a belated application for a senior demyship – Magdalen terminology for a graduate scholarship that was halfway to a fellowship. BJ was in the theatre audience, and sought guidance from a reluctant Derek Kahn about her reviving interest in Thomas. For the second night of the play Thomas went with his parents and before the third night he was travelling across Europe on cheap tickets.

Chapter 2
Palestine, philosophy, politics and partnership: 1932-1937

Thomas with his Magdalen award went first to Nicosia in Cyprus, to visit his former teacher James Cullen, a Balliol contemporary of Christopher Cox, who had travelled with Cox on archaeological expeditions in Anatolia in 1918 and 1925. He caught up on Oxford news. The John Locke Scholarship had gone to a scholar of Corpus Christi College, Winston H.F. Barnes, who had a double first in moderations and Greats in the same years that Thomas faced the examiners. Lionel Hale wrote that Robert Lynd (BJ's father) was offering him a job as assistant literary editor on the Liberal-inclined daily *News Chronicle* and he would be taking this. Thomas wrote to give notice of his impending arrival in Palestine to Christopher Eastwood, an old Etonian from Trinity College, Oxford, whom Thomas had met at the Binyons. Eastwood was now serving as private secretary to the High Commissioner for Palestine, Lieutenant-General Sir Arthur Wauchope, who governed under the mandate of the League of Nations awarded to Britain in the 1920s. Magdalen dons met on 8 December and determined that Thomas should be elected to a senior demyship for one year from 1 January 1933 'to do work in certain branches of Near Eastern archaeology'.

Thomas planned to arrive in Jerusalem by Christmas. Eastwood was spending Christmas with Humphrey Bowman, the director of education in Palestine, and Bowman's wife. Through Eastwood Thomas was invited to dinner on Christmas evening when the guests would include the Crowfoots – Grace 'Molly' Crowfoot and John Crowfoot. Thomas hoped he could talk to Crowfoot about the possibility of going to him on a dig in Samaria in March to find Roman inscriptions, and to discuss his proposed thesis on the history of Roman Palestine. On Boxing Day Thomas would begin work with Garstang. He was trying to hatch another plan – for BJ to run away from home to join him in Palestine. Thomas had charged Derek Kahn with the task of making a case for this. A telegram from BJ to Thomas reached Nicosia late on the morning of 20 December and was forwarded to Thomas at the Othello Hotel in Famagusta next day, with the message: 'London twentieth not yet dear Thomas forgive miserable B J'. Derek wrote from Berlin on 21 December: 'I wrote to Maire and got what I expected – a muddled letter full of romantic excitement and indecision that was not really indecision, because as I said in my first letter the idea of her running away to you is an exaggeration – it is too much.'

As Christmas approached Thomas's departure was delayed by acute stomach-ache. He recovered enough to embark in the evening of Christmas day for Palestine. He reached Jaffa in the rain, caught a glimpse of a walled Jerusalem and on Boxing Day found Jericho – a bright green patch of orange and banana trees in a hollow in the mountains – and Garstang with his wife Marie. Thomas was lodged at the Winter Palace Hotel in Jericho. He met a tall Hertford College man, John Richmond, who as an Oxford freshman had been taken to meet Thomas by Pat Cotter (Thomas's close friend at the Dragon School) and who already had a season's experience of digging. Thomas sat down on his first evening – 'feels like all my first terms at all my schools' – to write understandingly to BJ about her failure to join him: '... we both hope, and I believe, that we aren't apart for ever ... I know it wasn't lack of braveness that made you not come.'

Thomas, still nursing an upset stomach, had a first day of light duties helping Marie Garstang arrange kitchen stores, and then began on archaeology. He wrote to his father on 29 December:

> On two days' experience I should say that Archaeology was a good career: it's reasonably simple and unconstructive work so far which is just as well – on the tombs – Richmond and I each have one. The Professor potters between them – looks at our notes – sits down on our sherds and jumps into our shafts. Mine has turned out to be a good little grotto tomb with a great stone in front – about a yard in each direction, which we rolled away from the tomb mouth with great pomp and excitement this morning.

Thomas was beginning to learn Arabic from the expedition surveyor, a Christian Arab Bulos al-Araj.

On 27 January 1933, Thomas received a letter from BJ with explanation of the botched elopement plan that might have taken her to Germany, Cyprus or Palestine. She had her own stomach pains on Boxing Day of 1932 and was admitted on 10 January to a nursing home in Hampstead where next day she had her appendix removed by Geoffrey Keynes (a brother of the economist, John Maynard Keynes). In London BJ was reading Thomas's contribution to *Red Rags: Essays of Hate from Oxford*, edited by Richard Comyns Carr and published by Chapman & Hall. The 18 essayists were all Oxford graduates or undergraduates, who had been invited to write on an object of peculiar detestation. Thomas, whose paternal grandfather had made his scholarly reputation as a historian of Italy, wrote a tongue-in-cheek diatribe against the tradition of grand tourism entitled 'Hating Italy'. He had wanted to be anonymous and he feared the title with his name would offend the paternal aunts – especially Violet Holdsworth, his grandfather's amanuensis.

General Wauchope, the High Commissioner, came on a Sunday visit to the dig on 5 February. Thomas learned that Wauchope knew from Ralph Furse that Thomas wanted to go into the colonial administration. Wauchope had questioned Garstang about Thomas's character. Thomas commented: 'It was rather like Herod noticing a likely looking Jew in a chain-gang at the stone quarries.' He wrote to his father that if the colonial service were taking a serious interest he felt encouraged to stay as long as possible and to learn Arabic as well as possible. He was hoping in May to ride through Syria to Aleppo.

The season's digging at Jericho ended on 15 March and Thomas gave a dinner of sheep roasted whole to about a dozen of the workmen. The writing up of records and notes was demanded before Thomas could leave. He planned that as soon as he could escape he would transfer to an Italian nunnery, the Tantur Hospice some three miles out of Jerusalem in the hills. By 26 March, he had packed his books and with his first archaeological earnings – a ten pound cheque from Garstang – he prepared the move to Tantur.

Thomas, mindful of the showing he must make in a second bid for All Souls, was ready to make his way in Jerusalem society, and wrote to Dorothy on 9 May: 'I ought to begin to know Jerusalem properly. I ought to begin to get to know some important Jews. How else can I face Sir John Simon over All Souls dinner table [if I do have to face him] unless I can gossip with him about what the Zionist leaders have most recently been thinking.' (Simon was Britain's Foreign Secretary.) Meanwhile he came into the ambit of the Antonius family. He had formed a good impression of Katy Antonius, daughter of a prominent Egyptian editor and political figure Faris Nimr. She was married to George Antonius, from a Greek Orthodox family in Alexandria, who was a graduate of King's College, Cambridge, and had been assistant director of education to Humphrey Bowman from 1921 to 1927. In Jerusalem they lived in a stylish house at Karm al-Mufti, where Thomas was a guest at a small dance held within a few days of his meeting with Mrs Antonius. In a letter to his mother on 16 May he described the host George as 'a man with rather the manner of a young fellow of All Souls and a mysterious profession of controlling governments – travelling expensively round, interviewing Amirs, Sultans, Grand Rabbis and Secretaries of State – and opening all their eyes'.

Thomas put the sociable Katy almost on a par with Helen Sutherland who was the exemplar to the Hodgkin and other families of stylish hospitality – 'platefuls of truffles and asparagus-tip sandwiches'. The Chancellor of the Hebrew University in Jerusalem, Judah Leib Magnes, wrote to Thomas on 23 May saying that he would be glad to see him, and on the same day Katy Antonius was writing to Thomas to encourage a plan of going to the pictures with him – '1st house and we could eat sausages at the Vienna or German Café…'.

Thomas was still in the job market and following up a proposal made by Colin Hardie who had left Balliol early in the year to become director of the British School at Rome, where Nicolete Binyon was studying. Colin wrote on 9 April to Thomas with a suggestion that he consider being librarian of the British School: 'The duties are not really very heavy, really only half-time … You would have ample leisure to work at what you wanted and to know Rome and its many grades of society and Italy too.' The post would make Thomas second in command of the school, pay a salary of £300 and provide free rooms, food and services. Colin suggested that Thomas consider the post from October or after the All Souls examination (to allow six months notice to the incumbent).

The Rome letter sent to Jericho was slow to catch up with Thomas in Jerusalem. In late May he replied to Colin that he would stand for the librarianship. Thomas spent 2 and 3 June at Sebastiya, Samaria, where John Crowfoot was conducting a successful archaeological dig jointly with Harvard University and the Hebrew University. Crowfoot was joined by Molly Crowfoot who had become an authority on ancient weaving, and by their second daughter Joan Crowfoot, who gave up reading medicine at the Royal Free Hospital in London because of eye trouble and became extraordinarily skilled at classifying flint instruments. Thomas described his reception in a letter to his mother on 6 June: 'Crowfoot delightful – friendly in a rather gnarled way – gave me very kindly almost a day of his time showing me buildings and explaining them – which is more than that old curmudgeon Garstang would have done for anyone short of a Duke: and the people seemed pleasant there – mostly young women. The daughter seemed a gay and well-featured young woman. I don't think that she can have been the one you had out to tea, who I think you called mute.' (Dorothy Hodgkin in the summer of 1932 entertained Joan's older sister Dorothy Crowfoot in Oxford to ask about Thomas going to Samaria).

Thomas left Jerusalem and arrived on 8 June to stay in Beirut with Robin Hodgkin's former pupil Raymond de Courcy Baldwin, who had been serving in the consulate since 1927 and was recently confirmed as vice-consul. Thomas took a look round Damascus and gathered advice on the journey he wanted to make through northern Syria – on horseback for a month's 'dirty travelling', to be followed by a week of 'clean travelling' with John Richmond and another Oxford friend, Tom Boase.

While Thomas was on these travels the librarianship committee for the British School at Rome met in London on 26 June to consider an appointment, and chose a New College graduate from the National Gallery, Ellis Waterhouse.

Thomas reached Aleppo on 7 July and leaving Richmond and Boase he returned to Jerusalem for a hasty final packing of his possessions from the Tantur Hospice and farewells to acquaintances in the administration. After a sluggish train journey he took ship from Alexandria for five days of sailing to Europe.

Thomas's return to Europe had been the topic of a convoluted correspondence between family and friends. He planned to spend a week with some of the Lynds, for Teddy to join him somewhere in Europe where they would see Derek, and for the family to reunite in Northumberland at the end of August, first as guests of Helen Sutherland at Rock Hall and then in the Neville Tower of their favoured Bamburgh Castle. What was intended as a week in Portofino turned into a scramble around Italy. The Lynd sisters were travelling in Italy chaperoned by a widowed novelist, Frances Harrod, a sister of the actor Sir Johnston Forbes-Robertson and mother of a brilliant Christ Church don, the economist Roy Harrod. Harrod with Isaiah Berlin made up the holiday group in Portofino (where Derek Kahn was planning to join Thomas about 5 August). The visitors found the Hotel Splendide perched too steeply above the sea and the Portofino beach over-crowded.

By the time Thomas arrived at the end of July the others had already decided to move on to Lake Garda on 2 August – to a resort where the Lynds had stayed en famille during the previous summer. At short notice Leonardo Walsh the hotelier of the Locanda at San Vigilio could provide rooms only for the Harrods; the others stayed in the Eremitaggio, an annexe along the lake shore, and returned to the Locanda for all their meals. Sigle and BJ were due to return to London on 6 August and little time was left.

In this company Thomas and BJ – between the swimming and rowing and seemingly endless amusing conversation over leisurely meals – were almost never alone to rebuild an understanding. Roy Harrod was showing BJ how to dive. Thomas and BJ managed one boat ride on the lake and a pre-breakfast walk up a hill where they saw a golden eagle at the top. On BJ's last full day of the holiday they took a walk back to the Eremitaggio along the shore; they were not close enough for a renewal; there seemed no way forward. She and Sigle left next day for London. Thomas reviewed the situation in a letter to Robin on 7 August: 'This has been a necessary time but not an easy one. The distance between Maire and me has grown greater since last winter even – though we both wish to be together we remain apart. I don't see how that can ever now be remedied. This week in each other's company had to be in order to find that out.'

Thomas and Teddy went to the village of Patsch in the Tyrol near Innsbruck and took the cheapest rooms in a modest boarding house, the Gruenwalderhof, so that they could study quietly for a few days. They were invited by Isaiah to join him in Salzburg from 20 August where they could have study and music.

Thomas was thinking about his own future career now that the Rome offer had fallen through. He was keen to settle an alternative before the All Souls examination and to arrange interviews before going to Northumberland. He thought the possibilities were something in the Near East (improbable but possibly worth the effort of arranging an interview with Furse for 25 August when he planned to be in London), or WEA work or some form of adult education. After Salzburg he returned to England and was soon on familiar ground in the Neville Tower of Bamburgh Castle.

Thomas sat for All Souls in early October, sent a report to the President of Magdalen on his year as a senior demy and explained his decision not to apply for an extension. With Oxford obligations settled he went north, essentially as a volunteer in his first job in England – treading a path reminiscent of his maternal and paternal grandfathers. Working-class adult education had been one of Oxford's concerns since the late nineteenth century and a keen interest of Dorothy's father AL Smith. Thomas's venture into adult education was with the Unemployment Committee of the Cumberland Friends or Quakers and in the Cumberland port and industrial town of Whitehaven where Robin's father Thomas Hodgkin had gone in 1856 to work in a bank. The flourishing mining and fishing centre of the mid-nineteenth century had become a place of exceptional unemployment in the slump of the 1930s. Lindsay, Smith's successor as Master of Balliol, bestowed his benediction on Thomas's task and wrote about Thomas to the Unemployment Committee's organising secretary, Wilfrid Lunn, and to Cumberland gentry including the Bishop of Carlisle at Rose Castle.

Thomas was put into lodgings at 7 West View, Hensingham, Whitehaven, then taken by Lunn for an overnight stay at the Friends' School at Wigton where the committee's chairman and paymaster, David Reed, was headmaster. Thomas warmed to Reed's Quaker wisdom and to Lunn – 'his reticence reasonableness and intelligent revolutionariness seem perfectly suited'. Thomas wrote to Robin on 22 October for books on German history – Frederick the Great and Bismarck – and on 25 October gave his first talk – on Palestine – to a group in Whitehaven. Despite the hilly countryside he hired a bicycle so that he could visit clubs on his own. He was hoping to talk about Germany and had begun to struggle through *Mein Kampf* by Adolf Hitler, who had recently come into the limelight as that country's Chancellor. Thomas wrote to Robin on 27 October with a further request for a quantity of spare books from Oxford – 'thousands rotting there unread' – to add to the sparse collections in the workmen's clubs, and for old boxing gloves. The book requests were promptly met.

He played football on 2 November – in shorts and boots against men in corduroy breeches and clogs. He was discounting to Dorothy her high expectations for All Souls, and urged against attempts to find out how he fared if not elected.

Dorothy waited at home in Oxford on 3 November for the telephone that did not ring. All Souls elected only one prize fellow for 1933 – another Balliol classicist, John Austin, whom Thomas had earlier described to his family as by far the cleverest man he knew. Dorothy, although bidden by Thomas not to probe into the All Souls decision, could not help hearing the conjecture and gossip proffered by family friends among dons and undergraduates. She gave a lunch party on 6 November for Helen Sutherland who was spending a few days with her and the guests included Felix Markham and Isaiah Berlin. Isaiah disclosed that the five examiners had submitted only one name – Austin's – for election.

Isaiah wrote later that day direct to Thomas in detail:

> Let me tell you all I can without breaking my oath of secrecy. You weren't elected because the examiners recommended only Austin. Consequently all those who either had no chance of reading the papers or trusted the examiners voted for Austin alone. A large party mustered round you including the most distinguished names you could wish for. There was a long and closely run contest in which you lost by literally the narrowest possible margin. Everyone old and young made speeches about you, whether they wanted to have you or not, saying how nice you were, how well you got on with everyone you met, how anything you said was bound to be original and interesting, and how fond of you everyone who knew you was. This went on for a very long time. The Warden was in tears after the result was known.

Isaiah urged a third attempt – on recent experience third tries did better than second tries. Thomas replied on 8 November that the previous year was ill planned – he should either have worked much harder or not at all. He deserved and expected this result – and though it was beautiful to hear of all these great men taking his part, he ruled out a third attempt at All Souls: 'At the moment I think of trying to be a Labour Exchange official – learn about the Means Test by applying it.'

The All Souls outcome rekindled the discussion between Thomas and his close family about longer term career prospects. Thomas expected to remain in Cumberland until about April of 1934. Robin noted from the Oxford Calendar that All Souls had rights to make appointments to the Delegacy for Extra-Mural Studies (heir to the extension teaching schemes inaugurated in 1878), and he was looking out for openings in WEA work. He relayed to Thomas on 19 November an interview he had with M.B. Hutchinson at the Delegacy about work prospects in tutorial classes: a full time staff member with four or five classes could earn from £450 to £500 a year, with very hard work during the winter months that could not be kept up for long. A provincial university post might be appropriate, but a junior lecturer was set to do the dirty work.

Thomas cabled on 20 November to Teddy at Balliol for books on Lenin's Russia on his Blackwell's account. Teddy responded by sending books including Lenin's *State and Revolution* and the first volume of Stalin on *Leninism*. Thomas gave his Russia talk in Maryport on 24 November – after three days of reading hard, mostly Lenin.

Robin was returning to Oxford on 23 November from a visit to the British Museum and by chance was joined in his railway carriage by Sandie Lindsay to whom he recounted Thomas's interest in the new unemployment scheme. Lindsay through his chairmanship of the unemployment committee of the National Council of Social Service was much involved in the issues, but said that Thomas had been suggested as a possibility for a teaching and organising post they were thinking of creating in North Staffordshire. Robin and Lindsay agreed that Thomas and Lindsay should talk at Lindsay's vacation cottage in Eskdale.

Thomas visited his Gresford Jones aunt and uncle at Winwick Rectory, who were keen that Thomas in pursuit of employment should see their friend Walter Moberly, the Manchester University vice-chancellor. Thomas assented, despite some doubt about things being done unofficially through aunts and uncles. Robin had another straw in the wind as he heard a rumour of a temporary vacant post in philosophy at Manchester University. He went on 28 November to an official tea-party at Oriel and sought more information from a former Balliol classicist, the philosopher David Ross, now Provost of Oriel College. The rumour was confirmed: Manchester was seeking a temporary replacement for J.L. Stocks (Stocks was going to spend a term in the West Indies) and Ross was willing to recommend Thomas. Stocks sent to Thomas a meticulous account of the courses and classes to be covered – for which he would provide his own lecture notes if Thomas were available and met the requirements of a small appointments committee (the job would pay about £100).

Thomas travelled to Manchester on 6 December, and spent the evening with Moberly in a discussion he found encouraging. He felt that a university like Manchester would give him the discipline of associating with people from whom he could learn and scope to try to interest people in philosophy apart from the actual teaching of it. He spent the morning of 7 December with Stocks who showed him lecture notes and explained the sort of people and subjects he taught. Thomas thought there was a good deal of nineteenth-century political theory and political history of which he was ignorant but at which he was very willing to work. He met another of the selectors and gathered that only one other candidate was in mind – the appointment might be made at once or the alternative candidate might be called for interview.

Thomas spent 10 December walking in the Lake District hills with Geoffrey Cross and climbed to the top of Scafell Pike. On return to new lodgings he had taken on the High Street of Cleator Moor, he found the Manchester University response. Stocks wrote that the selection committee had met on the afternoon of 7 December and decided to recommend Thomas for the job. There was no likelihood of the recommendation being rejected and he could act as if it were settled. Stocks invited Thomas to come and stay with him in Manchester for a day or so in the coming week for a handover of all the notes.

In the New Year of 1934 Thomas transferred to Manchester and joined Geoffrey Cross (now a schoolteacher at Manchester Grammar School) in lodgings at 20 Longford Place, Manchester 14, although he did not find the landlord and landlady congenial. His university teaching schedule bequeathed by Stocks covered six tasks: three small groups and three large classes. Half a dozen students had three hours a week on the history of modern philosophy – covering Descartes, Leibniz and Kant. An essay class of four considered nineteenth-century political thought. Four classical honours students were on a refresher course in Greek philosophy for one hour a week. A class of 30 had a weekly introductory class based on Bertrand Russell's *Problems of Philosophy*. A class of 40 had a weekly hour on the history of philosophy, and a similar course was given as an evening class to some 45 participants. The tasks fell from Monday to Thursday at mid-day, leaving a long weekend for further lecture preparation and for country air, although Thomas soon took on additional weekend commitments.

He wrote to William Temple proposing a visit to the Archbishop's Palace in York, as he had been encouraged to do after Robin had talked to Temple at a dinner of the Queen's College Association in London. Temple replied on 13 January offering the following weekend in January or a choice of three in March. They agreed to meet at the Archbishop's palace in York for the weekend from 24 March. Meanwhile Temple asked Thomas to look over the manuscript of the Gifford lectures on 'Nature, Man and God' he was preparing for publication, so that they could discuss them during the March visit.

At the end of the first week of teaching Thomas wrote to Robin on 18 January that he felt 'as if he had just run 40 miles – but that is a pleasant feeling'. The Descartes class – 'six embryo Methodist ministers and a scientist' – had the most carefully prepared lecture. Thomas went armed with six typed foolscap pages. He returned the following day to Cleator Moor to give the first in a fortnightly series of classes and stayed over to meet friends among the unemployed. After the third round of Manchester lecturing, he went again on 1 February to

Cleator Moor for a session on the Pope. He stayed in Cleator Moor with an unemployed miner, John Farrell, with Thomas in one room and Farrell and his wife and five children in another. The morning brought a country rinsing in a cold bucket with the family before breakfast.

He snatched a fleeting visit to Oxford to take his degree on 3 March – and for a glimpse of his family – and was back in Manchester in time for his lectures by catching a train at three in the morning. Thomas's parents received on 19 March a bombshell of a letter – as they saw it – affecting Thomas's career prospects. The Colonial Office was renewing an interest in Thomas of which he was unaware. General Wauchope who met Thomas at the Jericho dig in February 1933 had been alerted to Thomas's presence there in a despatch from the Colonial Office. About a year later Wauchope wrote on 12 February 1934 to Sir Philip Cunliffe-Lister, the Colonial Secretary, requesting revised budgetary provision for the engagement of two additional British cadet officers (he pointed out that there had been no such appointment to the Palestine Government since 1929 when Hugh Foot, one of five sons of a Liberal MP Isaac Foot, was posted there). The Colonial Office supported the request but recommended to Wauchope that to secure the best candidates he should wait if possible for the annual selection process due in August. Wauchope replied that Hodgkin, if still available, could be appointed at once and that he would wait for a second cadet in the annual selection.

Furse was instructed on 13 March to sound out Thomas and submit his candidacy if everything was correct. Accordingly, Furse sent an official letter inviting Thomas for a discussion in the following week if possible. The letter went to Bamburgh (where Thomas had been at the time of the abortive Gold Coast appointment in September 1932), and was forwarded to Oxford and then to Manchester. Thomas had no doubt that he did want to attend an interview at the Colonial Office (and had a tip-off from Eastwood about the possibility of Palestine). He wrote to Dorothy immediately that he had been happy as a temporary assistant philosophy lecturer, but was attracted by more practical work: 'Palestine remains the pinnacle of my hopes – not permanently but say for ten years … It would be miserable to have another long parting: but my heart leaps at the thought of Arabs and my tongue tries to shape Arab remarks.'

Thomas had breakfast in London on 23 March with Helen Sutherland and they walked down to Whitehall together for Thomas to visit the Colonial Office and meet Furse. Furse asked him if he were certain that he wanted to go to Palestine but would not take an official answer until Thomas had talked to Eastwood. Thomas went through the motions of half an hour's talk to Eastwood about Palestine. He telephoned Furse to confirm that he would like to apply for the vacancy in the Palestine administration. Furse explained that the decision went before a selection committee but as the members had seen Thomas two years before they would probably not want to see him again, and a decision could be expected before Easter.

A letter from Downing Street, dated 20 April 1934, advised that Sir Philip Cunliffe-Lister proposed to select Thomas for probationary appointment to the Colonial Administrative Service as a cadet in the Palestine Civil Service – subject to his being passed as medically fit by the department's consulting physician. Thomas must indicate the earliest date at which he would be prepared to leave for Palestine. In the last days of April Thomas packed his Manchester possessions and moved back to Oxford for the preparation.

Robin and Dorothy waved him off on 12 May as he sailed from Southampton on the S.S. Rajputana on the India mail and passenger run. On arrival in Palestine, he lodged in the old city of Jerusalem at the Austrian Hospice. He could walk through a warren of little streets a quarter of a mile to the Secretariat opposite the Damascus Gate where he worked. He felt his own obligatory tidy dress an obstacle to chatting with the beautiful slovenly people he walked past.

He was introduced to the task of drafting official letters. At dinner with Wauchope on 25 May he voiced respectable opinions, and wrote to Dorothy: 'In fact sheepishly and treacherously Tory, so that I was ashamed of myself … of course I should never have the courage or folly to label myself Communist here (knowing what a red rag that is to people – nor even Socialist – which means the same but is a degree less)'. Thomas went to a Sunday lunch with Katy Antonius and found himself dragged awkwardly into argument as she became passionate about the Arab cause and Thomas felt obliged to make the balancing Jewish case. The advent of Hitler's power in Germany had led to an increase of legal and illegal Jewish immigration into Palestine and to concerns of Palestinian Arabs over the rights and future of their community.

Thomas understood that he was expected to make formal calls on the wives of a dozen British officials – and even to leave cards though he had none. He found and made friends of his own. During Thomas's first days at the Austrian Hospice he saw a strange great bearded man like Tolstoy dressed in yellow and black striped silk, an Arab skirt, with Arab headdress who could talk English only. This turned out to be the sculptor and calligrapher Eric Gill, who had been invited by the government architect Austen Harrison to carve panels for the walls of the Rockefeller Museum of archaeology to be constructed in Jerusalem.

Gill spoke of a friend flying in from Cairo. Thomas eavesdropped and guessed correctly that it was the artist David Jones whom he knew through Helen Sutherland. (Helen bought a portrait of Thomas painted at Rock Hall by Jones and shown in 1930 at the Wertheim Gallery in London). Jones arrived by the end of May and Thomas began to meet him and Gill for dinner and to talk and drink with them in his room afterwards. Jones was in poor physical and mental condition and found the streets of Jerusalem stressful. In Thomas's room, he would talk until 11 or so at night.

Thomas renewed contact with the Bowmans, went to them for Sunday lunch on 3 June and was forgiven for a rather disorganised departure from Palestine nearly a year earlier. He broke away in time to take Gill and Jones for tea at the Tantur Hospice and to see Sister Matilda with whom he had tried out his Italian during a previous stay.

He wrote to Robin on 14 June about his long conversations with Jones at the Hospice (where food was troublesome) and dinner with Arthur Wauchope. Jones was 'learned and wise and interested in the things that I am interested in, Jews and Crusades and the British empire, and makes admirable judgments about all of them, having Catholic wisdom without those particular Catholic prejudices that one doesn't like'. At dinner with the High Commissioner, he was regaled on Moselle and old brandy, roast pigeon and crème brulée and could impress his host by boasting of a family connection to Johnny Jameson's older brother, General Sir Andrew McCulloch.

Thomas accompanied the Gill family in late June on a journey to Lake Galilee (Eric Gill had been joined by his wife and the youngest of his three daughters, Joan Hague). Thomas in Jerusalem again on 26 June attended a Christian conversazione and found himself in discussion on Oxford philosophy with the Jewish philosopher Leon Roth (as he recounted in a letter to Isaiah Berlin who was due to visit Palestine in September and to whom Thomas promised a bevy of notables: 'I know you expect to be critical but it would be much easier to understand or attempt to understand Zionism in your company and with your comments and explanations than it could be on my own'.)

Wauchope's private secretary left for England at the end of June – mysteriously, wrote Thomas – and Thomas after just a month in post found himself as acting private secretary to the High Commissioner, feeling rather as he had in his first term at Winchester, and sharing a little room of maps, red and blue pencils and telephones with ADCs, one moderately kind and the other simply cold and handsome, a Seaforth Highlander of alabaster. From 1 July, letters home were written on the crested writing paper of Government House and Thomas had to leave the day-to-day life of living with the Gills and David for the last ten days or so of their visit to Jerusalem, except when he could snatch a break to creep back like a reformed Prince Henry.

He thought the official position rather terrible as it brought frequent official dinners and entertainment, much dressing up in ready-made tails, and no time to himself, especially to read, to write letters or to reflect. Thomas was not used to diplomatic discretion. 'I cannot help first beginning to talk politics with every foreign stranger I meet, second, always running down the country which I imagine he wants me to run down', he commented to Dorothy after a fortnight, but he was learning how to avoid Palestinian politics.

Thomas was already looking forward to returning to routine obscurity and the Austrian Hospice when Wauchope would go on leave in late August. When Wauchope was away to celebrate 12 August by shooting sand-grouse at Beersheba, Thomas astonished the staff at the vast Government House by planning a long walk from Hebron to the ancient Herodium that would dispense with any of the three stately well-bred Humber cars garaged in the stables. On 25 August Wauchope wrote Thomas a warm letter of thanks for his two month stint as acting private secretary, described as no easy job taken on at short notice: 'Apart from your work as private secretary it has been the greatest pleasure to have you as a companion in this house. … I hope I may think that we have made good friends this summer and will continue to be so.' He gave the letter to Thomas at the airfield where Thomas waved him off next day.

Wauchope during his home leave accepted an invitation from Helen Sutherland and made a brief stay in early October at Rock Hall, where David Jones and Thomas's father and brother were also guests. Helen was preparing to visit Thomas in Jerusalem on her way to Kenya where Heinrich Enderle, a German protégé who had long been under her roof, was to be set up on a coffee farm. Wauchope invited Helen – with Thomas – to stay at Government House for the Jerusalem days. Thomas, writing to Dorothy on 5 November, reported a rumour in Jerusalem that he might have to do another spell as private secretary when Wauchope returned from leave: 'I pray not though I love him: I am bad at the job and I want to be independent.' The rumour was confirmed but for only a fortnight pending the arrival of an appointee and by 13 November Thomas was writing again from Government House where he had moved back to prepare for Wauchope's return. It was convenient that Helen Sutherland, who was on her way by ship, could be spared the chill of the Austrian Hospice and its poor cuisine. Thomas went hunting on 18 November when Wauchope attended the opening meet of the new season, hurried back for a walk with the Professor of International Relations at the Hebrew University of Jerusalem, Norman Bentwich, whose book *The Promised Land* he had been reading, and attended a dinner party of soldiers during which he went to sleep but was forgiven.

Wauchope's flurry of nightly dinner parties was soon compounded for Thomas by Helen's arrival by train at Lydda on 22 November for her visit to Jerusalem. Thomas snatched moments to show her the old town, the Damascus Gate and the Church of the Holy Sepulchre. She was impressed at Thomas's ease of contact in Arabic with street traders, but was finding the obligations of conversation at frequent meals with Wauchope to be a strain. Within a couple of days she thought of moving to the Austrian Hospice but Wauchope pressed her to stay on. Thomas had a further week of Government House official entertaining and more agreeably a long walk with Wauchope on 8 December to mark the end of the acting assignment – with the post now held by the young High Church Ralph Poston (Wauchope was a member of the Presbyterian Church).

Thomas was resettled at the Austrian Hospice, at peace but feeling the cold and wondering whether in the long term he should move to somewhere warmer and equally peaceful. He had made a new acquaintance, an architect Pierce Hubbard – young handsome and revolutionary – a Rome Scholar who had run away from the British School at Rome, unhappy to work on imperial monuments rather than Byzantine churches. Thomas sensed friction with the British School director Colin Hardie and recounted his own mild quarrel over the abortive offer of appointment as librarian.

In the New Year of 1935 Helen, on her way back from Kenya, spent a week at the Austrian Hospice and startled the nuns with her expectation of hot water four times a day and other comforts, but exercised beneficent pressure on the standards of cooking. Thomas and Helen went on to visit Pierce Hubbard at a hillside village some four miles from Jerusalem, Ain Karim. Thomas looked at a house that he thought he might rent as more satisfactory than continuing hospice life – although the house had an elderly Greek nun as a sitting tenant in one bedroom. Thomas went on leave and on return he took on the Ain Karim house and as servant and cook a Bethlehem Christian, Michail Jadallah Jagoman, while planning to keep a foothold at the hospice.

Thomas began with the untried cook some ambitious entertaining: on 15 March dinner guests included John Richmond and his mother Ann Richmond, Laurence and Cecily Binyon passing through after a lecture by Binyon in Egypt, and Robin Furness, the Palestine Government press officer. Michail, the cook, made an omelette in the morning that he proposed to dish warmed up for the dinner guests and Thomas persuaded him to prepare the food fresh. He gave Sunday lunch on 31 March to Furness again and his artist niece Diana Furness who was on a visit to Jerusalem and to the Chief Justice Sir Michael McDonnell and Lady McDonnell. Diana Furness went back to England on 15 June after some ten weeks' visit – she had made a strong impression on Thomas but their encounters had been argumentative.

Thomas's work changed briefly in July when he was assigned to a district for three weeks to stand in for a newly-appointed cadet Christopher Pirie-Gordon in Haifa. Thomas had doubted the usefulness of his Secretariat work and was stimulated by the taste of responsibility for a district. He travelled by train to

Jerusalem on 21 July first class on an official ticket and had time to read, but regretted missing the people he might have met in the third-class carriage. He returned to Ain Karim on 22 July after a day in the office. It was a kind of homecoming to the clerks, the bus driver, and to a colleague Max Nurock who was sensitive to the satisfaction Thomas had derived from the work in Haifa. Thomas, writing to Dorothy from Ain Karim on the evening of 22 July, reported: 'From today I have started smoking cigarettes when, as a moment ago, I feel myself falling asleep: a good plan I think, though I have not learnt to keep the smoke out of my eyes.'

Thomas's anxieties continued. Some 14 Communists held in the Jerusalem were on hunger strike. They saw themselves as political prisoners rather than criminals but were forced to wear prison clothing rather than their own clothing since English law did not recognise a distinction. Thomas went to the prison and saw the prisoners through the bars but did not speak as he thought they would not listen to his views. He wanted the hunger strike to stop but knew no Communists in the country who might be effective intermediaries. He went with John Richmond on 29 July to Tel Aviv to the Habimah theatre group, thinking that some of the players with their Moscow Arts Theatre background were partly sympathetic with Communists and might be listened to by the prisoners if the Government would let any of them visit. He attended a play and sat afterwards with the actors drinking beer out of cups. The talk was inconclusive.

Thomas read T.E. Lawrence's *Seven Pillars of Wisdom* – he found lacking in Lawrence the appreciation that British Imperialism was bound to have no use for Arab independence except as an idea to stir up Arabs for its own imperialist ends. He included a poem mildly derisory of Britain and of Lawrence in a letter for Teddy's birthday on 25 August, and commented that though in contemporary Palestine the High Commissioner had a sense of obligation 'that doesn't have any effect on the broad national policy, in this country or elsewhere – for which I think a Marxist explanation (in so far as I know what that is) is the truest that can be got'. Thomas proposed from the end of August to begin inviting half a dozen Secretariat clerks to Ain Karim once a fortnight to discuss non-Palestinian politics. He wrote to Robin on 26 August that he would begin with Abyssinia about which he knew little: 'Manchester and Cleator Moor have made me believe that you can have a fairly satisfactory discussion without much knowledge – more satisfactory of course if you have some.'

Thomas travelling with an Arab companion, Salim Husseini, visited Beduin tents on a three-day journey between Hebron and the Dead Sea. One purpose of the ride was for Thomas to consider his future in the colonial service against a background clouded by Italy's impending invasion of Ethiopia and a glimmering of war in Europe. His mind was in turmoil and he felt the likelihood of war compounding the contradictions between his own beliefs and the obligations of government service. He decided to continue with his government duties until faced with a duty that was so intolerable it was clearly better to resign than carry it out. He thought the breaking point might be years in the future and in a letter to Teddy of 4 October concluded wryly that from a Communist point of view he ought to stick at his desk until the Colonel of the Berkshires and all his men had begun to fraternise with the workers in front of Government Offices.

Arab workers and shopkeepers went on strike on 26 October against Jewish immigration – and the smuggling of arms into Palestine. Since the buses were not running Thomas walked to Jerusalem from Ain Karim and spent a Saturday evening in a long discussion with Katy Antonius. Thomas spent the evening of 6 November in a discussion with Jews in Jerusalem who were of Zionist sympathies but he deemed too intelligent and sensitive to feel altogether comfortable about living a practically segregated life among hostile Arabs protected by British bayonets. Thomas imagined them on the edge of a bonfire or volcano and that the remedy lay in Communism or Socialism.

He was also discussing politics with Arab interlocutors: Sami Sarraj, a Syrian expelled from several neighbouring countries for writing articles against European intervention; Musa Alami, a Palestinian 'dispossessed landowner' who had served as Wauchope's Arab private secretary. He noted an incident on 20 November when five Arabs and one English police officer were killed in a fight in the hills near Jenin. 'Truly, all imperialism is fundamentally alike, I think – imposed by force and maintained by the fear of force and from time to time by actual force.' He suggested the distinction between Italian and English imperialism was only a difference of degree. He was also beginning to think that even if he secured a transfer to the district administration it would be better not to stick for much longer in work that was on a small scale contradictory to his beliefs since it could lead to something contradictory on a larger scale and being 'responsible for Police firing on Arab crowds for instance – not at all an impossible event if one was in a District'.

Katy Antonius remained the person with whom he found it easiest to talk politics, and he found some congenial minds among the English. The circle was broadened with the arrival on 21 November of a close friend of David Jones who recommended her to Thomas (and to Teddy). She was the personable Lady Prudence Pelham (younger daughter of the sixth Earl of Chichester and three days younger than Thomas) who through study under Eric Gill had become expert at letter carving. Jones had taken her in the summer to stay with Helen Sutherland where her exhilarating character made her an incongruous guest for the refined delicacy of the hospitality at Rock Hall.

Prudence followed up the introduction to Thomas and wrote to Jones from the Citadel Hotel in Jerusalem on 22 November: 'We talked and talked till it made us quite ill – I hadn't talked to anybody in English since the two buglers.' Thomas took to Prudence instantly: 'She has been travelling with beautiful independence through Syria, in the best way, meeting the human beings she happens to come across, staying as long in a place as she likes it – the only check on her is how long her money will last out.' Teddy was arriving in Palestine on 28 November. Thomas set out on the first bus of the day from Jerusalem for Jaffa intending to meet the boat early in the morning, only to find that the boat would not dock until mid-morning so he returned to work at the Secretariat where Teddy found him in the afternoon. They went off to talk over beer and sausages, had tea with the Bowmans, and supper with Furness and Prudence on Teddy's first evening in Jerusalem.

Teddy, Prudence and Thomas settled to use Thomas's three weeks of leave to ride to Petra and Aqaba and into the Sinai – this meant braving winter cold. They grappled with bites from bed bugs, with Prudence's malaria (as it turned out to be) and an unidentified sickness that ailed Teddy (later diagnosed as jaundice). Thomas rushed reluctantly back to work in Jerusalem on 15 January 1936. Prudence and Teddy returned to Jerusalem early in February and shared their time between the city and the village house at Ain Karim. Prudence with a commission from Wauchope carved an inscription stone for an extension to the agricultural school at Tulkarm.

Dorothy and Robin travelled to Palestine later in February, taking Mary Jameson with them, and reached Jerusalem early on 20 February. The purpose was not only a family reunion after some twenty months' absence from Thomas. It was a clear understanding on both sides that this would be the opportunity to discuss Thomas's future and whether he would choose to continue in his job with the colonial administration. Thomas was wavering between an early resignation and waiting to try the experience of a district assignment in Haifa. Dorothy, Robin and Mary left on Good Friday 10 April in little doubt about the choice he would make. The Secretariat officials already had a sense of Thomas's disquiets; verses he wrote and left in his office had in February fallen into the hands of a senior colleague. Thomas discussed his thoughts of resignation with Nurock who in turn alerted Wauchope. Wauchope let it be known through Nurock that he was sympathetic and would not put pressure on Thomas to remain. Nurock relayed this to Thomas on Easter Sunday, 12 April.

Thomas worked on the text of a resignation letter and by 14 April, he had a complete draft for Teddy's approval. Thomas was on the eve of a temporary transfer to Haifa to replace a colleague suffering from scarlet fever. A year earlier he had pined for a district but this sudden assignment meant going away from Ain Karim, from Teddy and from Prudence who had just returned from another bout of travel in Transjordan. Thomas took a room in the German Hospice at Haifa and began working under the acting District Commissioner for the Northern District, Morris Bailey.

In a hold-up incident in Nablus on 15 April, one Jew was killed and two seriously wounded. The killing on 17 April of two Arabs was, according to news agency reports, believed to be a Jewish reprisal. At this critical moment in Palestinian history an 'Arab Revolt' was signalled in a call for a general strike of Arab workers. Thomas's letter of resignation, prepared before the outbreak, was dated 20 April and sent on 21 April from Haifa. He applied formally to the Chief Secretary, John Hathorn Hall, for permission to resign from the public service of Palestine with three months' notice. He asked for leave to remain in Palestine and Transjordan privately for about six months after his resignation had taken effect – partly among Arabs in a village or among Beduin and partly in a Jewish settlement.

Thomas wrote at length to Wauchope to explain the reasons that had made him decide to resign. He argued that the previous two years had confirmed him in Socialist views that he had held more vaguely when he came to Palestine. If he had been sure of them earlier, he hoped he would have been sensible enough not to apply for a Colonial Office appointment. He regretted that he had partly misled the Colonial Office. What now interested him was the establishment of Socialist societies in countries that presently had capitalist societies. Living or working in a capitalist country was bound to make one to some extent the servant of capitalism, but it would be possible to find a job that gave more opportunities of working towards a Socialist society or making conditions more tolerable for people within the existing capitalist society.

The volatile situation in Palestine and strike action on 19 and 20 April spread to a general strike by the Arabs from 23 April. Thomas in the District Commissioner's office in Haifa found himself with the unpleasant task of receiving and writing and passing on telephone reports on the opposition action. Wauchope replied privately to the resignation letters: 'I am no lover of the capitalist system: but I don't feel capable of even helping to put another in its place. So I try to lessen the evil I find.'

Official action against the strikers made Thomas thankful that he would soon end his participation in the Palestine government. Crowds were fired on; prison sentences up to six months were given for picketing, and up to three years for stone throwing at policemen. He wrote to Dorothy on 30 April about arrests without charge of 75 Communists 'on suspicion of being the sort of people to cause a breach of the peace'.

The Chief Secretary sent an official reply on 2 May to Thomas's formal resignation. The application was granted and he was permitted to resign, but expected to remain in the public service until arrangements had been made for the arrival of a successor. The request to be given leave to remain in Palestine and Transjordan for six months was rejected because it could cause embarrassment to government and give rise to local comment and surmise as to his objects and intentions.

For the closing week of Teddy's visit to Palestine Thomas moved briefly to the Stella Maris Carmelite monastery overlooking the sea to be joined by Prudence who had delivered the inscription stone, the Ain Karim schoolmaster Abdurrahman Sinokrot whose pupils were on strike, Michail the cook and again by Teddy who had collected his luggage from Ain Karim. Teddy sailed from Haifa on 6 May.

Thomas with much hesitation responded to the Chief Secretary's letter of 2 May and confirmed his willingness to remain in public service until the arrival of a successor. On 11 May he rented two stone-floored rooms (at one pound a month each for himself and for Prudence) in the house of Butrus the potter and his wife Dora on the Khayat beach some two miles southwards of Haifa. He spent as little of the day in the office as possible and as much of it as possible with Prudence in these new surroundings. In the light of the government's handling of the strike and the disturbances Thomas was reconsidering his undertaking to remain in the service by working out his notice or until he was replaced. He felt that the ordinary work of administration was reduced almost to nothing and that he was being forced into what was virtually War Office work. On 26 May, Prudence took the train to Jerusalem to settle her accommodation bills and pack up her belongings. Dorothy was uncomfortable about the propriety of Thomas and Prudence sharing a house.

Thomas had already decided it was time to leave his appointment in Palestine: he wrote letters to the most senior Palestine government representatives asking to be allowed to resign at once. On 27 May he handed to Bailey his letter to the Chief Secretary with its argument that as long as the government's attitude to the Arabs was mainly defensive he had thought it possible to remain, but now that the government appeared to have taken up the offensive against the Arabs he found it not only repugnant but morally impossible to participate in government's repressive measures. He instanced deportations of political leaders and punitive raids against villages carried out by police or troops or both. Since a decision on his remaining in Palestine or Transjordan was deferred, Thomas proposed instead to stay some time in Syria or the Lebanon.

Nurock telephoned Thomas on the evening of 30 May to say that a letter was being sent from Jerusalem to Bailey in Haifa that Thomas was released from the government. The violence of military raids against villages in the Northern District in the preceding days made Thomas more than ever certain of his decision: 'I feel that when a Government behaves as this Government is behaving the only sensible course for me is to desert it,' he wrote to Robin on 31 May. He had half-finished an article that could be sent to the newspapers now so deluged with the Zionist and Imperialist statements of the case.

Wauchope was still taking a personal interest in Thomas and wrote again privately on 31 May: 'I look back on the months you worked with me here with nothing but pleasure and memory of happy hours. Bless you my dear Thomas – a French woman once said of me Arthur, coeur de chrystal. I do not deserve that. I believe you do.' George Antonius arrived in Haifa, en route from Turkey to Jerusalem, and when they met on 1 June Antonius supported Thomas's resignation decisions and the article he was writing and offered hospitality in Jerusalem. Thomas finished the article and at the end of the first week of June he sent it to Sigle Lynd (she now worked for the publisher Victor Gollancz who, with John Strachey and Harold Laski, had just initiated the Left Book Club to oppose Nazism and Fascism).

The Arabic press reported Thomas's resignation and he was billed as a noble great Englishman resigning for the Arab cause. Thomas's own article had already found a home in principle. Sigle wrote on 12 June: 'I have immediately placed your excellent article, and the paper has asked me to ask you at once what should be done about mentioning its authorship' (she did not identify that she was dealing with Hugo Rathbone for the July issue of *The Labour Monthly*, a Communist journal founded by Rajani Palme Dutt).

The Palestine authorities were already reacting. Thomas was instructed by Bailey to leave Palestine within two days. Thomas left for Sidon on 15 June and booked into the Hotel Phoenicia. He asked Sigle to let the article appear without his name but with a note to the effect that the writer of the article had lived in and been closely acquainted with Palestine for some years. The journal chose 'By British Resident'. Thomas was drafting another article about Zionism in Palestine. He wrote to Robin on 22 June that he was thinking of coming home in September and seeking information about the chances of teaching in a grammar school or possibly an elementary school.

Thomas travelled on to Beirut at the beginning of July and stayed with the British vice-consul Baldwin (whose guest he had been in June 1933) whom he found intelligent, especially about Arab matters. Prudence arrived in Beirut suffering from fleabites, which had given her a poisoned leg. Thomas disclosed to Teddy (to be kept quiet from parents already anxious about the journalism and Prudence) that Baldwin had told him that his consulate for Lebanon had instructions from Jerusalem not to give Thomas a visa for Palestine if he applied for one: 'So I am banished. Banishèd. It is a nuisance – I don't know the reason. But I seemed to be very much under suspicion the last fortnight when I stayed in Palestine after having resigned…'

Prudence had a notion of going to Jebel Ansariya in Syria, a centre of worship for the goddess Ashtoreth or Astarte, and was making the journey by car. Baldwin thought she should not go alone and Thomas accompanied her, although he planned to go only as far as Aleppo. They made a round of crusader castles – to Hama through Markab, Kadmous (staying in the house of a Christian gendarme) and Massiaf (after a car break-down that made them, and a hitchhiker, sleep out under the cover of bushes with a fire all night to keep off hyenas, wolves and lions).

Dorothy and Robin house-hunted for a permanent home to replace the house at 20 Bradmore Road in Oxford (his retirement was close and they expected both sons to be living elsewhere). They had been thinking since 15 July of an old house on the outskirts of Chipping Campden and had almost decided to take this despite its expense and defects (no back stairs and only one bath). Dorothy planned to type Robin's letter of offer for the early morning post on 23 July when the breakfast post brought particulars of another house that seemed a better proposition.

This property was on offer as a principal residence, three cottages, four garages and gardens with orchard paddocks, or as an entire estate with an additional four secondary residences. Robin was keen to view but Dorothy was hesitant since it was a wet day. Robin's sister Violet, who was staying with them, recounted the outcome in a letter intended to be passed along her close family network: 'So we went off to see it in the rain and R and D felt at once that it was THE ONE they have been waiting for all this time: "Just dropped from Heaven" D says. Robin's face was all wreathed with smiles coming home (most lovely to see) and he had actually bought it – and three cottages – before I came down for tea!!!' Robin had telephoned the agent with an offer of £6,250 and a return call was made with the seller's acceptance.

The house that had gone through several transformations since its sixteenth-century origins was Crab Mill, named for crab apples in the orchard, in the Warwickshire village of Ilmington. It was a substantial house built of Cotswold stone, with six main bedrooms and three double bedrooms for servants. Dorothy and Robin returned to Crab Mill on 25 July and met the barrister owner. They looked at the other houses on offer and Robin decided to raise his offer by some £5,000 and buy the whole estate of 11 houses and cottages to include rental property as an investment for retirement. Robin wrote on 27 July to Cyril Humphries about this purchase of 'a permanent home in the country with some nice cottages attached to it'. He asked if Cyril and Annie (with their small daughter Christine, Teddy's godchild) would like to try the country instead of the town life in Oxford – with Cyril helping with the garden or the car. This would make them neighbours and helpers for Cookie (still May Fox). Dorothy and Robin showed the Humphries couple the estate and their prospective cottage on 2 August and they accepted. Robin took from St John's College a three-year lease on an Oxford flat in Belsyre Court from the end of September.

Thomas proposed to return to England by mid-September to begin a teacher-training course. He was corresponding with the University of London's Professor of Education, Sir Percy Nunn, who assured him that he could do a month's teaching practice in a London school without committing himself to the full year's training. Thomas left Beirut to make his way back by way of Turkey but his aim of being in London by 14 September was thwarted. As he travelled into Turkey from Syria, the police on the train took his passport for checking and failed to return it. He had to write to Sir Percy Nunn apologising for a two or three days' lateness in arrival for the teaching course.

The England to which Thomas returned on 17 September 1936 after twenty-eight months of Palestine and related travels was greatly troubled by the growing threats of Nazism and Fascism. German troops had occupied Rhineland in March. Civil war emerged in Spain from General Franco's Fascist coup against the leftist Popular Front government in July. Nazi triumphalism was manifest in the Berlin Olympic Games in August.

Thomas went straight into his teaching practice of several lessons a week with boys at the Brecknock Elementary School in Holloway. He had arrived in time for a mass event organised for 20 September by the London District Communist Party and under the aegis of the CP leaders Harry Pollitt and Willie Gallacher. The procession with an accompanying pamphlet – 'The March of English History' – was from the Embankment to Hyde Park. BJ (who had joined the CP in 1934 and was in the Marylebone branch) was surprised to see Thomas on the corner of Baker Street and Marylebone Road as she set off for the procession. They marched together on the demonstration (with a reported 20,000 participants) – and afterwards went their separate ways (BJ suspected that her sister Sigle had tipped off Thomas where he might find her).

At the weekend Thomas and Teddy were together with their parents for the night at their weekend cottage in Broad Campden. It was a moment of change for all the family. Dorothy and Robin had their furniture moved from Broad Campden to the flat they had taken at Belsyre Court and Robin offered the house at 20 Bradmore Road to Queen's College for the Michaelmas term to house undergraduates. Thomas went into lodgings at 32 Holford Square, London WC1. Teddy took a flat at 9 Oak Road, Withington, Manchester, after Margery Fry had provided an introduction to the *Manchester Guardian* editor

William Percival Crozier who was willing to give Teddy a trial at leader writing for a month or so.

Thomas postponed a visit to Oxford as he had corrections and additions to make to his draft pamphlet on Palestine for *The Labour Monthly* and he wanted to see how the Fascists, the anti-Fascists and police would interact in Oswald Mosley's proposed Blackshirt march through the Jewish quarter of the East End. He went on 4 October with Diana Furness on the demonstration to oppose the march. He witnessed a great deal of shoving by the police and one or two baton charges in what became known as the 'Battle of Cable Street'. Thomas decided to pursue his teaching course with history as the main subject – in one of his last classes at Brecknock he gave a lesson on Roman Britain drawing on a text by R.G. Collingwood secured from a Bloomsbury bookseller on tick on the strength of the Hodgkin name and Robin's recently published first volume of *A History of the Anglo-Saxons*.

Thomas spoke about Palestine in the evening of 5 October to the Wood Green branch of the CP and next day he transferred for trial teaching at Marylebone Grammar School where a relative, Peter Maclean, was on the staff and proved to be friendly and helpful. Thomas prepared a school lesson as a conversation about the Renaissance with the St Marylebone boys ('better that the boys should talk considering how ignorant I am about the subject', he wrote to Dorothy). Thomas's next school lessons were on the disparate topics of trade unions and Babylon. From his modest lodgings in Holford Square (where he had no bath), he secured the privileges of the London Library with an application of 28 October and introduction by Derek Kahn, who had recently changed to the English surname of Blaikie.

Thomas had a crowded Sunday on 1 November seeing Teddy in the morning at the comfortable open house Margery Fry kept at 48 Clarendon Road in West London after her retirement as Principal of Somerville. He met a friend at lunch and went on to a meeting in Hyde Park calling for arms for Spain. He saw the Jarrow hunger marchers arrive in Hyde Park and unexpectedly ran into his Winchester contemporary Randall Swingler, now helping to edit *Left Review*. Stocks wrote suggesting that Thomas could return to Manchester in the temporary post of university philosophy lecturer for the next two terms – with the hint of a subsequent permanent appointment. Thomas had a dual hesitation: he regarded himself as a Communist (he was a member of the Holborn Branch) and thought this might be unacceptable to Stocks, and he wondered whether the work would be compatible with his new political perspective. He rejected the Stocks proposal.

Thomas's second article on Palestine that he had worked and reworked since the middle of the year now appeared in two forms, as an extract 'Is Palestine

Prosperous?' in the November issue of *The Labour Monthly* and as full text in a *Labour Monthly* pamphlet 'Who is prosperous in Palestine?' Thomas for both versions continued with the pseudonym 'British Resident' but made no secret of his authorship and sent copies to friends and former colleagues. He was trying to explain the causes of the Arab strike movement in Palestine from April to October 1936 and to counter the Zionist argument that unrestricted Jewish immigration would bring prosperity and a higher standard of living to the whole of Palestine. Thomas's case was that the immigration would lead to further impoverishment of the Arabs. He cited three Arab demands: the stoppage of Jewish immigration, legislation to prevent further sales of land by Arabs to Jews, and the setting up of a responsible national government.

Thomas went on 13 November to a meeting in support of the Jarrow hunger marchers and then for a weekend visit with Prudence Pelham to Eric Gill's home and workshop at Pigotts near High Wycombe. At a workers' theatre in London on 16 November he heard recited what he thought an admirable poem on Spain – then found with additional pleasure that it was written by his friend Randall Swingler.

Teddy had met and drawn to Thomas's attention the Secretary of the British section of the League Against Imperialism, Reginald Bridgeman, who had been in the Foreign Office but become converted to communism. Bridgeman had links with the African political and student lobby in Britain. Thomas sent Bridgeman an essay on T.E. Lawrence that he had written over the previous summer months. He was finding himself in modest demand as an authoritative source on Palestine, speaking to a WEA class in Worcester on the weekend of 21 and 22 November; and to Jewish Communists at Oriel College, Oxford, on 25 November. Hugh Foot, a former colleague in Palestine, read Thomas's pamphlet and wrote from Westminster on 30 November seeking a meeting later in the week.

On a suggestion from Teddy, Margery Fry wrote to Thomas on 4 December inviting him to come to stay with her for a while at Clarendon Road. Thomas accepted and on 9 December prepared his few possessions for a move from Holford Square to Margery's. The family all change was continuing: Dorothy and Robin made what they believed to be the transition from Oxford to Ilmington as their principal residence and slept at Crab Mill on 12 December for the first time. Thomas continued his teaching until 22 December before going on 23 December with Diana Furness for his first sight of Crab Mill.

In the New Year of 1937, Thomas went up to Cumberland for a brief visit and into a lodging arranged by John Farrell. Thomas discussed work prospects in Cumberland with Wilfrid Lunn as an alternative to pursuing a full teacher-training course at London University. Literary journalism offered partial escape. Thomas's connections through Robert Lynd and Lionel Hale had brought book reviewing assignments for the *News Chronicle* – assorted new fiction. Thomas briefly considered going to the conflict in Spain (possibly with Prudence and by borrowing a car from his parents) but returned instead to teaching at Marylebone Grammar School – mainly history classes. He wrote on 21 January to Teddy: 'I find myself getting worse at teaching boys. At times I much regret not having accepted Manchester. However, it probably does me no harm. I am learning a little history, but I doubt if I should ever be able to manage these young fiends, or teach them anything.'

Thomas's political frankness on his visit to Cumberland rebounded. Lunn wrote on 29 January to say that the Cumberland Friends' Unemployment Committee had just met to consider if a post could be found for Thomas in the distressed area. The committee members all recognised the inspiration and value Thomas could bring but thought employment of a member of the CP would prejudice the work especially in the Roman Catholic districts. Lunn suggested that if Thomas could find a formula to cover the position he should write to the committee chairman David Reed for reconsideration.

Thomas sent a formula for consideration by Reed in Cumberland that would make his employment feasible. Reed wrote on 11 February that he would be putting a favourable recommendation to the committee due to meet on 14 February in the light of a Thomas proposal that should meet the difficulty: 'By this, whilst not working with the local party, you would not be prevented for instance, from writing for reviews etc. or doing other literary work, or even speaking, I should think, in other parts of the country.'

Thomas's parents were anxious about his apparent poor health and a recent smoking habit that had become heavy since his first cigarettes in Jerusalem as a form of self-medication against unexpectedly falling asleep. Thomas, in response to prompting by Robin, had been the previous November to see a doctor about his sleeping disorder, whose symptoms had shown since his school days. The doctor was Dr George Riddoch, from Aberdeen University and the London Hospital, who specialised in diseases of the nervous system. Riddoch wanted Thomas to undergo further extensive tests after the initial examination pointed to narcolepsy, a condition characterised by recurring moments of uncontrollable daytime sleepiness. This was a little understood disorder described and named in 1880 by a French clinician Jean Baptiste Edouard Gelineau. The causes even after half a century remained unknown. Thomas was prescribed a new treatment in the form of an amphetamine. Dorothy found in early February when she took a prescription of Thomas's to a pharmacy in Oxford that the pharmacist and his supplier had never heard of the amphetamine being prescribed for internal use. Thomas had a talk on 21 February with a distant cousin

Herbert Hodgkin who suffered from narcolepsy, and wrote next day to Teddy: 'I feel less annoyed with the disease now I know it's hereditary. The bourgeois equivalent of haemophilia among the Bourbons.'

He attended two Sunday conferences in London on 28 February. The first was held by the League Against Imperialism and the speakers included V.K. Krishna Menon, secretary of the India League. Bridgeman made what Thomas thought a convincing argument against colonies being returned to Germany. Thomas made a five-minute contribution to the discussion on Palestine, but had not been given notice that he was expected to speak and felt he had not done well. He went on to a Jewish conference, on Biro-Bidjan colonisation, in the afternoon but felt rather an outsider since the older men all spoke Yiddish rather than English.

Thomas went for a consultation weekend in Cumberland after the Cumberland Friends' Unemployment Committee confirmed that they would like him to work there again. He agreed provisionally with Lunn that he would go up to Cumberland late in March. He had not definitively abandoned the teaching diploma course but had reached the conclusion that he had better abandon it.

Among personal obligations Margery retained from her years as Somerville Principal was one to the LMH lecturer Dot Wrinch who taught mathematics to women students from other colleges including Somerville. Dr Wrinch had moved from Cambridge to Oxford after marriage to a mathematician John William Nicholson. Margery was godmother to their daughter Pamela and kept a friendly eye on Pam when the mother was out of Oxford on research missions or conferences abroad. In August 1936 Dr Wrinch had sought assistance for Pam from the Oxford research scientist Dorothy Crowfoot (the eldest of four Crowfoot sisters). Since Pam was returning as a boarder to St Christopher's School, Letchworth, on 17 September and Dr Wrinch was sailing to the US next day for a tour of centres of protein studies, Dorothy Crowfoot had agreed to keep an eye on Pam, who would write a weekly letter from school.

Margery was particularly fond of Dorothy Crowfoot, had interviewed her in March 1928 for entrance to Somerville and was Principal through her early undergraduate years. When Margery left Somerville, she encouraged this exceptionally brilliant student to keep in touch and offered her hospitality in London when she needed to be there for her work. Dorothy Crowfoot took Part I of the chemistry school in 1931. She returned to Oxford to begin research in X-ray crystallography and to complete the formalities of Part II, since it was a peculiarity of this subject that able students were expected to do a fourth year of research under supervision and to submit a thesis. She then went to Cambridge to continue her research, this time with John Desmond Bernal (Sage) in the crystallographic laboratory.

After two academic years in Cambridge Dorothy Crowfoot returned to Somerville in September 1934 to combine her research with being a chemistry tutor. On 25 October she was given shining colourless crystals of insulin to examine (that were too small to X-ray) and insulin became one of her central research interests. The significance of insulin was the discovery by Frederick Banting and Charles Best in 1921 that diabetes was the result of the inability of the pancreas to produce insulin and process the glucose that the human body needed for energy. Dorothy Crowfoot knew about insulin from a book she had read as a schoolchild – the second edition of *Fundamentals of Biochemistry* by T.R. Parsons, who described it as a hormone active in treating diabetes.

She had continued to read about insulin; from 1934 she began to grow insulin crystals and from 1935 to publish her own findings on the subject. In early 1937, one of the leading scientists of the time, Sir William Bragg, suggested that she bring her crystals to the Royal Institution in London to photograph them with the powerful X-ray tube that had been built there. She stayed at Margery's house when taking her insulin photographs and met Thomas, who was living there. The two adults were of an age – he about to turn 27 on 3 April and she on 12 May – and were Oxford contemporaries although they had not known each other there. Each knew something of the other. Thomas's mother in the summer of 1932 had invited Dorothy Crowfoot to tea in Oxford to sound out the possibilities of Thomas joining an archaeological dig with the Crowfoots in Palestine, but this was when Thomas and Teddy were travelling on holiday through Europe. Thomas had met the Crowfoot parents and their second daughter Joan in Palestine early in 1933 and on several subsequent occasions, but this was during Dorothy Crowfoot's research in Cambridge. Margery had spoken to Robin of Dorothy Crowfoot's splendid qualities on hearing years before that Thomas was going to Palestine and had thought they should meet.

On this first evening at Margery's they went on talking very late, filling in the gaps. Thomas read aloud extracts from the novels he had been sent for review. The Alicia Markova-Anton Dolin ballet company was dancing 'Swan Lake' from 8 March in the second week of a season at the King's Theatre, Hammersmith. Margery treated her houseguests to tickets for one of the performances (through much of which Thomas seems to have slept). Dorothy Crowfoot returned to her routine of that time: in the Oxford vacation Patterson function calculations for insulin; or on visits to Cambridge to keep in touch with Bernal's group of scientists. She would also go to the Norfolk village of Geldeston where she had spent her late childhood and where her parents lived in the Old House. She helped cope with the personal crises of her younger sisters: Joan (whom she sometimes called Jo); Elisabeth (with an early career in repertory theatre and known there as Liz Bayly, although at home as Betty); and Diana (known as

Dilly), who was thinking of coming up to Oxford. Dorothy (who was not keen on the form 'Dot' and was conscious that Dot Wrinch – some 16 years her senior – had that name in university circles) was known within the Crowfoot family circle as Dossie.

Joan Crowfoot was the focus of a difficult courtship by Denis Payne, who was from an Oxford family and had met her in Cambridge where he worked in a bookshop. In March 1937, Joan was away on an archaeological expedition and Denis sought advice from the older sister who deferred any decision to Joan. Denis, in a letter from Cambridge on 18 March, wrote: 'Dear Dossie, Travelling back in the train this morning I realised that you're inevitably right.' He had written to Joan so that she might decide: 'It was difficult to avoid asking her outright to come back on the one hand, and seeming indifference as to her return on the other: and I'm not sure that I've succeeded.'

Thomas returning to the familiar ground of Cleator Moor took lodgings with a Mrs Scrogham and her husband, an iron-ore miner, at 149 Ennerdale Road that were more slap-up than he had intended. Margery spent the weekend of 3 to 5 April with Robin and Dorothy Hodgkin and they talked further about Thomas's state of physical health. The parents were glad to hear that Thomas had promised Margery and Prudence to see another doctor. Thomas came back to London in June to stay again at Margery's and to follow the round of medical tests discussed with her general practitioner Dr William Alexander Hislop, who brought three specialists into the task. They were: Gavin Livingstone (an ear, nose and throat surgeon); a consultant physician Dr Frank Patrick Lee Lander (who had published on anaemia and rickets); and Dr Desmond Curran, a psychiatrist and specialist in diseases of the nervous system (British trained and with experience at the Johns Hopkins Hospital in Baltimore in the US). Lee Lander required Thomas to have a chest X-ray to exclude the possibility of tuberculosis of the lungs.

The medical men would discuss and prepare a formal written report, but Thomas collected initial verbal opinions. One tonsil was infected; Hislop did not think this could be enough to affect Thomas's general health and he would indicate what treatment was advisable. Thomas had a sore throat and must give up smoking (he did so from 23 June). Thomas might have some mild sort of bronchitis, hence the X-ray photograph of his chest.

Thomas's interest in WEA work had led to his being asked to take a pupil in philosophy at the Oxford summer school in the period from 15 to 29 July. Formal details were sent in a letter from Edward Stuart Cartwright, who was organising secretary for the Tutorial Classes Committee of the University of Oxford Delegacy for Extra-Mural Studies based at Rewley House in Wellington Square. Thomas was to give his student a total of four hours' tuition a week, preferably in the mornings but at convenient times that he could work out with the student. His first student McVittie was a postman from Dumfries. Thomas was offered a second experienced tutorial class student interested in taking the political thought of Plato and Aristotle who would require a separate four hours of tuition during the week. Thomas would be paid the usual fee of 10 shillings an hour.

The Delegacy for Extra-Mural Studies was the institutional structure from 1924 of earlier university extension work and a summer school at Balliol was heir to a tradition initiated by AL Smith. Smith wanted participants in extension tutorial classes to be in touch with Oxford University and arranged hospitality at Balliol for a summer school for WEA students in the long vacation of 1910. The school became an annual event where Smith taught regularly and he insisted on individual tuition as the chief means of teaching. Thomas wrote to his grandmother Mrs AL suggesting that he should stay with her for the first few days of the 1937 summer school.

In correspondence from John Crowfoot it had been agreed that Thomas should visit Geldeston for the first weekend in August. Dossie wrote from Geldeston on 13 July indicating a possible change of timing since she was due to leave England on 28 July for a vacation in Yugoslavia. Her father suggested Thomas might rather come some other time before then, say 26 July. She would be coming to Oxford for a week from 15 July (her undisclosed thinking was to go on from Oxford to Cambridge on 22 or 23 July to see Sage – to walk and talk about their scientific work).

Thomas wrote on 15 July a cordial reply explaining that he could not change the weekend that he had planned to stay at her home since he must be in Oxford from 17 to 31 July, working at the WEA summer school including weekends, but since she would be in Oxford from 15 to 22 July he asked if they might meet for supper on 19 July when he could call for her at Somerville at about seven in the evening, and she could reply to Balliol. Thomas was in Oxford in time for a preliminary meeting of the summer school students and tutors held at Rewley house on the morning of 17 July. He was staying with his grandmother at 14 Banbury Road but went during the weekend to Ilmington where Helen Sutherland was visiting.

Thomas had letters to write and after tea went for a walk with Helen. Helen had an impression that Thomas felt he should not have left Palestine, which was much on his mind. Thomas went back to Oxford early on 19 July to agree his tutoring timetable with his first two students. He saw Dossie in the evening. Thomas, writing to his mother on the night of 20 July, noted that he and his grandmother were getting on without quarrelling though he was out of the house for most meals. He had decided to stay in Balliol for the second week of the school.

Dr Hislop provided a confidential report dated 20 July on the medical examinations Thomas had undergone in June. The cautious main finding read:

Mr Thomas Hodgkin is suffering from symptoms very suggestive of narcolepsy. Narcolepsy is produced by different causes and an attempt is being made to discover the underlying cause here. A general examination showed him to be thin and there was evidence of undernourishment. There was also some bronchial irritation, apparently of fairly long duration. Beyond these, there was no obvious physical disability detected.

Livingstone reported infected tonsils and slight pharyngitis (throat irritation) – probably due to over-smoking, and considered it would be wise to have the tonsils removed. Dr Lander corroborated the diagnosis of narcolepsy. The chest X-ray did not show any evidence of tuberculosis. Lander recommended several months of fresh air, good food, moderate exercise, etc. in order to get rid of the bronchial irritation. Dr Curran gave similar findings to Lander, but he suggested treating the existing narcolepsy with Benzedrine. Benzedrine was a new medication (beta-phenylisopropylamine) that in recent months had been under trial at the Mayo Clinic in the US with a hundred patients and a broad range of conditions including depression and exhaustion. The Mayo patients took tablets of 10 to 20 milligrams.

Thomas with two tutorial students, family visits and London commitments was finding difficulty in matching his timetable with Dossie's. She was characteristically working late night and early morning hours in the laboratory (for her first major paper on the crystal structure of insulin) so that even a meeting at midnight was a possibility. Thomas conducted a whirlwind wooing, partly in the form of notes exchanged from 14 Banbury Road and through the college mail services for Balliol and Somerville.

After the meeting on 19 July, he missed finding Dossie on 20 July. He rearranged his appointments in London on 21 July so that he could spend the evening with her rather than in London. Dossie was unsettled by the attention, and wrote to Thomas: 'I'll come with you tonight and stay with you tonight but I won't promise anything more because I feel all perplexed in myself and a little troubled by your urgency – but not fully knowing you or understanding it's too difficult to be sure.' They went to a country inn (the Rose Revived near Witney, a haunt of his undergraduate years). They exchanged letters next day: he to her 'Last night was deeply happy. I am thankful you burnt our boats and came. And you're happy about it too. This does seem a beginning, don't you think?'; she to him: 'I'm feeling still very exalted though also really incredulous.'

Thomas, who was going back to his parents at Crab Mill for the weekend and for a family outing to 'King Lear' at Stratford-on-Avon, wrote to Dossie in the few minutes before seeing his student on 23 July: 'I feel very contented about us really. And I don't mind much it being three days until I see you again.' He promised to do as much work as possible so as to have more time free during the next week. Dossie postponed her departure for the journey to Yugoslavia.

Thomas surprised his mother on 25 July by asking for some flowers to be picked that he could take back to Oxford. Dorothy tried unsuccessfully to buy Benzedrine for Thomas in Stratford and wrote to Dr Curran for some to be sent to him. Thomas found a Benzedrine supply in Oxford but was glad for Curran to send more. He wrote to Curran about experimentation in the dosage. Dr Curran wrote on 29 July with a prescription for Benzedrine tablets and advice: 'Some people find it makes their heart palpitate if taken in doses which are too large; but I see no reason why you should not go up to 25 milligrams a day, or even more should the effects not be unfortunate, and I should really be most interested to hear how you feel it works with you.'

Thomas spent much of the bank holiday weekend at the beginning of August with the Crowfoot family in Geldeston, although in different circumstances from when the plan was made. The hasty, snatched encounters of the few days in and around Oxford and experimental lovemaking had shown Thomas and Dossie that they wanted to marry. What had been envisaged as a routine social call to Geldeston turned into an idyll. They paddled along the canal cut from the River Waveney to Geldeston (for the maltings). They walked and sat in the sun. They went along a lane and looked for livelong – the flower one may sleep with on Midsummer night and dream of one's lover. They found only the willowherb growing in profusion over the marshes.

Their decision to marry was allowed to trickle out to their families and friends. The Crowfoot parents were the first to hear and then Thomas wrote to tell his parents that he and Dossie loved each other. Robin and Dorothy received the news well and on 4 August sent a congratulatory telegram and letters to Thomas. Dossie wrote to Sage breaking the news of her feeling for Thomas and pointing to a sudden dreamlike quality of two nights together with Thomas in strange country places and days wandering through woods. Dossie left London on 6 August for her delayed vacation of four weeks in Yugoslavia.

Dossie was returning to England in time for the annual meeting of the British Association for the Advancement of Science in Nottingham – and particularly for a session on the structure of proteins on 3 September. Thomas arranged that he and Dossie should spend the first weekend in September with Helen Sutherland at Rock Hall so that she could come to know his family circle. Thomas had not found an opportunity in his few meetings with Dossie to talk about his own sister Betty and her childhood death in 1927. He wrote to his mother on 18 August suggesting that she bring to Rock a copy of the memorial volume to Betty so that Dossie could see it, especially as they would be visiting Bamburgh (where Betty was buried).

In his letter to Dossie on 19 August he suggested a Christmas wedding to be discussed when they met and on 8 September arranged that Dossie be sent as a gift from him a set of artist's proofs of David Jones's engravings illustrating 'The Rime of the Ancient Mariner'. Thomas had them with him in Palestine and they were left behind with other possessions when Thomas was barred in 1936 from returning. Eric Gill, who had rescued the set on his 1937 visit to Palestine, sent the pictures to Dossie. Thomas sent Dossie a book he had received from the Left Book Club *Modern Marriage and Birth Control* (by Edward Fyfe Griffith). Dossie received the Jones illustrations and the marriage book and sent Thomas presents she had chosen for him: a volume of Yeats and a green and grey tie. When Dossie was changing library books in the last minutes before closing she had chanced on Léon Blum's *Marriage,* newly translated by Warre Bradley Wells, and took that with her.

Robin had resigned from Queen's and this was due to take effect on 29 September (a farewell garden party he gave in Queen's in mid-June had brought nearly four hundred acceptances). His and Dorothy's contemplation of their life of retirement at Crab Mill was jolted when the Provost of Queen's Canon Streeter was killed in an aeroplane crash into a mountain near Basel in Switzerland on 10 September. Robin had been a possible alternative to Streeter in the election of 1934 but his reaction now was to urge the possibility of electing a young don Oliver Franks, who had gone recently to Glasgow. Robin sought the advice of his sons and with their encouragement informed his colleagues that if they wanted him as provost and did not think Franks would be better he could not refuse. Queen's had a college meeting on 22 September and agreed unofficially to support Robin Hodgkin as provost and Robin was elected Provost of Queen's on 5 October.

Thomas travelled to London on 9 December, dashed to Oxford for a suit fitting and a brief meeting with his mother. Then with Dossie he went back to London where they saw the clergyman chosen to perform the marriage, the Reverend John Cyril Putterill, Vicar of St Andrews in Plaistow in the far east end of London, to discuss variations on the conventional marriage service. They stopped at a jeweller's and bought a wedding ring. They agreed afresh on a honeymoon destination – Margery Fry's suggestion of La Croix – dined with Margery, Prudence Pelham and David Jones. The Habimah theatre group from Palestine were playing a short season at the Savoy Theatre. Thomas and Dossie, joined by Derek Blaikie, went to a performance of 'The Dybbuk'. After the play

they sat talking at the Strand Palace Hotel with Abraham Baratz and other per-
formers.

Thomas returned to Cumberland on the night sleeper. Dossie stayed overnight
at Margery's and then went back to Oxford to devote half a day to spinning a
centrifuge in the laboratory to measure the molecular weight of the vitamin E
derivative she had been given. Thomas's last lecture of the year was on Monday
13 December and he travelled to join his family in Oxford on 14 December.
They went on to the village wedding at St Michael's Church in Geldeston on
16 December. Teddy was Thomas's best man and they wore what one guest
described as 'un-wedding-y' clothes, Thomas in a grey-blue-green lovat tweed
and Teddy in a darker roughish blue tweed. Dossie wore a flowery brocade of
blue and green threaded with gold (like the background of mediaeval pictures
of Paradise, as a guest described it). Jack Putterill spoke informally about the
couple and instead of the first book of Corinthians he read Shakespeare's sonnet
116 'Let me not to the marriage of true minds Admit impediments'. The first
verse of William Blake's 'Jerusalem' was sung as a solo during the signing of the
register and the congregation joined in as a chorus for the second verse.

Thomas and Dossie went to London and then to France for the start of their
honeymoon in the Villa St Michel at La Croix, Valmer, in the Var. Sage wrote to
Dossie from Hampstead that he would have liked to have been at the marriage
ceremony: 'I do wish you and Thomas the greatest satisfaction and understanding. I don't feel and won't feel cut off but rather released to meet you evenly.'
Dossie and Thomas returned from La Croix on 26 December overnight by train
to Paris and London where they went for a night's rest to Margery Fry. They
made another night train journey to Cumberland for a few more days together
before the start of Oxford term.

Chapter 3
Adult education, war and peace: 1938-1952

In the first days of 1938, Thomas and Dossie found new lodgings for Thomas with Mrs Philipson, a Scottish-born Cumbrian, at 53 Church Street, Whitehaven. The new lodging offered a more accessible bathroom and hot baths at will. Mrs Philipson had other lodgers: a building engineer, a master tailor and travellers going about to canvass newspaper subscriptions. Dossie left on 7 January for the start of term and the couple planned to try to meet at fortnightly intervals (and for longer spells when vacations allowed); they began to correspond more or less on alternate days. Thomas was busy with his classes and drafted a fresh article on the conflict in Palestine for the WEA journal *The Highway* (highlighting the impossibility of a united front of Arab and Jewish workers so long as the organised Jewish working class supported demands for further Jewish mass immigration into Palestine).

Thomas's parents, newly installed in the Provost's House at Queen's, were looking for a country cottage near Oxford for Dossie and Thomas to rent as a temporary home. One possibility was a house at Shotover, Elder Stubs, that had been the rented home of the art historian Kenneth Clark and his wife Jane when he was keeper of the department of fine arts at the Ashmolean Museum. He had moved in 1935 as director of the National Gallery in London and received a knighthood in the New Year honours of 1938 when the Clarks were living in Kent. The Elder Stubs garden had gone wild from neglect and Lady Clark said they would let the remainder of the Clark tenancy rent-free on condition that the Hodgkins spent at least £30 on doing up the garden and would leave the house in reasonable decorative repair. Thomas and Dossie agreed to take on Elder Stubs for the summer.

Dossie suspected she might be pregnant. Thomas discussed with Dossie and with Margery his own career plans – both of them believed it would take several years to achieve anything substantial in educational work in Cumberland and that he might consider alternatives. Thomas in Cumberland went to Wilfrid Lunn on 21 April and explained his desire to broaden his experience. Lunn agreed that Thomas should apply for a University of Manchester post as resident tutor.

Dossie, Thomas, Teddy and Prudence converged on the hastily furnished and equipped Elder Stubs on 30 April – in the light of Jane Clark's request a gardener, Finlay, had been engaged for the summer months. Thomas initially spent only two nights in the first home of the marriage before returning to Cumberland, and with no indication from Manchester of an early appointment, he looked in mid-May at advertisements for other possibilities. He applied for posts in Bristol and Gloucester and summed up his year's employment as education officer for the Cumberland Friends' Unemployment Committee. He had been responsible during the past winter for the organisation of 18 lecture courses in 12 unemployed clubs. At the same time he had taught seven lecture-courses (five of 12 lectures and two of six lectures), mainly on international relations and social history, and given single popular lectures on different subjects, including some to women's groups.

He was called for interview for the Manchester tutorial post on 16 June – without success. He was asked to tutor two students in philosophy at the WEA's Oxford Summer School in the first fortnight of July, with the possibility of some work in the third week. On a two-month break from his duties in Cumberland he could live for a while at Elder Stubs, do his tutoring in Oxford as required and go to London to maintain his political contacts and interests. The third week of WEA work in Oxford materialised. Then Thomas went up to London to see George Mansour of the Jaffa Labour Party, exiled from Palestine and teaching in Iraq. Thomas invited him to the cottage, along with other colleagues, friends and acquaintances of the couple. He wrote to his mother on 22 July that Dossie enjoyed the visitors and 'is almost as rash about inviting people as I am'. He felt able to assure her that Mrs Bye who did the cooking at Elder Stubs was almost on the level of May Fox who cooked for his parents: 'She makes beautiful soups, summer puddings, etc. and we get all the credit.'

Thomas returned to his Cumberland work in mid-August refreshed by the summer months with Dossie and ready to look for somewhere more agreeable than his Whitehaven lodging as a place to live with her and eventually with the child they expected at the end of the year. He moved on 8 October to new lodgings with a Mrs Robinson at 19 The Promenade, at the northernmost end of Maryport, where he enjoyed being able to look out on the seas and mountains. He found Mrs Robinson's cooking to his taste since she baked good cakes and bread and provided meals including kippers, fish cakes and fish pie.

Dossie, who was in London on 17 November to make a presentation to a Royal Society session on protein molecules, stayed with Margery Fry and wrote next day to Thomas: 'I had a very good talk with Margery. She made one suggestion for the child's name if a boy – that he should be called Luke after Luke Howard, your great grandfather who was an FRS and named the clouds. I rather like the name. Do you?' Luke Howard, born in 1772 and actually Thomas's great-great-grandfather, was a self-taught scientist particularly known for a paper 'On Modification of the Clouds', which he read to the Askesian Society in 1802.

Dossie went to Geldeston a week later to await the birth of their child. Thomas joined her at Geldeston in mid-December for their first wedding anniversary, and found her cheerful and unfussed, spending most of the day finishing the protein paper that she had been working at all summer. Dossie's labour pains began on 19 December. On the afternoon of 20 December as Thomas waited in John Crowfoot's study Dossie gave birth – to a son just under 7 lbs in weight and given the name Luke Howard in line with Margery's suggestion. Thomas and Dossie were firm that the birth should not have a ritual announcement in *The Times*. This caused a mild flutter in the family since Thomas's mother felt she had to write numerous letters to family and friends and reported to Thomas that his aunt Violet Holdsworth feared people would think the child illegitimate.

Thomas and Dossie parted on New Year's Day of 1939. Thomas sat in the Great Hall at Euston waiting for a late train to the north and wrote to Dossie of the prospect of being reunited with her and Luke in Cumberland within some three weeks. Dossie wrote to him from Geldeston that the baby's nurse had chided her for gently crying into the remains of her soup after Thomas's departure. The nurse declared that weeping would spoil the baby's milk. Thomas arranged with Mrs Robinson for his family's arrival in Maryport. He was promised the larger of the two bedrooms with a second bed and a gas fire. Dossie wrote on 17 January that she had developed a breast abscess. Thomas's plan to go to Geldeston to fetch Dossie and Luke was put on hold when Dossie's condition persisted with complications.

Thomas was in London on 29 January in transit between Geldeston and Maryport and called on his Jerusalem friend, the architect Austen Harrison, at his flat in Lincoln's Inn Fields – for supper and talk about the Arab and Jewish delegations to an official conference in London on Palestine. Thomas thought that the choice of George Antonius as secretary-general indicated that the British government meant business. He was looking forward to bringing Dossie to London where he might meet some of the Arab delegates to the conference and Luke might be shown off to Sage and other of Dossie's London colleagues and friends. The second plan to collect Dossie and Luke was frustrated – this time by a driving accident for Thomas in which the car's windscreen was smashed and he suffered a severe cut in his neck. He made his way to hospital and described the event to Dossie in a pencilled letter of 2 February from Whitehaven Hospital: '… a cut in my neck from the broken glass (like the advertisements for

Triplex), which went a little deep in one part and so made it difficult for them to stitch it up. However with the help of chloroform they stitched it satisfactorily and I am now lying in this ward full of chaps with broken legs from pit accidents and things…'

Thomas had also contacted Teddy about the accident. Teddy took advice from the wealthy Morton family – of Jocelyn Morton who had been under Robin Hodgkin's moral tutorship at Queen's – who lived near Carlisle at Dalston Hall. Teddy arranged for Thomas's transfer from the ward in Whitehaven Hospital to Dr Hartley's nursing home in Carlisle. By 5 February, Thomas's wife, child and mother were travelling to Cumberland. Dorothy reported to Robin that Thomas was in a good nursing home and that she, Dossie and Luke were comfortably entertained by the Mortons. Dossie visiting Thomas was advised that she should be admitted for treatment for her own health problems and that she must stop breast-feeding Luke.

Thomas was moved on 10 February to write verses on Dossie's distress including the lines:

> Dejected she sits in her room
> And tries to occupy her mind with scientific perplexities.
> They have taken from her her seven-weeks son,
> And bound her breasts with plaster.
> Her milk, say the Mandarins of Carlisle, is contaminated,
> An ill diet for the babe.

Thomas made a speedy recovery in the nursing home. He turned his mind to house hunting in Oxford, where Dossie for the first fortnight of March was a patient in the Acland Hospital. He prepared too for job-hunting and told Wilfrid Lunn on 21 March that he was resigning. Dossie identified a house in Oxford that might serve as their new home: 315 Woodstock Road in North Oxford with a view towards the countryside round Wytham. The existing tenant offered the assignment of the end of a lease. Thomas recruited a young Maryport woman, Renée Hyde, as a helper for the baby. He was in Oxford again at the tail-end of April to assist in setting up their new home in Woodstock Road, with a Mrs Townsend as cook, a Mr Gee as an occasional gardener and the French Laundry to call for the heavy washing. Mrs Townsend turned out to be difficult as cook and when she sent a note that her own small son had measles Dossie turned to a Mrs Arnold from Cutteslowe as an alternative.

Thomas attended a job interview in Birmingham on 18 May without success. He renewed his application of a year earlier to the University of Manchester for the post of resident tutor. He then applied to Rewley House in Oxford for a post as organising tutor in the North Staffordshire district of the WEA. Ties of long standing bound the interests of Oxford and the Potteries in extramural and workers' education. Oxford regularly sent staff tutors to North Staffs and two vacancies were due to be filled. The North Staffs district secretary was George Edward Cecil Wigg who on appointment in 1937 retired from the army to take on the task. In May 1939, Wigg became an advisory member of the Oxford University Tutorial Classes Committee.

The North Staffordshire Sub-Committee met at Rewley House on the afternoon of 31 July to appoint the two organising tutors for North Staffs. The key Oxford figures on the panel were Sandie Lindsay, Master of Balliol, in the chair, Charles Morris as secretary of the Extra-Mural Delegacy and Stuart Cartwright as secretary of the Tutorial Classes Committee. Wigg was one of four Staffordshire guests in a consultative capacity. In a short-list of eight, they interviewed Thomas, from Oxford, and candidates from Loughborough, Liverpool, Dartington, Cambridge, Manchester, Sheffield and Stoke-on-Trent. The panel decided to offer appointments to Thomas Hodgkin and to Miss Gladys Malbon, from Dartington in Devon. The tutors were to take up their duties on 1 September and were appointed in the first place for a probationary year.

The post meant that Thomas would be lodging in the Potteries but was within reasonable reach of Oxford, which could remain as the centre of family life. He began making connections in North Staffs. His friend Randall Swingler had a brother Stephen Swingler who lived in a country cottage at Gnosall some six miles from Stafford and without being a staff tutor took WEA classes in the North Staffs district. A Cumberland friend, the Frizington vicar Alan Ecclestone, wrote to congratulate Thomas on the appointment and recommend his friend Harold Mason, vicar of one of the Burslem churches.

Thomas's parents were offering as an Oxford base for Dossie and Luke (with his nursemaid Renée) part of Thomas's own childhood home at 20 Bradmore Road converted into flats two years earlier. In Britain as a whole, the prospect of a war that might involve massive air bombardment was impelling some three million people to move or contemplate moving from potentially vulnerable target areas to what might be safer locations. Thomas's parents were expecting Queen's College to be requisitioned, at least in part. Dorothy, with the help of an Austrian refugee she was housing, worked at darkening the windows of Crab Mill with makeshift curtains and brown paper. She believed that her grandson Luke was safer in Ilmington than he could be almost anywhere in Britain.

Thomas went to Staffordshire for the official start of his new job on 1 September. With Dossie's help he had picked pleasant rooms with Mrs Poole as landlady at 2 The Avenue, Harpfield, Hartshill in Stoke-on-Trent. His first preparatory task was collating information for a Citizens' Advice Bureau (CAB) due to open that week. He went to Oxford to collect clothes and books for the Staffordshire lodgings and spent the night of 2 September at Crab Mill with his parents and wife and child. They were together when the British ultimatum to Germany against Hitler's invasion of Poland expired at 11 next morning. A quarter of an hour later Chamberlain, almost reluctantly, broadcast a declaration of war on Germany.

Thomas moved into Mrs Poole's. He had a spacious allowance of a bedroom and two sitting rooms, although was almost instantly apprehensive about the beta standard of his new landlady's cooking. He could however go into the kitchen with the Poole family to listen to news on the wireless. On the first day of war he went out for a walk in the evening and caused a mild sensation by carrying a gas-mask as about the only person who did. He reported to Dossie: 'Almost everyone I passed I could hear saying – "Oo look, he's carrying his gas-mask".' He spent the morning of 4 September visiting class secretaries to see what they thought about classes carrying on. In the mining villages, the miners expected to go on mining as usual and wanted classes to continue. In towns with more unemployed or middle-class people, there was less certainty. He spent the evening visiting a veteran of the Tunstall tutorial class, Elijah Sambrook, and they called on two more village class secretaries, who expected to be going on working much as normal under wartime conditions.

He had lunch next day with the Swinglers (Ann and Stephen and their child) at their cottage in Gnosall. Stephen and Thomas talked about the war prospects, with Stephen sympathetic to the Non-aggression Pact between Germany and the Soviet Union of 23 August and Thomas remaining unconvinced. George Wigg was negotiating for a special petrol ration for WEA tutors under the forthcoming rationing scheme. Thomas bought a bicycle and was finding it not too difficult to ride in the blackout although disconcerted by the rumble of lorries coming up behind him.

He was beginning to know WEA colleagues in the area: his fellow recruit Gladys Malbon, John Rhodes the district treasurer and active over the new CAB, Harold Marks, who as an undergraduate at University College, Oxford, was tutored by the Socialist economist G.D.H. Cole, and recruited as a WEA tutor a couple of years before Thomas. Thomas formed an impression of Gladys Malbon as chatty and cheery and of Harold Marks as inclined to be gloomy.

Thomas followed up the introduction from Alan Ecclestone to Harold Mason by going on 12 September to give a talk in the vestry of the Sneyd church on the familiar topic of Palestine. He tried to connect Palestine with the international war situation, arguing that the interests and aims of colonial peoples should be remembered during a war and the colonial peoples should not be regarded simply as a means for winning the war of the colonial power. The Palestine talk was one among several individual current affairs lectures Thomas was to give in his first year as a staff tutor. However, his main responsibility was to conduct long-running sessional classes.

His regular Tuesday night class at the Audley Social Service Club from 19 September looked at the rise and development of the British Empire. Tutors could also conduct terminal or informal short courses of three lectures, or half a dozen or more. Thomas had nine of these requiring over the year several dozen lectures – often on themes woven around the war and war aims, although Thomas felt confused over current war issues and preferred a more reflective historical approach to Britain's foreign policy. He was also to participate in one-day and weekend schools. The tutoring and lecturing took him over the Five Towns of the Potteries and the mining areas – including clubs, meeting halls and homes in Brindley Ford, Burslem, Kidsgrove, Leycett, Longton, Middleport, Rookery and Shelton. The principal lectures were concentrated in the first three working days of the week.

Thomas's mother intended to keep open Crab Mill and the Provost's House at Queen's since the college would continue to have a core of undergraduates and she wanted to be in Oxford with Robin. Dossie would remain with Luke in Oxford provided that the city did not become a target for German bombing and on 26 September, with professional movers and the help of a friend and the cook, Dossie made the move from 315 Woodstock Road to the top flat at 20 Bradmore Road.

Thomas wrote to BJ – with whom he had been out of touch since before his marriage – about his dispersed family life. She had become a publisher's reader for Heinemann and in 1938 married Jack Gaster, a Communist Jewish lawyer and one of numerous children of the Haham (head of the Sephardi community in Britain) Moses Gaster. BJ replied on 10 October to Thomas about occasions when she had been meaning to write to him but had not – 'your marriage, your son, my marriage – all of them made me tremendously happy and longing to write'. She now wanted to meet Dossie and Luke and she wanted Thomas to meet Jack who at 32 was not in the conscription age group, but did night and morning war service as an air-raid warden and worked as a lawyer in the afternoons. They lived in a London flat at 94 Baker Street high above ground level with a bathroom window opening towards the Classic Cinema next door. Her publishing office had moved to the country where she went every Tuesday and Friday. Jack's mother was living at Appleton near Oxford and BJ wondered whether it might be possible to combine a visit to her with a meeting with the Hodgkin family, petrol rationing permitting. Thomas relayed the suggestion with approval in his regular letter to Dossie.

Wigg, as an enthusiastic and exacting taskmaster, had asked Thomas to go round miners' welfare groups to try to fix up lectures, and Thomas sought advice from Bridgeman of the League Against Imperialism on Indian and other colonial speakers who might come to Stoke. Bridgeman recommended 'the very active and able' Krishna Menon as a speaker on India; Desmond Buckle for West Africa, Peter Blackman for the West Indies and Johnstone (Jomo) Kenyatta for East Africa. The colonial pressure groups in London were in more than their accustomed turmoil as they balanced the political opportunities the war might bring to their cause against loyal restraint in pressing their demands in wartime.

The address for Buckle, Aggrey House in Doughty Street, was in itself a sensitive barometer since it had been opened five years before in October 1934 as a hostel for African students and was operated with financial support from the Colonial Office. From the outset, some African students, especially from West Africa, had argued that Colonial Office tutelage would rule out Aggrey House as a centre for revolutionary propaganda or even ordinary criticism of British government measures. However, in the late 1930s, the Aggrey House Committee included personalities with links to the conservative League of Coloured Peoples (LCP, founded 1931) and the more radical International African Service Bureau (created in 1937 from an Abyssinia lobby). Buckle was from the Gold Coast and associated with Gold Coast student politics and with the Negro Welfare Association. Blackman in October 1939 was drafting a moderate statement on wartime restraint for the LCP. Kenyatta, who had come to Britain in 1929 and represented the Kikuyu Central Association, had early links with the League Against Imperialism and with the CP.

Thomas pursued the political concerns on 2 January 1940 through a day of encounters in London. He began about noon with Krishna Menon, who was willing to come to Stoke in February and thought it possible to establish a local group to support the aims of the India League. Menon and Thomas explored the possibility of forming a small committee of Arab, English and possibly Jewish representatives along with other activists on colonial issues to work on Arab questions on a broader basis than the Arab Centre. Thomas went on to Bertorelli's in Soho for a pasta lunch with Bridgeman who was careworn by constituency difficulties with the Labour Party over his critical attitude to the war: Thomas thought Bridgeman was being rigid and suspected that Bridgeman thought Thomas inclined to hedge.

After lunch, Thomas made telephone calls to see how he might spend the evening: Margery Fry was out of London, John Richmond and Diana Furness no longer on the telephone. He found BJ in and arranged to go round to the Gasters' Baker Street flat for supper. He walked on to Aggrey House to meet

Blackman and Buckle who were also willing to come as speakers to Stoke. They talked about African questions. He tried to visit the London Library and found it closed for the New Year holiday, and went on to BJ. They talked about a child she was expecting in July. Jack Gaster arrived and Thomas showed photographs of Luke and offered a Moses basket as a belated wedding present. They talked of the war and workers' education. Thomas was pleased to find that Jack had an ILP background and had been to Cumberland to do ILP meetings. Thomas was easily persuaded to stay the night since he had an unfinished call to make to the London Library.

Thomas returned to his lodgings with Mrs Poole and the round of lectures interspersed with fleeting visits home to Oxford. By mid-February, he gave up the lodgings (warm fires, but indifferent meals ill-adapted to his teaching schedules). He moved temporarily into a small hotel and had the occasional use of Gladys Malbon's flat in which to prepare lectures. Krishna Menon drew about forty people to a meeting at Stafford and half a dozen said they would join a local branch of the India League if one were formed.

Thomas made spasmodic efforts during the week to find new lodgings. A member of Thomas's Stoke class – a pacifist-Socialist schoolteacher Leslie Charles – suggested Thomas might lodge at his parents' house at 245 Prince's Road in Stoke-on-Trent. Thomas visited the house and decided he would like to lodge there. BJ wrote on 23 February that she and Jack would be going next day to visit Jack's mother in Appleton near Oxford and to inquire if there was a possibility of seeing the Hodgkins on the way. The date did not fit: Dossie – leaving Luke with Thomas's parents – joined Thomas on the evening of 24 February for a weekend in the Potteries, bringing a letter from Teddy, who had joined the army in September, saying that he was being posted to India. Dossie helped Thomas settle into the new lodgings that both thought a considerable improvement on the previous ones. Not only was the Charles family friendly and intelligent, but David Charles had in his time stayed in some ninety separate lodgings and Thomas saw that this gave him a particular understanding of a lodger's circumstances. Thomas thought it auspicious that he and Dossie shared the new room as Dossie wanted, rather than going away for the night, as he had initially suggested.

George Wigg (mindful how British armies had been transformed by the demands of the first world war) had been battling for a year in favour of education in the armed forces. He believed this to be an essential concomitant to conscription. He mobilised support among educationists and politicians. Under the 1939 statutes, adult education was nominally mandatory. However, army education was virtually stalled on the outbreak of war in September 1939 through the dispersal of the personnel of the Army Educational Corps to other duties.

Civilians, including Wigg from the WEA and Sir Walter Moberly and Sandie Lindsay from the universities kept up pressure. Wigg, in discussion with Gladys Malbon and Thomas on 6 March, suggested that effective adult education in the army was in the offing (Wigg through Lindsay knew that members of the war cabinet had promised support).

Thomas walked near Trentham Park on 9 March, in the company of the Sneyd schoolteacher Doris Pulsford whom he had met through Alan Ecclestone's recommendation of local churches. Thomas recounted the conversation in detail in a letter to Dossie next day:

I started by trying to find out what it was she really needed – whether a lover or a friend – but she didn't like that way of dealing with things – thought it too rational and cold-blooded. And I found myself in the position rather of talking as though she had all the needs and I hadn't any – superior-like – which isn't of course a true picture, but (since I have you and she hasn't a husband) has a sort of truth in it. Anyway she talked about herself a bit – as I'd asked her too – and things got plainer that way. She hasn't had a lover, though one very important friend, as Sage might be to you – a might-have-been. And she doesn't now want me for one – partly I think fear that she'd be doing it for the wrong motives (desire to be made a fuss of and that sort of thing) and would be sorry she had afterwards, partly having known me such a little time and not knowing you at all.

Thomas's dialogue with Doris continued (as he meticulously reported back in almost daily letters to Dossie). Doris was concerned whether Dossie would mind about the incipient relationship. Thomas responded: 'I said that there from my knowledge of you and how we felt together about these things you wouldn't – though one could never absolutely see ahead. Also I mentioned your sleeping with Sage, and that that had genuinely not made me feel jealous or unhappy – only a little odd – liking moving into a slightly new kind of world.'

Thomas was given a chore by the Association of Tutors in Adult Education, whose honorary secretary Henry Hardman in Leeds was married to Thomas's Hodgkin cousin Diana Bosanquet. Hardman was asking Harold Marks to revive the association's activities in North Staffordshire and hearing from Diana that Thomas was working in the area asked him to help. A revival meeting of the Tutors Association, called for 20 April, tied Thomas to the Potteries for a weekend when he had intended to go to Oxford. He and Doris took camping equipment away to Offleybrook and spent the Friday and Saturday nights together there, with Thomas devoting much of Saturday to meetings with other tutors and to calls on WEA matters.

The countryside excursion was cold and rainy, but avoided the question of concealment of their conduct from their respective landladies and a prospect that Thomas much disliked of hotels and disguised names. They took another Sunday afternoon walk in Trentham Park on 21 April and went on to a political tea party of the Sneyd Group and ILP members in the Potteries.

Thomas spent the last days of April and first days of May in Oxford at the Bradmore Road flat. BJ wrote on 30 April with May Day greetings and to say that since Jack's mother had died the chances of her being in Oxford had grown smaller. She followed up with an invitation for 7 May for Dossie and Thomas to have supper at the Baker Street flat and to stay the night if it suited them. The two couples discussed the course of the war: Jack saw prospects for an early peace; Thomas thought the war would be intensified.

Almost immediately the war did seem to be coming much closer as British troops went into Belgium to meet the German invasion and in Britain a coalition government was formed on 10 May under Winston Churchill. Anthony Eden in the Churchill war cabinet announced on 14 May a new force of Local Defence Volunteers for British men between the ages of 15 and 60 who were not on military service. Thomas called at the Stoke Labour Exchange on 10 June where a clerk confirmed that Thomas was by age and occupation in a reserved category but must still register for military service. That day, Italy declared war on Britain and France. Thomas took on another new commitment: to stand by to drive an ambulance on Sunday nights, with first aid and gas training thrown in. He enrolled for Local Defence Volunteer duties.

Thomas registered on the afternoon of 22 June for military service. Wigg found yet another task for his staff after four battalions of French soldiers were stationed at Trentham Park, to which they had been diverted (from fighting in Norway) on the decision of France to seek an armistice with Germany. WEA lecturers took turns to staff a French Soldiers' Bureau to provide news and information. Hitler signed a directive on 16 July to prepare for an invasion of Britain. The Battle of Britain was waged in the air through the summer and early autumn months. A Balliol friend of Derek Blaikie's, Guy Branch married to Prudence Pelham, was killed in action on 11 August.

In September, Wigg assigned Thomas lectures on food and suggested that these might open the way for new short courses. Wigg was pressing for more lectures to the army and he was called up at the end of November to be commissioned into the Army Educational Corps (Gladys Malbon with Elijah Sambrook's daughter Mary Stringer became joint acting secretaries in his absence).

In the New Year of 1941, Thomas sustained the civil defence tasks that Wigg had urged on him. Thomas spent much of the night of 15 to 16 January trying to put out a fire started by an incendiary bomb next door to his Stoke lodgings, but did more damage than the bomb. He took sand up into the loft to quench the fire, put a foot through the ceiling and brought down a shower of plaster onto the landing below. 'The ceiling seemed to be made just of cardboard – not of wood like our solid bourgeois ceiling,' he wrote to Dossie.

Dossie was pregnant and the expectation of a second child set Thomas and Dossie house-hunting in the Potteries. By late August, they agreed on a change of lodging from the Charles family to a Mrs Layne at 10 Bramfield Drive, Newcastle. Thomas took leave of Mrs Charles on 8 September and settled books and papers into his new home. Dossie's Austrian nursemaid Olga Weiss was joined by an additional helper Edith Mutters, an East London evacuee. The second child, a daughter, was born on 23 September in the Oxford Radcliffe Infirmary and the parents wanted the name Elizabeth (evoking Dossie's friend Betty Murray and Thomas's sister lost in childhood). Thomas wrote to the recently widowed Prudence Branch saying that the child would be named Prudence and asking her to be godmother. Prudence wrote on 4 October asking to be excused from godmotherhood, but as a childless widow expressed delight that this child should carry her name. The daughter was duly named Prudence Elizabeth, but dandled as Lizzie Prue.

Thomas took up again with Doris Pulsford, confessing to Dossie in a letter from Newcastle on 29 October: 'It's rather on my mind to tell you that I went home with Doris last night after the Sneyd class and made love to her – I felt it all right myself but wanted you to know and to know whether you feel it all right too.' He sought to excuse himself: 'And in these absences from you I find I get pretty browned off and needing company and affection. Well you know all that. And part of me must feel it wrong or I wouldn't feel the need to justify it.'

BJ sent Thomas a Christmas letter confirming a plan she had outlined a year earlier several months after the birth on 17 July 1940 of a daughter Lucy – of setting up a shared household in the country with her school friend Diana Hubback, now Hopkinson, and her own sister Sigle, now Wheeler, as young mothers. The families were now living in Kiln Copse Cottage at Marcham near Abingdon within bus distance of Oxford – Jack came from London at weekends and her brother-in-law Peter Wheeler was stationed nearby. BJ invited Thomas to visit with his family, and they took the bus to Marcham during Thomas's brief break for the New Year of 1942.

Wigg, although on military service, had his family living in the Potteries. He drew on Thomas's family friendship with Archbishop Temple to go with Thomas on 18 March to Bishopthorpe in York and to lobby Temple over the civilian side of education in the armed forces. They found Temple (a former president of the WEA) sympathetic to their concerns and plans, and willing to take soundings and to pursue the matter with Sir James Grigg, responsible for the War Office in Winston Churchill's war cabinet appointments of 19 February (Temple was moving to London at the end of April on becoming Archbishop of Canterbury).

Thomas took on additional voluntary tasks through the Association of Tutors in Adult Education, as editor of the association's newsletter and as one of its representatives on the joint publications committee of the national WEA. This involved him in preparatory work for pamphlets on current problems to be used by discussion-group leaders and members. The publications meetings held at WEA headquarters in London brought Thomas into close contact with Harold Shearman, the WEA education officer, and to a lesser degree with the WEA general secretary, Ernest Green. Thomas commissioned and edited material for the Tutors' Association newsletter that he sent on to the honorary secretary F.J. McCulloch at Leeds University for a mimeograph edition to be distributed to members.

Thomas was writing a pamphlet of his own on colonial empire for a WEA series of study outlines to support adult study circles. *The Colonial Empire: A students' guide* was in print on 16 October as a 40-page pamphlet of the WEA, price fourpence. The book list covered advocates and critics of empire and noted the advent of nationalism in the colonies: 'The national movements which have shattered the traditional political framework of the colonial and semi-colonial countries of Asia during the inter-War period, and have already begun to develop in the African colonies, are in reality simply one aspect of the whole process of social and political awakening of the common people throughout the World, which has been in progress since the American and French Revolutions at the end of the eighteenth century.' On this analysis, colonial rule could be seen by the colonised as an obstacle to social progress.

McCulloch was talking on 24 October to a Yorkshire MP Arthur Creech Jones who was a member of the Colonial Office Advisory Committee on Education in the Colonies (ACEC) and the first chairman of the Fabian Colonial Bureau. McCulloch asked Creech Jones to write a review of Thomas's study outline to appear in the Tutors' Association newsletter. Creech Jones sent to McCulloch on 5 November a review welcoming the study: 'The discussion is realistic of the problems which the liabilities of empire create for us ... you will be aware of the alert and well-instructed mind behind the Outline, seeking no easy explanations and purple evasions and not lost in a welter of emotional gush about empire.'

Thomas was surprised to receive – from a Colonel in the War Office whom he had known in North Staffordshire army education – a letter on 9 November asking him to serve on a committee to prepare an Arabic phrasebook for the Forces. He decided to accept, although this involved him in journeys to London for meetings of the committee – in addition to WEA meetings on publications.

In the New Year of 1943, Thomas continued work with the Arabic Committee although he could find little time for his contributions to the phrasebook. Wigg was asked to stand as a prospective parliamentary candidate for the Common Wealth Party of the Liberal MP Sir Richard Acland, opposing the wartime coalition between the major parties. Wigg and Thomas had an hour and a half discussion in Newcastle on 18 April when Thomas argued that this would be a mistake and that Wigg should remain with the Labour Party and movement.

Thomas's appointment as an organising tutor in the North Staffordshire WEA District was renewed for three years from 1 October 1943. After the death of Dossie's maternal grandmother, who had taken the ground floor at 20 Bradmore Road to escape the London bombing, Thomas and his growing family moved from the top floor to the larger ground floor flat. Thomas went on 16 December to bid farewell to Doris Pulsford leaving for a new school post at Beccles. He had formed a sentimental friendship with a member of his Stoke Class Audrey Calveley, a twenty-five year old who did nursery school work and was active in the local Nursery School Association.

In the New Year of 1944, Dossie was being considered for a readership at Oxford, and possibly for a Cambridge appointment, and Thomas was looking for ways of being closer to home. But when he read a newspaper report of Winston Churchill's speech to Parliament on 22 February about the parachute mission by the Oxford don F.W.D. (Bill) Deakin to Marshal Josip Broz Tito in Yugoslavia during 1943, he felt regret that he was not playing a more active part in the war. He was saddened on 1 March to see that Derek Blaikie was killed in action, and remembered him as his closest friend of the 1930s.

Thomas's North Staffordshire assignment was being modified. The Burton WEA branch wanted to extend activities and was considering establishing an adult education centre. The North Staffordshire district had agreed that Thomas would give more attention to Burton, and would be resident there (this would test whether appointment of a full-time tutor for Burton was justifiable). Thomas retained his other classes in the district so while preparing to move to Burton had also to maintain a foothold in Newcastle and could be in Burton only part of the week.

He had first to meet Wigg on 8 October in Dudley where Thomas booked himself into a hotel to allow for a long and late talk with Wigg. Wigg had a complex agenda: political work in Dudley where he hoped to fight for the Labour Party as parliamentary candidate, adult education in the area, and a recent tour of Africa where he made a reconnaissance of education schemes for British and African troops. Wigg wanted Thomas to apply for a forthcoming vacancy as secretary of the University of Oxford Delegacy for Extra-Mural Studies. The application list was being opened about a year before the new secretary would take up the duties. Wigg urged Thomas to contact friends among the Balliol fellows – Charles Morris who had held the post in the pre-war years and would have a say in the selection and another committee member John Fulton who might provide a testimonial. Thomas was already sleepy when Wigg turned to his concerns over West Africa (where Wigg was keen to promote English as the working language among African troops).

Thomas unpacked books and papers on the afternoon of 11 October in his lodgings at 337 Shobnall Street, Burton. Since Dossie was likely to remain in Oxford and they were taking steps for Luke to be admitted to the Dragon School in Oxford, he was paying close heed to the Oxford appointment that Wigg was urging on him. It was a pensionable post with a salary in the range £1,000 to £1,200 and recognised by the university as of professorial rank (Thomas's annual salary in North Staffordshire was £400 augmented by a war allowance and some additional fees for special tasks). The delegacy was looking for a candidate with experience of adult education for civilians and soldiers, and as the official notice of November 1944 indicated it was 'specially important that he should have those personal qualities of sympathy and imagination which will enable him to get on easily with people of all classes and creeds'. Wigg provided a reference on 22 December testifying that Thomas closely met the requirements: 'Hodgkin has as many qualities for the job as are likely to be found in one human being.'

Thomas received a letter from L.K. Hindmarsh, a joint honorary secretary to Oxford's Tutorial Classes Committee, inviting him for interview in Oxford on 24 April. He had his tidy suit patched and cleaned. Thomas had a WEA branch meeting in Burton on the evening of 23 April and intended to travel on to Oxford afterwards. Wigg took command. He spoke to Thomas about the Oxford interview and Wigg's idea of developing Oxford extra-mural centres in the African colonies. Wigg had a hardheaded view of British influence continuing after the end of colonial empire and thought Thomas's views on the subject sentimental. On the practical side Wigg insisted that Thomas should miss the Burton meeting, should travel to Oxford on 23 April for a good night's sleep to be settled and refreshed before the interview next day, and should have his hair cut and a new shirt – with a detachable collar! Thomas was hesitant about missing the Burton branch meeting, and then acquiesced.

Thomas attended the interview in Oxford and returned to North Staffordshire thinking he was second to John Hampden Jackson from Norfolk (who was some three years older than he was). When he heard that Hampden Jackson might not take the offer he raised his hopes again, and by the end of the first week of May he was after all offered the Oxford appointment along with a professorial fellowship at Balliol. Thomas was replacing Hindmarsh in the twin tasks of secretary to the delegacy and organising secretary of the University Extension Lectures Committee.

The war in Europe ended with formal German surrender in early May. Britain's wartime coalition government ended on 23 May and Winston Churchill headed a caretaker Conservative administration in preparation for a general election on 5 July. Thomas became quickly embroiled in North Staffordshire where several colleagues and friends were contesting seats for the Labour Party. In the first weekend of June he and Gladys Malbon met Wigg to go through Wigg's election address for Dudley. Thomas took a canvassing team there on 4 June. Thomas went to speak in Stephen Swingler's campaign for Stafford and by the closing days of the month was largely organising the canvass in Swingler's constituency. The election results were delayed for three weeks to allow time to collect and count service votes including overseas voters. The outcome brought the first clear majority ever for the Labour Party, with some two-thirds of its candidates entering Parliament for the first time. Within this Labour majority (by a margin of 146 seats) Thomas found himself with what he felt to be a good number of friends and acquaintances in the new Parliament: they included George Wigg in Dudley, Stephen Swingler in Stafford, Barnett Stross in Hanley, Harold Davies in Leek and Albert Davies in Burslem.

Cartwright had retired and his successor as organising secretary of the Tutorial Classes Committee was the former assistant secretary Henry Percival Smith. Thomas attended an appointments sub-committee in Oxford on 21 September to designate Smith's assistant. This post went to a former member of a Longton class, Francis Vincent Pickstock. Thomas took up his new responsibilities as secretary of the Delegacy for Extra-Mural Studies on 1 October. His return to Oxford meant that for the first time since his marriage eight years earlier he was living with his wife – plus now a young family, and Dossie was pregnant again. His appointment gave him a high profile in the debates on post-war adult education. He was expected and invited to visit centres in several regions, to lecture at national level and to attend WEA and other educational policy discussions in London. Thomas inherited Hindmarsh's preparation for post-war activity including a course on 'Great Buildings'. One of the lecturers was a Dominican scholar from Balliol, Gervase Mathew, with a breadth of learning from theology to archaeology that Thomas found impressive – he became a friend and mentor.

In the New Year of 1946, Thomas was considering how WEA organisation could be strengthened, especially after the 1944 Education Act required local education authorities to provide an adequate adult education service. The CP had resolved to encourage Marxist education and the publication of Marxist studies of British history. Thomas agreed to draft for the CP education sub-committee a paper on Marxist education and the working-class movement. He was in touch with the head of the CP's education programme, Douglas Garman from Wednesbury in Staffordshire and a graduate of Caius College, Cambridge.

Thomas's draft paper went to the sub-committee for discussion in February and was predicated on a duality of working-class and adult education developing on a mass basis. Garman thought the document suffered from confusion between the development of adult education and the task of educating the working class. Thomas revised his paper and a second version to be circulated in April opened explicitly: 'There is clearly an urgent need at the present time for the extension of working-class education.'

Thomas in his delegacy role in early March was laying the ground for university extension courses in West Africa, the innovation for which George Wigg had pushed him towards the Oxford post. The project would require joint and simultaneous support from the dons in Oxford, the mandarins at the Colonial Office in London and the officials serving in the colonies. The matter was due for discussion at a delegacy meeting in Oxford on 9 March. Thomas sent a copy of the proposal to Creech Jones at the Colonial Office. Creech Jones had been vice-chairman of the Elliot Commission on Higher Education for West Africa in 1943 to 1944 and was current chairman of the ACEC. In the Labour Government of August 1945, he became a junior minister as Parliamentary Under Secretary in the Colonial Office. Creech Jones found Thomas's memorandum on 8 March when he returned to the Colonial Office from opening and closing a House of Commons debate on Malaya. He hastily sent a handwritten note to urge caution on the Oxford meeting due to be held next day and to ask that no decision be taken on a proposal needing considerable care and consideration 'before action of the right kind can be taken'.

The delegacy gave agreement in principle for the West Africa courses without approving the detail. Thomas sent the proposal to a New College don Christopher Cox who had been a friend and confidant since Thomas's undergraduate days. Cox had been education adviser to the Colonial Office since 1940 and he asked Thomas if he might circulate the West Africa proposals to the Mass Education Sub-Committee and its parent ACEC. Cox's deputy Frank Ward, who had been senior history master at the Achimota School in Gold Coast from 1924, wrote to Thomas on Cox's behalf on 3 April to say that the main committee would be likely to consider the proposals on 27 April. Ward by the end of May was able to inform Thomas that the Colonial Office's Mass Education Sub-Committee had given a warm welcome in principle to the proposal to send an experimental team of tutors to West Africa. Work pressures in Oxford kept Thomas from going with Dossie to Geldeston for the christening on 4 August of their second son, born on 16 May and given the forenames John Robert Tobias, the first two after his maternal and paternal grandfathers, who became known in the family by the third name shortened to Toby.

Thomas and Frank Ward met on 8 November at the Colonial Office. Ward reported that the Gold Coast colonial administrators had given a favourable response to the Oxford scheme, would welcome an exploratory visit from the delegacy and would pay their share of the total cost of the scheme if implemented. Thomas was given the go-ahead to discuss the scheme with those who would be interested or who could give advice, including other academics and West Africans in Britain. Ward recommended a Gold Coast student in Oxford, Kofi Busia. Another Colonial Office official wrote on 2 December that the Nigerian colonial government had cabled welcoming the proposal and a projected visit by Thomas to Nigeria.

The official blessing was going to a provisional scheme of what the Colonial Office preferred to call study courses. The experiment was to stimulate the local development of an adult education movement in West Africa by introducing among small groups of Africans the aims, methods and standards of adult education as they had emerged through the association between the universities and the voluntary student bodies in Britain. The essence of the scheme was the secondment by the Oxford delegacy of two of its experienced staff tutors to West Africa – one to Nigeria and one to the Gold Coast – with each tutor to conduct three study-courses of 12 weekly meetings in different centres. Salaries would be paid by the delegacy and the colonial governments would pay for food and subsistence.

Thomas cast his net for further contacts in Africa. He wrote on 30 December seeking a meeting with the historian of British Empire and Commonwealth, Sir Reginald Coupland. Coupland, with a Winchester and New College education, was at All Souls and since 1920 holder of the Beit professorship of colonial history. He also followed up the offer made by the writer Leonard Barnes to gather some West Africans to meet Thomas. He wrote on 31 December to a London University educationist Margaret Read for advice on organisations and individuals in Nigeria and the Gold Coast and about meeting some of her West African students. He saw on that day Margery Perham, the director of Oxford University's Institute of Colonial Studies. She referred Thomas to an anthropologist teaching at the London School of Economics, Dr Audrey Richards (a former pupil of Bronislaw Malinowski), who had been concerned with running courses for colonial teachers.

In the New Year of 1947 Thomas invited round Busia, who had been an assistant district commissioner in the Gold Coast and was at University College, Oxford, reading for a doctorate on the position of the chief in the Ashanti political system. Busia represented a conservative perspective on West Africa. Thomas was also casting around to see how the proposal to second two experienced staff tutors to West Africa could be met when tutors were already committed for the current session of classes in Britain. He had two colleagues in mind. John Anderson Mack was a Balliol contemporary of Thomas and as early as the 1930 session was teaching a Tunstall tutorial class on the history of scientific thought (from primitive magic to Newtonian science). J.A. (Tony) McLean was not a personal acquaintance but he had served in Spain in the International Brigade and had experience of the Army Bureau of Current Affairs and of tutoring in East Sussex and Kent. Thomas in his own and Smith's name wrote on 7 January to McLean in St Leonard's-on-Sea in East Sussex to alert him to the possibility of a temporary stint in West Africa.

Through Barnes Thomas had made contact with a Nigerian lawyer, Godfrey Amachree, who was active in West African student politics in London. Amachree was secretary of the West African Students' Union and sat on its joint committee with the West African National Secretariat (WANS). WANS had been formed in December 1945 in the wake of the Pan-African Congress held in Manchester in October of that year. These students seemed intent on freedom in the form of independence and self-determination. Thomas spent 14 and 15 January at a succession of meetings with Amachree and other West African students collected by Barnes, with Margaret Read and with a Colonial Office official. John Mack wrote from Glasgow turning down Thomas's 'flattering invitation' to spend a term in Africa because he had taken on writing that would fill up the whole summer. Thomas wrote to the Oxford economist Peter Ady, whom he knew from her lectures in the Potteries in 1943, to draw on her knowledge of the Gold Coast where she had done research. She telephoned the anthropologist Meyer Fortes and sent on the names of a dozen Africans whom Thomas should try to meet. The Colonial Office arranged for Thomas to see the Gold Coast director of education Tom Barton on home leave. Ward, to whom Thomas sent the draft programme of his Gold Coast journey, made his suggestions.

Thomas – after nearly a year of piloting the scheme through official channels – flew on 6 February 1947 from snow and ice in a Britain suffering an exceptionally hard winter for his venture into Africa. He took a trundling flight that hopped to Bordeaux and Lisbon and through the night to Africa via Casablanca and Port Etienne where one of the twin engines was repaired. During the wait, Thomas heard Saharans speaking an Arabic dialect, introduced himself and found they were able to understand one another. Passengers made an overnight stop at a rest house in Bathurst, then a breakfast stop at Freetown and went on to Takoradi and Accra, where Thomas by the evening of 8 February was installed at Achimota with a large room in which to work.

Thomas's groundwork paid off and within the fortnight he had allowed himself for the first stage of his mission he made a round of visits including Accra, Cape Coast, Sekondi, Tarkwa and Kumasi. He had talks on the delegacy's scheme with more than sixty people over a broad range from colonial governor and paramount chief to lawyers, trade unionists, journalists, teachers and their pupils.

Thomas was struck in the first few days by the extreme beauty of the Africans and wrote to Teddy on 12 February of 'very regular clear-cut sort of faces'. Among his African interlocutors were Joe Annan, a former trade union organiser now in the colonial labour department, and J.C. de Graft Johnson (Annan attended the Pan-African Congress in Manchester in 1945 for the African Railways Employees Union and Johnson for the African Students' Union of Edinburgh). He met the scholar and nationalist Dr J.B. Danquah.

Thomas encountered some scepticism about adult education among expatriate officials and among the Africans he met – but he found sufficient understanding that adult education was more than a luxury to feel able to press on. He wrote up his notes on interviews as he went and over the weekend of 22 and 23 February he wrote a report of what he had in mind: 'The term "adult education" is here used to describe education in "liberal studies" (with special reference to History and Social Studies) through the medium of classes or study-courses for literate men and women who are normally in employment during the day – the students taking an active part in the work of the class both through their contribution to discussion and through reading and written work.'

He delivered the report to key people on the Sunday evening of 23 February and spent the next day and a half arranging that study courses could go ahead and that an Oxford tutor should be brought out to Gold Coast in April. Two of Thomas's allies in overcoming the stasis of indefinite postponement were friends of Peter Ady with Oxford backgrounds. Peter Canham in the colonial secretariat had been at Pembroke College and become a colonial service cadet in the Gold Coast in 1930. Modjaben Dowuona had been awarded the first Achimota Council scholarship for further education in Britain, studied at St Peter's Hall and then returned to Achimota as a teacher.

Thomas, waiting for a delayed flight from Accra, cabled to the delegacy in Oxford: 'Gold Coast arrangements reasonably firm, in circumstances probably best McLean comes here, please consult H.P. and inform McLean.' Thomas was expecting a mid-April departure date for Tony McLean. On this visit Thomas changed his view of the Gold Coast that he had described as 'a country with no past and no history' when he turned down the offer of a colonial appointment in 1932. Thomas was impressed by another Achimota teacher, Miguel Augusto Ribeiro, who attended the Institute of Education at London University from 1938 to 1939 and on return to Achimota became senior history master. Ribeiro was teaching a history syllabus that was not confined to typical themes of European conquest but looked back to a pre-colonial past of the break-up of Sudanese Empires and the beginnings of the 'Guinea' Kingdoms. The school used recent textbooks taking into account the oral traditions of the Gold Coast peoples, dating back several centuries, and drawing on new findings in anthropology to supplement history.

Some of this embryonic work had been done by Ward during his Gold Coast years and Ribeiro was among his African colleagues who had given assistance. When Thomas asked where he could learn more about the kingdoms he was recommended to read E.W. Bovill's *Caravans of the Old Sahara* published in 1933. Bovill's introduction to the history of the Western Sudan and of trans-Saharan trade was prefaced with a late fourteenth-century map of a Kingdom of Mali. Bovill had been inspired to his study by reading Flora Shaw's 1905 book on northern Nigeria, *A Tropical Dependency*.

Thomas reached Lagos at the beginning of March for another intensive round of visits and talks, and again used his personal introductions to avoid too close an identification with colonial officialdom and to meet independent Africans who impressed him more than the officials. Such contact was neither automatic nor easy in a Nigeria where an informal social colour bar obtained in colonial circles. Thomas found a favourable reaction to the delegacy scheme when he put it to a leading Nigerian nationalist Nnamdi Azikiwe, an Ibo newspaper editor and proprietor. Thomas went to a Lagos bar for a drink with the first secretary-general of the Nigerian Trade Union Congress M.A. Tokunboh. They witnessed a demonstration against the Bristol Hotel. A crowd emerged from a protest meeting over the hotel manager's apparent colour discrimination against a guest refused accommodation as an African (Ivor Cummings, who was born in West Hartlepool to a Sierra Leonean father and British mother, was on a visit as a Colonial Office student liaison officer). After police dispersed the crowd, Thomas walked down the street with an African on each side. Tokunboh introduced him to a journalist and lawyer H.O.D. Davies, who had recently been studying law in Britain (Davies attended the Pan-African Congress in 1945 for the Nigerian Youth Movement). Thomas was impressed by the pertinent questions Davies raised.

Back in Oxford, Thomas's prompt action on the Gold Coast study courses was causing a flutter; Lindsay at Balliol seemed unprepared for events to move so quickly. Delegacy staff advised that Thomas had acted within the limits of his jurisdiction by sending for McLean. The delegates met in Oxford on 8 March and confirmed Thomas's detailed strategy – just a year from their agreement in principle.

Thomas on return to Oxford followed up his visit to Africa. He sent out his Gold Coast report and by 15 April completed a report on the Nigeria mission. The editor of *West Africa*, a journalist of West Indian origin George Hunte, wrote on 17 April asking about the delegacy scheme and about McLean's expected departure for the Gold Coast. Thomas replied on 23 April that he would send Hunte his Gold Coast and Nigeria reports after they had been approved by a delegacy meeting in June and that McLean had already left to conduct study courses at Accra, Kumasi and Cape Coast.

Cox wrote on 14 May that he had been fascinated to read Thomas's two West Africa reports and thought it excellent that the 'Gold Coast show' had begun. He wanted to hear Thomas's background impressions of the two countries and invited 'Dear Tommy' to dine in hall at New College on the following Saturday or Sunday. (Thomas had to decline since he had promised to help with a weekend school at the Wedgwood Memorial College in North Staffordshire.) Thomas received a Colonial Office imprimatur on 7 July when Cox invited him to sit in on discussions in the Mass Education Sub-Committee.

Thomas now wanted a tutor for the scheme in Nigeria. He thought Leonard Barnes, with long experience of WEA lecturing and with international knowledge, would be the best person the delegacy could find. The study courses were likely to run during the British winter lecture session when it was unlikely that any full-time tutor could leave. Barnes agreed in principle if the beginning of the courses could be postponed until Christmas since he wanted time to finish a piece of research. Barnes was then offered the post of secretary to Oxford's Delegacy for Social Training, which he accepted. Thomas had reluctantly to put the Nigeria plan back until April of the next year when another tutor would be free after the winter session.

Thomas proposed to the Colonial Office (where Creech Jones was now Secretary of State) the possible secondment in April of Henry Collins; he was an experienced full-time Oxford tutor in North Staffordshire who had spent time in Nigeria in the army during the war. He brought background knowledge of the country and, with a degree in Philosophy, Politics and Economics (PPE), could teach applied economics and politics. Thomas, in London for a meeting of the Universities Council for Adult Education, had lunch on 21 October at London University with Margaret Read, recently returned from a visit to Nyasaland, and with Tony McLean whom he was meeting in person for the first time, after they had corresponded over the Gold Coast.

Thomas had an approach from the principal of Gordon College in Khartoum, Lewis Wilcher, a Rhodes Scholar from Australia who had been a junior contemporary of his at Balliol, to explore the prospects for extra-mural study in Sudan. This would involve a visit in March 1948 and he was hesitant whether he would want to go. He was lobbied in Oxford on 11 November by the vice-principal of Makerere University in Kampala Thomas Reginald Batten who, as a social scientist, was interested in the prospects of extra-mural work in Uganda. Thomas said tentatively that it might be possible to consider sending a tutor or two.

Thomas in early 1948 was preparing to visit Sudan in response to Wilcher's invitation. He set off in March just as the delegacy and the colonial secretariat in Accra agreed on the first resident tutor in the Gold Coast. The appointment went to David Kimble, who was coming up to his twenty-seventh birthday and who had become a delegacy tutor in 1945 after education at Eastbourne Grammar School and Reading University and two years' wartime naval service.

Thomas on arrival in Sudan was stepping into a network of family links through the Hodgkins and the Crowfoots. When he visited Gordon College he found a bust of Dossie's father John Crowfoot and he met leading Sudanese who had personal memories of John and Molly Crowfoot. Thomas had an initial talk with the Gordon College vice-principal Ibrahim Ahmed who had been an inspector of schools under Crowfoot as director of education. Thomas went on to spend a few days at the Sudan Institute of Education at Bakht-er-Ruda. His host on the staff was his first cousin Robin Allason Hodgkin (Robin was a son of Thomas's paternal uncle George Hodgkin and Mary Wilson and had been brought up by Thomas's maternal uncle Lionel Smith who had married Mary when she was widowed young with three children). Robin opened the way to many young and intelligent Sudanese among his former pupils.

Thomas went back to Khartoum and visited Omdurman where on 24 March he met a pioneer of education for girls in Sudan Sheikh Babikr Bedri on a visit to his son Yusuf Bedri, who was running the Ahfad School for women. Sheikh Babikr in his ninetieth year was between fund-raising tours for the school, and told Thomas stories of Dossie's parents in the Sudan, especially of what he described as the heroism and daring of her mother.

Thomas went on to Wad Medani, where he saw more of the education system and to the railway centre at Atbara to meet trade unionists, although some activists were unwilling to meet him after the arrest of a Workers' Affairs Association leader Suleiman Musa whom Thomas had been hoping to see. Thomas had found the Sudanese receptive to the idea of extension classes, but many of the academics were apprehensive of additional pressures on the staff of Gordon College, which was in transit to university college status. He wrote a report in favour of tutorial classes in Khartoum, Omdurman, Wad Medani and Atbara, with an expatriate and a Sudanese lecturer to initiate the scheme. Students successful in the Sudan classes might carry on to degree courses.

Thomas had missed stormy moments at a trade union course organised by Pickstock for the Tutorial Classes Committee from 3 to 10 April. The course for tutors and trade unionists was organised in conjunction with the Workers' Educational Trade Union Committee, but was seen in some WEA circles as an Oxford intrusion on WEA responsibility. Participants included young economic historians Hugh Clegg, Ron Bellamy, and Alan Flanders. It brought a clash of styles between trade unionists with political attitudes affected by the post-war Cold War rivalry between the US and the Soviet Union and the academics who believed in following an intellectual argument wherever it went. Ernest Green, the WEA general secretary, complained to a meeting of the Tutorial Classes Committee on which he sat of allegations against delegacy employees that some of those holding teaching appointments were engaged in Communist propaganda in their teaching. Green called for a private investigation to be made and he offered to collect illustrative material.

The Tutorial Classes Committee agreed to conduct a private investigation through a special sub-committee chaired by the Principal of Brasenose College 'Sonners' Stallybrass with three other college heads (Sandie Lindsay, Lucy Sutherland and Henry Clay) and G.D.H. Cole as members. Green supplied written allegations from a dozen persons whom Green declared to be occupants of responsible positions in adult education or the trade union movement and whose names Green offered to show in confidence to Lindsay.

The sub-committee found the written allegations imprecise and they eliminated allegations that assumed that no member of the CP or someone with similar views could hold a teaching appointment under the delegacy, or allegations that assumed that the Communist point of view could not be put forward or discussed at conferences organised by the delegacy to discuss contemporary problems. The sub-committee did not believe that the delegacy should impose restrictions on the freedom of academic discussion.

The experiments in West Africa were not the subject of inquiry but despite the collective view individual dons had their own Cold War anxieties. Some shared them with Christopher Cox who took soundings in Oxford in mid-summer on rumours of Communist leanings in the delegacy environment. Cox saw Thomas, Lucy Sutherland and Stallybrass. Stallybrass in July made a point of seeking out Cox to put his concerns that charges of undue Communist presence could affect Oxford's extension work in the colonies and with the army. Cox understood that the army authorities were excluding Thomas personally from work among the forces. The Colonial Office ministers and senior officials were taking a view before the Oxford committee completed its findings, but they believed it would do more harm than good to recall McLean and Collins from Nigeria in the middle of what was a spell of only four months in the colony.

With the advent of the Michaelmas term in Oxford Lucy Sutherland succeeded Lindsay as chairman of the Tutorial Classes Committee. Creech Jones sent Cox a private handwritten note on 10 October asking what should be done about Oxford tutors and West Africa: he did not like the idea of condoning in West Africa three out of four tutors who were Communists; the Colonial Office could not easily go witch hunting but the scheme could be suspended to enable them to think again.

Cox replied on 14 October with a long memorandum sketching how Oxford could be made to fade out of the picture. Kimble, who had gone to Gold Coast on a two-year assignment to put the work on a permanent basis, was a Liberal. The University College at Ibadan would have its own extra-mural studies department, although there were short-term difficulties over deciding on the suitability of the Gold Coast African Robert Gardiner as the leading applicant for the post of director. On Nigeria, Cox reported from his discussions in Oxford that Collins was confidentially admitted to be a member of the CP and McLean was admitted to have been so in the past.

Cox advised: 'I really think we can hardly acquiesce in a further appointment or appointments from Oxford at this stage unless we can depend on the University authorities not this time to select Tutors in respect of whom they and we are running such political risks.' He had confidence that Stallybrass and Lucy Sutherland could be relied upon from this standpoint. Cox proposed using his weekend in Oxford to press home the message, to see how the charges against the delegacy stood and 'make it clear we should find great difficulty in agreeing to any fresh appointment to Nigeria being made if these are Communists, in the present circumstances'.

Cox was somewhat reassured by his further soundings in Oxford: the senior members of the delegacy would not send further tutors to Nigeria except after consultation with the Colonial Office and at the wish of the Nigerian authorities – and any tutors sent out to bridge the gap until Ibadan was effectively functioning would not expose the Colonial Office to 'political embarrassment' (meaning would not have Communist affiliations).

Meanwhile Green had taken his attack on Communism and Oxford to Creech Jones. Creech Jones in a note to Cox on 27 October disclosed that Green was arguing that Oxford should cry a halt to allow an evaluation of the programme. Thomas, who had not been alerted to Cox's political anxieties, discussed the Nigeria programme informally with Stallybrass, Lowe and Lucy Sutherland and wrote to Cox on 29 October reassuring him that they agreed that the delegacy if asked for any more tutorial assistance should co-operate further in Nigeria, as it had done in Gold Coast. Stallybrass died suddenly and unexpectedly on 28 October. John Lowe, who had originally come from Calgary in Canada to Christ Church as a 1922 Rhodes Scholar, became vice-chancellor unusually below the age of fifty and without some of the usual preparatory Oxford university appointments. Cox, who had previously been writing his letters to 'Dear Tommy', replied cautiously on 11 November to 'Dear Hodgkin' saying he was 'glad to know of the upshot to the informal talk you had with the late V-C and others just before his death'.

Lowe's new office made him chairman of the sub-committee investigating the allegations against the delegacy whose work ground on into the Hilary term of 1949. The results of the investigation of Green's statement concerning tutors were reported back to the Tutorial Classes Committee in March. The members found no evidence that any tutor had turned classes into instruments of party propaganda, although on some occasions a few tutors may have displayed warmth that was not discreet. They noted that of 16 full-time delegacy appoints made in 1946, 1947 and 1948 only two had been even criticised in the material placed before the committee. They had found in the course of their investigation nothing that might shake their confidence in the integrity and devotion to duty of the Delegacy staff at Rewley House.

Kimble travelled in Sierra Leone from 15 to 20 April to scout prospects for adult education and in May he helped appoint in Gold Coast four African adult education organisers who went initially on a study visit to Britain. McLean in May went again to teach in Nigeria along with two newcomers to the Nigeria programme: Stephen Coltham, who had shared lodgings with Thomas in the Potteries, and Marjorie Nicholson. Kimble, who was based in Accra, was establishing a team of resident tutors at regional level – Dr Joe de Graft Johnson, an African Thomas had met soon after arriving in Accra, one of Thomas's tutor-trainees Lalage Bown and Dennis Austin.

Thomas now formally gave up membership of the CP, where he had long been inactive. This was to clear the way for his work as a teacher and his growing interest in Africa. Thomas wanted also to talk to Cox after they both returned from holiday. He wrote to 'Dear Christopher' asking for an hour in late September to discuss three matters: Sierra Leone practically, Nyasaland tentatively and his personal plans for the future on which he wanted Cox's advice.

Kimble on leave in Britain was married on 20 August to the first of Thomas's tutor trainees Helen Rankin, appointed in 1946 initially in Lincoln and later working in Rewley House. Helen and David went from their wedding to Accra where the mood of Gold Coast politics was changing. The Convention People's Party (CPP) was formed in June with Kwame Nkrumah breaking away from the more conservative Gold Coast African leadership who had paid for his passage back in December 1947 to serve the United Gold Coast Convention. A new Gold Coast governor Sir Charles Arden-Clarke was appointed from 11 August.

Cox agreed to a meeting at the Colonial Office on 21 September – and for another official to attend the formal part of the discussion on Kimble's report on the April visit to Sierra Leone. Cox told Thomas that he had talked over Kimble's proposals with the Governor of Sierra Leone, who did not think that it would be desirable for Sierra Leone to have any direct assistance from the University College of the Gold Coast in the extra-mural field. Any work in adult education should be under the auspices of the reconstituted Fourah Bay College, where there was a new principal; the existing close connection between Fourah Bay and Durham University pointed to Durham rather than Oxford. Thomas ruefully accepted the line of argument. Oxford's direct part in the West Africa programmes was ending since responsibility for extra-mural work in the Gold Coast and in Nigeria was transferred to the two University Colleges, where full-time directors of extra-mural studies were in post (to Kimble in Accra and to Robert Gardiner in Ibadan).

Thomas when alone with Cox asked for a frank personal opinion on the possibility of the delegacy opening up exploratory work in any other colonial regions. Thomas had in mind Nyasaland, Northern Rhodesia and Tanganyika as colonial territories that might be considered. Cox argued that there were existing universities or university colleges who would want to undertake extra-mural work from the outset rather than have the agenda set by a virtually independent tutor responsible only to a remote body in Britain. He pointed to the factor in East and Central Africa of a resident European public opinion that strengthened the case for any such programme being under the control of a local institute. The personal plan Thomas disclosed was to give up his work with the delegacy before very long in order to write something substantial about Africa after further African travel.

Cox was responding personally as asked, and said that he would have to consult the head of African affairs in the Colonial Office, Andrew Cohen, on official policy implications. Thomas did not fully catch that Cox was intending to say that the delegacy's pioneering job in the colonies was now over. By the beginning of November, the Colonial Office mandarins had taken a firm view on their policy towards the Oxford delegacy. Creech Jones, after a discussion with advisers, gave instructions that university colleges were to be encouraged to draw upon other universities than Oxford; and the tendency to build up an Oxford monopoly of colonial interest in the extra-mural field should now be resisted. Cox was nudging the lay advisers towards the British Council as the body underpinning the educational institutions in the colonies – one more aligned with government policy.

Thomas was invited by Kimble to assist with residential schools in Gold Coast in the coming year. George Wigg alerted the recently appointed editor of *West Africa* magazine, David Williams, to Thomas's interest in Africa. Williams and

Thomas met in Oxford in early November and Thomas agreed to write ten articles on the national movement in the Gold Coast when he travelled.

When the Colonial Office's adult education sub-committee met in London on 22 November, Margaret Read and Leonard Barnes asked that the position on adult education in East and Central Africa be discussed at the next meeting, due in the second week of January 1950 (for Read at least this was in response to Thomas's talk with her). It was agreed at Cox's suggestion that the discussion include the type of informal adult education that the British Council would be willing to promote. At the end of the meeting, Barnes, knowing of the Communism scare, told Cox about Thomas's proposals for an Oxford delegacy role in East and Central Africa, and that these proposals might cause embarrassment to the Colonial Office.

Cox, after telephoning Cohen with an alert and to confirm that they took the same view, sent a detailed account and a minute with an advisory condemnation of the Thomas plan: Hodgkin and the delegacy should if necessary 'be pulled up with a round jerk'; the Colonial Office lay advisers and Lucy Sutherland and John Lowe should be told once and for all, and Creech Jones should if necessary see Wigg. Before the sub-committee met in the new year the Colonial Office should be clear what suggestions it would welcome for East and Central Africa and what suggestions it was determined to discourage.

Kimble had invited Thomas to the Gold Coast after Christmas for three or four weeks to help with a residential course for part-time tutors and another for people prepared to undertake work in adult education. Thomas's second West Africa journey was geared to the educationists and much less than his first journey to colonial officialdom. He was met on arrival in Lagos on 29 December by the general secretary of the Nigerian Union of Teachers Eyo Esua and accommodated at the Bristol Hotel. He took a train next day to Ibadan to visit the University College and to meet several academics including Robert Gardiner and his family. Gardiner took him to Abeokuta to meet the principal of the grammar school Israel Ransome-Kuti and his political activist wife Olufunmilayo Ransome-Kuti.

Gardiner on New Year's day of 1950 drove Thomas back to Lagos where Thomas had arranged to dine with his colleague of Palestine days Hugh Foot, who was now Chief Secretary and acting Governor in the Nigeria administration. Thomas felt that Foot approved of the work the Oxford delegacy had been doing in Nigeria. Thomas flew on 3 January 1950 from Lagos to Accra and joined the Kimbles on the final stage of a volunteer project to improve the water supply to the village of Komenda. Thomas mucked in by carrying pans full of the clay that was dug out and then by moving stones to build a ramp. This project between students and villagers was a preliminary to the training course for tutors in adult education at Komenda College from 7 to 21 January led by Thomas and by Kimble.

Thomas taught on the adult education course and started a study group on the Gold Coast national movement (in Accra a general strike was being called by trade unionists from midnight on 6 January and the CPP called for Positive Action from midnight on 8 January to support demands for Gold Coast self-determination). Thomas in a lorry-load of Africans and Europeans from the course went on 11 January to the centre of the strike movement Sekondi to see the effects. He met supporters and opponents of radical action and he returned there on 15 January, by which time colonial officials were speculating whether Komenda was a centre of subversive influence. Thomas began his return on 21 January to Accra hoping to meet Nkrumah, only to hear on the way of Nkrumah's arrest in the Labadi neighbourhood of Accra (in the subsequent trial of CPP leaders Nkrumah was sentenced to a total of three years imprisonment).

Thomas was due to leave Gold Coast on 1 February but he acceded to a plan of Kimble's to stay on a few days. Thomas with Dennis Austin held a one-day school in Kumasi on 28 January on 'The meaning of democracy'. Thomas was to speak on 'Problems of modern government', although the colonial administration's public relation officers raised an objection to announcing this subject on radio. When the school was held, three British officials turned up with some fifty local participants. The British general election of 23 February cut the Labour Party's parliamentary majority to five, and cost Creech Jones his Shipley seat. He was succeeded as Secretary of State for the Colonies by the trade unionist James Griffiths.

Thomas was finding a new platform and context for his increasing interest in Africa through the Union of Democratic Control (UDC) under the chairmanship of the *New Statesman and Nation* editor Kingsley Martin. The UDC had been formed in protest against the war in Europe, with largely Quaker support. The general secretary, whom Thomas met in March 1950, was Basil Davidson, born in Bristol on 9 November 1914 as Basil Risbridger and later given the name Davidson from a stepfather. Thomas and Basil came from different backgrounds but converging interests and they quickly formed a close bond in their respect for Africa and African aspirations. Basil, leaving school at 16, was a journalist in the 1930s and had a distinguished military record in the Second World War including service as liaison officer to Marshal Tito's partisans in Yugoslavia. He returned to journalism after the war – and began writing books of fiction and non-fiction – and in 1949 took on the secretaryship of the UDC. He wrote advocacy pamphlets such as a critique of political repression in Greece.

The UDC, with a long-standing interest in Asia, was turning its attention to the issues of African advance towards freedom and equality of opportunity. Basil sought Thomas's advice on people who could help with a conference in October on the theme of 'The Crisis in Africa'. Thomas recommended an official of the Nigerian National Union of Teachers, Fidelis Ayo Ogunsheye, now at the London School of Economics, and other friends and colleagues. Just as Cox, unbeknown to Thomas, was sending a Colonial Office minute to exclude Thomas from the process in Africa, Basil on the same date of 4 April wrote to Thomas from the UDC that he had fixed a meeting at the House of Commons on 27 April for 'the preliminary get-together which is to discuss our Conference on the Crisis in Africa'.

By 15 April Thomas was mobilising the interest of Ogunsheye, Tony McLean, Michael Carritt, a critic of Empire, and Leonard Barnes. In the ensuing weeks Thomas and Basil were in touch on an almost daily basis by letter, telephone or meeting as they prepared a conference programme and recruited participants. Thomas's connections were strong in the academic field and among Africans currently in Britain.

Thomas in the summer wrote and delivered the series on the national movement in the Gold Coast for *West Africa*. Ten weekly articles were published as 'Background to Gold Coast nationalism' from 9 July to 2 September 1950. They were seen as both scholarly and topical and in combination with the conference confirmed Thomas's deepening involvement in Africa. The conference was to be held at the convent-like Elfinsward in Haywards Heath, Sussex, during a long weekend of 20 to 23 October with the working sessions on 21 and 22 October (with dates misprinted by one day in much of the original documentation).

In the event about a third of some seventy-five participants were Africans in Britain and the others drawn from a broad left front of academics, activists, journalists, politicians and scientists from Britain. Basil Davidson chaired the economic session, with Henry Collins and Peter Ady as main speakers. Fidelis Ayo Ogunsheye was lead speaker in the political session. Thomas wrote a keynote paper on international relations: 'If by imperialism we understand a state of affairs in which one nation is subject to the political control of another nation, is economically dependent, and enjoys unequal rights and opportunities – then it is surely clear that imperialism does continue to exist throughout Africa.' Leonard Barnes responded and supported Thomas's paper: 'I cannot persuade myself that basic relationships have changed. The old relationships are still the same governing relationships. Imperialism still exists, and the problem of its removal is still before us.'

Africans in the Elfinsward discussions included Adenekan Ademola from Nigeria, A.M. Akinloye from Nigeria, A. Amponsah from Gold Coast, Okoi

Arikpo from Nigeria, Hastings Kamuzu Banda from Nyasaland, Ignatius Musazi from Uganda, Charles Njonjo from Kenya, E. Obahiagbon from Nigeria and Bankole Timothy from Sierra Leone. The British personalities included J.D. Bernal, Fenner Brockway, MP, Ritchie Calder, Wilfred Le Gros Clark, Kingsley Martin, Reginald Sorensen, MP and David Williams.

Thomas, in the New Year of 1951, planned a further journey to Africa. Williams had asked for ten articles on Nigerian nationalism along the lines of the articles on Gold Coast. Thomas wrote on 1 February to 'Dear Christopher' Cox (who had been awarded a KCMG in the 1950 honours) that he was hoping to go to Nigeria for a few weeks again towards the end of February to prepare the articles. The journey would not be to do with extra-mural work but Thomas foresaw chances of seeing Gardiner and the work of the University College of Ibadan where Gardiner was looking for full-time tutors. Thomas tentatively proposed meeting Cox before his journey and possibly in Oxford. Cox's secretary wrote on 7 February that Sir Christopher was on leave after a visit to the Far East and would be shown Thomas's letter on 15 February when he was due back at the Colonial Office.

In late February Thomas plunged into his fourth African journey, without seeing Cox again but believing that he had Cox's sympathetic understanding of his journalistic purpose in visiting Nigeria, Cameroon and Gold Coast. Thomas, with only contingent official duties, stayed in Lagos with Ogunsheye in a Yoruba house out at Yaba and renewed acquaintance with other Nigerians including radicals and nationalists such as Azikiwe. In West African style Thomas sat late into the night of 24 February talking in the Lagos nightclubs. Cox – in Oxford for that weekend and intending to talk to Thomas – heard that Thomas had already left for West Africa.

Thomas welcomed the exciting atmosphere he found in Gold Coast where Nkrumah had been elected from prison to the Legislative Assembly in the early days of February and the CPP had won a clear victory. Nkrumah was released from prison and became leader of government business. Kimble laid on a weekend course or conference on legislative procedure for about fifty deputies and ministers, many of whom were already his former students. Thomas suspected it might be the first occasion in human history when a university had run an extra-mural course for the cabinet and members of parliament. Thomas went on 27 March to meet Nkrumah (a little more than a year after Nkrumah's arrest by the colonial authorities had blocked an earlier meeting) and found him approachable and friendly.

Thomas returned to Oxford at the end of March in time for his forty-first birthday on 3 April and for moving house on 4 April to Powder Hill in the Oxford countryside. The Hodgkin family gave up their Oxford flat (inadequate housing in the view of Thomas's mother – 'five rooms for six people', as she wrote to her sisters in February) to rent a large house on Boars Hill. Powder Hill had been the home of the All Souls Warden W.G.S. Adams who had been a friend of Thomas's Smith grandfather and had bequeathed his home to the college. It was a house near Oxford with a large wildish garden and surrounded by fields and woodlands, but problematic for service and transport for half a dozen adults and children whose working and school lives were centred on the city of Oxford.

Thomas and Basil met in London on 16 April to discuss the UDC's burgeoning Africa programme under an Africa Sub-Committee chaired by Harold Davies, MP, whom Thomas knew well from their North Staffordshire days. The programme included a pamphlet series on the theme of Africa and the future. Thomas was willing to write on the political situation in West Africa.

Thomas wrote on 19 April to Teddy that he was proposing to retire from the Oxford delegacy appointment as soon as he decently could and hoped this would be within the next twelve months. He was hesitant only in case he had been in the past over-hasty in resigning from the pre-war Palestine appointment, but he saw no point in marking time in Oxford: 'Eventually though I would rather go to Khartoum than Nigeria. I think – preferring the desert to the jungle.'

He had not yet written up his material on Nigerian nationalism but by mid-May had submitted to the UDC a draft pamphlet on 'Freedom for the Gold Coast?' Thomas hailed Nkrumah who as Minister for Government Business was for all practical purposes the Gold Coast Prime Minister. Thomas also predicted that what existed in the Gold Coast might soon exist in other parts of Africa: 'A popularly elected African Government in the Gold Coast is, by its mere existence, a challenge to those in the Union and in the White Settler territories of East and Central Africa whose main purpose it is to preserve White domination in Africa.'

While Dossie was abroad on a scientific tour Thomas and the children spent 24 June at Crab Mill where Robin was ill and stayed in bed for the early part of the day (Luke in early June had been first in that year's election of scholars to Eton). Three days later Thomas in Oxford heard that his father had a coronary thrombosis and was suffering from cardiac asthma. Thomas went again to Crab Mill but returned to Oxford on 28 June for a tutors' conference. Teddy arrived at Crab Mill in the afternoon and was there when Robin died in the evening. The funeral was in Ilmington on 2 July and by the time of the Robin Hodgkin memorial service at Queen's on 7 July Thomas was discreetly alerting delegates of his proposal to retire from the delegacy.

Thomas's professorial fellowship at Balliol was held by virtue of his delegacy appointment. Lord Lindsay in July ended a quarter of a century as Master of Balliol and soon moved to prepare to open the new experimental Keele University. Thomas broached with his successor – the constitutional historian Sir David Lindsay Keir – the possibilities of a research fellowship linked to his plans for independent travel in Africa. Thomas's series of ten articles on 'Background to Nigerian nationalism' began to appear in *West Africa* from 4 August. The UDC in August published as a sixpenny pamphlet Thomas's polemic on 'Freedom for the Gold Coast', in which he urged British support for 'an enthusiastic self-confident and democratic movement for national independence and for liberation from the colonial past.'

In late September, Thomas sent out to the academic community and at the request of the vice-chancellor a formal note on the conditions of appointment for a new delegacy secretary. Edward Birchall, who had been appointed to the delegacy in 1925 and with Hindmarsh sustained much of the task of forces' education during the second world war, had stayed on as bursar on the administration side. Birchall, whose sense of administrative order had been offended by Thomas's tendency to be lackadaisical, wrote privately on 21 November to Frank Jessup, who had been a candidate when Thomas was appointed, and urged him to compete again. Jessup did apply next day, giving as referees two of Thomas's mentors Charles Morris, now vice-chancellor at Leeds, and Sir Philip Morris, now vice-chancellor at Bristol.

Delegates met on 22 December to consider applications for the secretaryship by Hampden Jackson (Thomas's rival in the 1945 round), Jessup and Harold Wiltshire. It was agreed by a majority of six to two to recommend the appointment of F.W. Jessup. Thomas wanted this and he sent Jessup a personal letter of congratulation to which Jessup replied on 28 December: 'I hope you will always remain pleased about the result of your machinations, and that you will not regret opening the door to this violent reactionary!'

Thomas continued to nurture the interest Basil Davidson was showing in Africa and a plan of Basil's to begin a trek of his own through West Africa from February 1952. Thomas sent a detailed list of some fifty friends and contacts in West Africa who might assist Basil on a journey through Gold Coast, Nigeria and Cameroon. The names ranged from the 'incredibly vigorous and independent minded' David Kimble to the reputedly enlightened Emir of Katsina – 'about as enlightened as a German Prince of the eighteenth century'. Most were Africans engaged in education, labour relations and politics who had befriended Thomas during his delegacy missions.

Thomas at this time found out that Cox had made a fuss a year before in March 1951 over a misunderstanding in the delegacy that Cox had given

Colonial Office approval to Thomas's journey to Nigeria to write articles on nationalism. Thomas wrote on 25 February 1952 to apologise and explain that he had talked to Lucy Sutherland and that 'in no circumstances would I have said or implied that my journey to write these articles had any official or unofficial backing from you'. This was not sufficient for Cox who wrote on 3 March to Lucy Sutherland, with a copy to the vice-chancellor Maurice Bowra, to complain that his name had been used as vaguely supporting Hodgkin's recent journalistic activities in Africa. Statements as requested by Cox were made by Lucy Sutherland and by Thomas when the delegates met in mid-March, and Thomas sent Cox the minute recording the statements. For Thomas that was the end of a trivial misunderstanding. He prepared his departure from the delegacy on 30 April and his attention was turned to Luke's return to Eton and Elizabeth's progress through selection and interview for admission to secondary education at the Oxford High School for the coming school year.

Cox ground on in his anxiety to distance himself from a past friendship with Thomas and worked through several handwritten and typed drafts of an internal Colonial Office memorandum where he repudiated any guilt by association. The polished version was dated 2 May 1952: 'Without knowing Mr Hodgkin really well at any time I have seen something of him off and on since he was an undergraduate, though with very long gaps when I knew nothing of him...' The scholarly apolitical undergraduate had in his colonial service in Palestine gone through 'a violent change of attitude'. Hodgkin, seen at a college dinner in 1936, bore 'obvious traces of some embittering experience'.

Hodgkin at the delegacy and instigating extra-mural work in West Africa had struck Cox as being perfectly normal, candid, sensible and friendly, with no resemblance to the Hodgkin fleetingly glimpsed in 1936. It came as a 'a great shock' to Cox in 1947 or 1948 to be told through private Oxford sources that one and possibly two of the tutors lent by the delegacy for work in West Africa were members of the CP. Cox investigated and found that Hodgkin had been and still was a member of the CP. By December 1949 Hodgkin had formally left the party. Hodgkin's integrity was vouched for by three Oxford college heads: Cox thought that even so they might have been relieved when Hodgkin decided to resign.

Thomas at Powder Hill spent much of the days from 6 to 8 May writing for Jessup a long hand-over document about policy and staffing issues facing the delegacy – and offering to give a party on 7 June as a house-warming a year late for Powder Hill and to welcome Jessup. The colonial work had dwindled to an annual course in colonial adult education and Thomas advised his successor that all sorts of things might be done if he could win the confidence of Cox at the Colonial Office: 'I think they only sheered away from us for political reasons, and now you are there they might be willing to work with Oxford again. Worth trying anyway.'

Chapter 4
Wandering scholar: 1952-1964

Thomas's departure from the delegacy at the end of April 1952 gave him the freedom for more extensive travel in Africa. He had drafted a scheme of work for a historian's study of nationalism in West Africa, covering four British territories – Nigeria, the Gold Coast, Sierra Leone and the Gambia – and French West Africa; the Trust territories of Togoland and the Cameroons; Portuguese Guinea and Liberia. He expected to spend at least five years on a phased investigation of political, economic and social groupings; tribal associations and unions; and religious bodies. For financial and personal reasons Thomas continued to accept invitations and approaches to teach and lecture in adult education that could be fitted round a journey of several months in Africa and would allow him to spend time in Oxford with his family.

He used the library resources of the Oxford Union to which his father had given him a lifetime subscription and scoured the files held at the Institute of Colonial Studies. When on a visit to these files Thomas met by chance a graduate student from Princeton University in the US, David Apter, who was a guest at Nuffield College and of the Institute. Apter was inspired by Kwame Nkrumah's release from prison and leadership of the Gold Coast cabinet and told Thomas that he was preparing to go to the Gold Coast for field research for a dissertation on the shift towards African self-government. Thomas immediately invited him to lunch at Powder Hill, offered Apter advice and they began a friendship.

Thomas consulted widely on his own plans. David Williams used his Liberia connections to seek a visa for Thomas from the Liberian Consulate General. Kenneth Robinson at Nuffield recommended French Africanist contacts. In June he met Margaret Read at the University of London Institute of Education and had tea with Hugh Massingham of *The Observer* (a George Wigg connection) to see whether he might write articles for the newspaper.

He carried on to France where he presented a paper on 'Adult and Workers' Education in the Gold Coast and Nigeria' to a UNESCO gathering. Virginia Vernon of the *Daily Mirror* Paris office helped him make Paris connections and Claude Gérard, the courageous left-wing Catholic editor of *Afrique-Informations*, gave him recommendations to her politician friends in several

African countries and introduced him to others at a party she gave at the end of June. Thomas outlined his travel plans to Théodore Monod, the director of the Institut Français d'Afrique Noire (IFAN), who advised him to spend a week or more at Dakar before following the trans-Saharan route to Gao and visiting the French Soudan. Monod helpfully sketched on a piece of paper a possible itinerary beginning in Dakar and radiating in three directions from Bamako. Thomas enrolled as a member of the International African Institute, where Professor Daryll Forde was administrative director.

Thomas proposed a series on the ancient cities of the Western Sudan for *West Africa* magazine and a separate series on political developments in Francophone West and Central Africa. Williams and Thomas lunched together in London in August and they agreed a strategy for Thomas to write from Africa about eight articles on ancient cities, thematic pieces on the territories to be visited and occasional articles on current events and issues. The ancient cities series was to be completed and sent to Williams by early December. On Thomas's return to England he would write pieces on the political and social evolution of French West Africa, French Equatorial Africa, Portuguese Guinea, Liberia and Belgian Congo.

Thomas was acting as part scholar and part journalist, but remained ambiguous in both categories. Williams wrote to the Portuguese Consul-General in support of an application for a transit visa for Thomas to visit Portuguese Guinea in order to write articles on methods of government and administration; economic development, particularly rice growing; and educational development. The preparations were paying off. Thomas's new passport issued on 18 July was soon stamped with visas for Liberia, French African territories, Guiné and Belgian African territories.

Thomas had booked a passage on a ship leaving Bordeaux for Dakar in the second week of October – the sea voyage was found to be much less expensive than the overland travel of Thomas's initial intention. He drew a special foreign exchange allowance on 2 October of £500 and in the following week spent a couple of days in Paris. He had a long lunch with Leopold Senghor, who was a Deputy in the French National Assembly and founder of a centrist political party for Senegal, the Bloc Démocratique Sénégalais (BDS). Thomas took a night train to Bordeaux and at four in the morning of 9 October sat in the Bordeaux station buffet hoping to board the ship well in time for a supposed nine o'clock departure.

The Foucauld was not ready, and Thomas wandered about the town as a reluctant sightseer of old churches. He thought his command of the French language was feeble: at a little restaurant on the quay he was about to order escargots for lunch as one of the cheapest dishes listed, but on looking up the word in a dictionary changed his snails order to omelette. Thomas queued in the afternoon for customs formalities and met in the queue a young Frenchman who was travelling fourth class via Dakar to make films in Brazil. Thomas when he booked at his travel agency in England was told that fourth class was impossible for Europeans so he was travelling third. Thomas felt envious of the Frenchman but once the ship sailed forgot his regret. The third-class passengers slept in bunks – eight to a cabin – while fourth-class passengers slept between decks on straw bundles. Third class passengers ate in a dining room: fourth class fetched their food on platters and ate in their quarters.

He was unexpectedly hailed on the quay at Dakar on 15 October with a cry of 'Winchester' by the British Consul Douglas Gordon Pirie who had been with him in the boy scouts at school. Pirie saw him speedily through port formalities and took him by car into the city. When Thomas went to IFAN he found that Monod was away and there was no chance of a room on the premises. Thomas, acutely conscious of his tight budget, was installed in the recently opened Hotel La Croix du Sud in the centre of Dakar – albeit in the cheapest room – on a tariff where the guests were obliged to eat at least one costly meal a day, or incur a penalty of almost the same amount.

Pirie lent Thomas a car and a Gold Coast driver, and Thomas searched out the cheaper cafés in Dakar. The IFAN librarian set out a range of materials on the ancient cities of the Soudan and Thomas's reading was interspersed with visits to administration officials, trade unionists and to Joseph Correa, an African radical shopkeeper recommended by Basil Davidson. Within three days, Thomas's anxieties were eased with the arrival from a conference on Morocco of the IFAN archaeologist Raymond Mauny who could give further advice on Thomas's journey. Pirie arranged for Thomas to move from the hotel to free accommodation in a government guesthouse close to Government House. This brought the comfort of a vast bed in a Second Empire bedroom, a sitting room and a bathroom with a real bath – the first Thomas had enjoyed for about a fortnight.

The Great Council of French West Africa was due to meet in Dakar to vote the federal budget and the event drew together political leaders from some eight component countries of the vast territory. Thomas was intrigued by Senghor, finding him reminiscent of Nkrumah although pursuing a different political agenda. He followed Senghor's schedule on the evening of 18 October, including a mass rally called by the BDS and a social in the Dakar Medina held late in the evening (Senghor remarked that Africans seldom slept much since it was not necessary when it was warm), and they had a private discussion in a café overlooking the sea. Senghor put to Thomas that the ideology of nationalism was unsuited to the twentieth century and he asserted an interdependence of Europe and Africa.

Thomas decided to watch the Great Council meeting. He found it difficult or impossible to keep awake during the formal opening ceremony of the Council with soldiers in scarlet uniforms and politicians in a variety of European and African dress. He was more stimulated by the informal debate after the High Commissioner Bernard Cornut-Gentille had left the session and by opportunities in the breaks to meet African political representatives. However, Thomas was invited to a copious lunch on 22 October given by Cornut-Gentille for a visiting Air Vice-Marshal (showing off the Canberra aircraft, Britain's first jet bomber).

Thomas left Dakar on 25 October for a thirty-hour train journey to Bamako, travelling second class – 'a compromise between pocket and remaining reasonably bien vu' as he wrote in one of his frequent letters to Dossie. He spent the cool of the evening on the front of the coach chatting to a couple of young railway workers about their respective trade unions. Thomas's priority in Bamako was to meet the scholars at the IFAN centre. After two days with a Ukrainian archaeologist, Thomas was glad to escape to look up Africans recommended by Claude Gérard, beginning with Abdoulaye Singaré of the Union Soudanaise section of the Rassemblement Démocratique Africain (RDA).

The IFAN archaeological lorry, his local transport, broke down. Thomas stocked up with biscuits, oranges and Vichy water and took a seat on a commercial lorry taking passengers to Nara on 1 November – after Nara, motor vehicles might be abandoned for horses and camels. Thomas was seated in the driver's cabin and his chance travelling companion passenger was Mamadou Fadiala Keita, a founder member of the Union Soudanaise, so the three days of slow travel on sandy roads became a political exploration and an opening to hospitality from administration and party officials along the route.

From Nara he became part of a five-strong caravan with an interpreter Koulibaly Maury, two Mauritanians Mohammed and Omar attending the horses and Demba the Sarakolle owner of a baggage donkey. Thomas rode a horse but soon ached from an unfamiliar Moorish saddle. When they slept out at night by their campfire Thomas suggested that they take turns as sentinels to keep up the fire and guard against hyenas and serpents. When Koulibaly interpreted the suggestion, the owner of the donkey said it was unnecessary: he knew verses of the Koran that were completely effective against hyenas or serpents. He cried these verses aloud in every direction, dug up some sand and scattered it all around so that nothing harmful should penetrate the circle in which the travellers sat.

They did much of their riding in the cool of night or early morning and refreshed their water supplies when they struck a well. They roasted sheep bought on the way but Thomas's standby of tinned sardines was rejected by the horsemen. Thomas paid off his helpers when they reached Mauritania and stayed with a French administrator at Timbedra who found Thomas a lift in the lorry a merchant had freighted with sugar and tea for Nema. In Nema another French administrator offered to find Thomas a good camel and guide to Walata and to lend his own saddle. Thomas, with Mohammed Abdullah as guide, set off on the two-day journey. Thomas preferred the camel to the horse, but had difficulties in making his camel trot as he had on a camel ride in Sinai in 1935. He was out of practice with the kick. The solution was that one of his travelling companions rode behind him, and if Thomas's camel showed signs of slowing down the companion stirred it on from behind.

Thomas arrived in Walata where he made a round of Islamic scholars to gather material and was repeatedly entertained to dates, roast pigeons and sweet tea. He described the experience in a letter to Dossie: 'A mixture of Maryport (as we knew it before the War), Basra, and any Oxford (male) Senior Common Room. Highly civilised donnish characters, whose life seems to be spent almost entirely in food and prayer, and remembrance of things past.' He followed the relevant history in the London Library copy he carried with him of Bovill's *Caravans of the Old Sahara.*

Thomas made a rushed lorry journey from Nema to Bamako. His next target was to go northwards of Bamako to the city of Timbuktu, which he reached on 29 November by forms of transport that changed almost on a whim. He spent a couple of days on a boat from Koulikoro to Segou along the river Niger about half a mile broad at this point. He travelled by aeroplane from Segou to Goundam, whose administrator he had met in the Bamako hospital and who was on the same flight, without a clear idea how he would travel on the next stage. The Goundam administrator arranged for him to travel onwards with the luggage on the open back of a Dodge truck. They arrived in Timbuktu in moonlight and to the sound of tom-toms as the Muslims celebrated the prophet's birthday.

Thomas retrod the footsteps of nineteenth-century European explorers of Timbuktu, visited the principal mosques and wrote up the visit for *West Africa.* He took a lift back to Goundam in an army car on 4 December and from Goundam caught a flight on 6 December to Gao, to see the capital of the fifteenth- and sixteenth-century Songhai Empire, and a further flight to Bamako on 8 December. He spent an evening learning about RDA policy from Modibo Keita, the Soudan secretary. He took again the long train journey between

Bamako and Dakar and worked on his articles on the ancient cities for Mauny to check for accuracy.

He had missed the weekly flight to Bissau and found the next one fully booked. He was rescued by Mauny who took him to the Portuguese Consul in Dakar. The latter arranged a lift for Thomas in the camionette of a Portuguese agronomist who was returning to Bissau from a soil science conference in Dakar. The agronomist and his wife and a Portuguese district administrator travelled in front, and Thomas in the back with an African servant amid the tumbling baggage. When they had reached the Gambia river and were awaiting a ferry they were able to cross in style since Thomas's Wykehamist friend Pirie, who was visiting the Governor in Bathurst, signalled for the Governor's launch to fetch Thomas's party. Then the plan began to unravel when the owner of the camionette took to his bed with a fever. Thomas stayed in Bathurst meeting whom he could find including E. Lloyd Evans from a prominent Gambian family and the trade unionist Edward Small who had founded the *Gambia Outlook* newsletter in 1922.

When the Portuguese group continued to the Guiné frontier post at San Domingos on 17 December, Thomas, despite holding a valid visa for a 60-day stay, was refused admission. A letter had been sent a few days earlier to the local administrator with instructions from Lisbon not to admit Thomas Hodgkin. Thomas explained that the historian Avelino Teixeira da Mota was expecting him in Bissau. The administrator riposted that Teixeira da Mota was in San Domingos where Thomas could see him, but he could not go to Bissau. Teixeira da Mota was kind and hospitable, gave Thomas meals, arranged a bed and drove him in his car to Ziguinchor in Senegal. Thomas felt angry and frustrated and he cabled David Williams to take the matter up with George Wigg and Daryll Forde. He fumed for a day in Ziguinchor while he wrote up his travels, and consoled himself with a good dinner and wine.

In the New Year of 1953, Thomas spent ten days teaching on David Kimble's extra-mural studies school at Wesley College, Kumasi, in the Gold Coast and a few more days in Kumasi with Dennis Austin and his family. News filtered back about protests over the restrictions on his movement, After his exclusion from Guiné the State Department in Monrovia decided to cancel his visa without explanation. Williams interceded with the Liberian Secretary of State, who was passing through London in the first week of January, and was given assurances that Thomas would be welcome in Liberia. Williams asked Thomas to go speedily to Liberia and to cover an official visit to be made by Kwame Nkrumah as Prime Minister of the Gold Coast. Teddy, who was now an established member of the editorial staff of *The Times*, sent word that Prudence Pelham had died in the previous October with multiple sclerosis in an advanced stage.

Thomas arrived in Liberia on 19 January to an airport welcome of drummers and dancers, since he had been integrated into the Gold Coast Prime Minister's suite of a dozen Africans (and musicians and despatch riders) travelling on a Liberian National Airways DC3 to await Nkrumah. He went to the Monrovia harbour to witness Nkrumah's arrival in the yacht of Liberia's President William Tubman and had renewed encounters with CPP friends and the Sierra Leonean journalist Bankole Timothy. Thomas was able to grab one talk with Nkrumah. The Nkrumah visit ended on 31 January and Thomas stayed on in Monrovia. He hoped to go by truck through French Guinea to Abidjan and then by boat from Lomé to Pointe Noire.

The road journey was marked by broken nights and broken springs. He stayed up all night for fear of missing a lorry due to leave around three in the morning of 5 February. The French proprietor had errands in Liberia and the vehicle did not reach the Ganta frontier post with French Guinea until late that night. Thomas slept on the ground wrapped in a borrowed blanket and caught a heavy cold. They went through two customs checks early on 6 February when Thomas was offered a lift from a Corsican merchant on his way to Abidjan. This vehicle broke down with dynamo problems: Thomas had some sleep in an African hut, but was woken in the middle of the night by the hooting of a motor horn from a lorry leaving for Man and for Abidjan that would take him onwards.

After repeated halts to repair a broken spring, Thomas and a police corporal found another lorry bound for Abidjan. With more pauses for repair of its spring the lorry reached Gagnoa by the evening of 8 February – and drove the remaining 300 kilometres through the night to reach Abidjan at dawn on 9 February. Thomas reflected: 'I could have reached Abidjan in two hours by air on Thursday, but one does see the country and meet people in a way air-travellers never do.' He renewed contact with one of the RDA founding members Daniel Ouezzin Coulibaly whom he had met in Paris and rose at 6 a.m. on 11 February to visit the populous African neighbourhood in Treichville. Thomas cancelled the boat journey to Pointe Noire, and bought air passages. He went for the first time to the Legislative Assembly in Accra on 13 February and heard Kwame Nkrumah make a speech on the budget.

Thomas was taken in hand in Brazzaville by the British consul-general Robert Mason, who had been a colleague and friend of Thomas's brother Teddy at the British Embassy in Baghdad. He saw local scholars and the information director, visited the African quarter Poto Poto and spent a fifteen-hour day tramping around fields to see groundnut and manioc cultivation – at Nzaza, a three-hour journey southwest of Brazzaville. He crossed the river Congo into Leopoldville, but felt he had neither the time, nor money, nor energy to do serious work on the Belgian Congo this time round, and he had gathered enough material for the 30 articles he was expected to write for *West Africa*. On Thomas's last day in Brazzaville he met an African Catholic priest Abbé Fulbert Youlou, whom he thought vigorous and intelligent, and they discussed the Conseil Coutumier Africain whose purpose was to bring together educated young men in the towns to prevent the disintegration of traditional customs.

He was in Bangui on 28 February sitting by the river Oubangui, and feeling homesick. A helpful French administrator arranged a busy schedule of meetings with representatives of the African and French communities. Thomas's enthusiasm was reawakened, but he could not quite overcome his sense of absence from family. He went on briefly to Fort Lamy in Chad and then to Maiduguri in Nigeria and to Kano to meet Dossie arriving by air on the morning of 16 March. The magazine *West Africa* began publication on 21 March of Thomas's ten-part series of scholarly and descriptive articles on 'Cities of the Sudan'. Thomas and Dossie left for England from Kano on 29 March.

From the moment of his return a flow of invitations began from educational and political institutions seeking to draw on his enhanced knowledge of Africa gained from nearly six months of continuous travel. On 14 April Teddy saw Walter Taplin at *The Spectator* and suggested articles that Thomas might write. Taplin, who had been a pupil of their father, was amenable, though describing the journal's policy on Africa as 'chocolate' – i.e. not aggressively black or white, but middle of the road. Teddy was also arranging for Thomas to see producers in the Arabic and schools services of the BBC. On 1 May *The Spectator* published Thomas's article on 'The Leaders in West Africa', as the first in a stream of contributions.

Massingham had alerted a friend on the *Manchester Guardian* to Thomas's return from several months of travel in Africa. An assistant editor, Patrick Monkhouse, wrote on 14 May asking if Thomas would care to write something on French Equatorial Africa, an area rarely addressed in the British press. Thomas had a chapter on the movement towards self-government in British West Africa in *The New West Africa: problems of independence*, a collection edited by Basil Davidson and Adenekan Ademola and published by Allen & Unwin.

Thomas dashed over to Paris for a few days in mid-June to fill in gaps from his travel notes and to meet people whose views he needed for various articles. Virginia Vernon and Claude Gérard ensured that he lunched with African politicians, including a member of the French senate Mahamanne Haidara. Thomas wrote a brief note on political parties in British and French West Africa intended for *The Observer* but steered by Colin Legum to the *Information Digest* of the Africa Bureau, with Thomas's consent.

The invitations to teach and lecture in Britain continued, not least from the Oxford delegacy. The University Extension Lectures Committee sent a provisional programme for Thomas to give sets of up to 12 lectures in the Michaelmas and Hilary terms: at Brighton on Mondays, at Hanley on Tuesdays, and six lectures at Mold on Wednesdays. These were under a generic theme of 'The crisis in Africa', which meant that similar material could be used with different audiences, but the conjuncture would bring a schedule of travel between Sussex and the Potteries reminiscent of his train journeys of the war years. The Tutorial Classes Committee appointed Thomas to a more conventional task as tutor in an introduction to philosophy class to be held at Abingdon from the autumn of 1953. This was a substantial three-year commitment with annual sessions requiring 24 classes each of two hours' duration.

Thomas was approached by the editorial director J.C. Reynolds of Frederick Muller to write a book on colonial affairs for the publisher's 'Man and Society' series of new books for adult education. Thomas gave a cautious and conditional assent: he did not want to go outside African matters and could not do the writing until the following autumn. The book Thomas determined to write was essentially the project on nationalism he had nursed through his latter days at the delegacy and his recent months of travel in Africa. In the New Year of 1954, Reynolds sent a contract for a book to be delivered 31 December 1954 and for an advance of £50 payable on publication. The British journal *The Twentieth Century* recruited Thomas as an occasional contributor on Africa – on the strength of his writings in *The Spectator*, with aspects of the French and Belgian territories as an initial theme and a first article expected before Thomas's next Africa journey.

Thomas had gained a new reputation in British academic circles, and his work was being noticed in the US. From the University of California's political science department James Smoot Coleman, who was revising for publication his Harvard doctoral dissertation on nationalism in Nigeria, wrote on 24 January describing himself as 'a very avid reader' of Thomas's articles in *West Africa* and seeking Thomas's advice for sources on political developments in French West Africa. He read Thomas's series published in *West Africa* from January to March of 1954 and wrote to Thomas on 15 April that they answered many questions he was asking himself. It was the first information he had seen in English and he had drawn the series to the attention of Professor Rupert Emerson, who was interested in comparative nationalism.

Thomas prepared a sixth Africa journey to traverse from west to east. He began with a visit to Brussels in May to identify officials and institutions in the Belgian colonies and the territories governed under a League of Nations mandate who might help him in Africa. He went briefly to Paris to refresh his connections with Claude Gérard and her circle of African politicians. He had become a regular contributor to *The Spectator*, which entailed a leaning towards contemporary events rather than the historical background that *West Africa* magazine could encompass. He abandoned a camel ride to ancient cities of Mauritania (mapped out in discussion with Monod) in favour of looking at the second general election campaign in the Gold Coast. Thomas flew to Niamey and entered the northern Gold Coast at Navrongo on 20 May and travelled south. He had supper on 29 May – his last evening in the Gold Coast – with Polly Hill, who from 1951 to 1953 had been on the editorial staff of *West Africa* and was living in Accra since her recent marriage to the Registrar of the West African Examinations Council Kenneth Humphreys. The next day he left Accra via Lomé to Douala in the Cameroons. He typed his first on-the-spot article for *The Spectator* about the Gold Coast – sent off so that it could be published just after the first stage of voting due on 10 June.

He flew to Brazzaville on 6 June and made the boat crossing to Leopoldville in Belgian Congo. Thomas encountered de facto racial segregation – to which he was unaccustomed – although as he toured Leopoldville he noted some barriers being lowered cautiously. Away from the city he was impressed by the argument of a veteran administrator René Schillings, who feared that mission and other external intervention was permitting the rapid destruction of the balanced so-cial and moral order that people like the Bakuba built up over hundreds of years.

He took a three-day train journey from Mweka to Elizabethville and in his carriage began for *The Spectator* a piece on 'Congo Progress' that mixed trav-elogue with political analysis. He drew on mining community contacts he had collected in Brussels to conduct interviews over three days in Elizabethville that tied in with his long-standing interest in social change. He flew on 26 June to Usumbura in Ruanda-Urundi, where the colonial governor's office provided a car with a Congolese soldier driver to take him to a research institute at Astrida through densely populated mountainous countryside. Thomas had a long con-versation with a Belgian anthropologist Jan Vansina who was doing fieldwork among the Bakuba and they discussed the degree to which the Bakuba were resistant to European culture and ways of working.

The government car took Thomas to Bukavu. He contemplated going on by road through the Mountains of the Moon to Uganda, but opted for speed's sake to fly to Entebbe on 4 July. He made his way to the University College of East Africa at Makerere. He was on new ground but among familiar faces and lunched on 6 July with the college principal Bernard de Bunsen, a part contemporary at Balliol, and with Lady Cohen, the wife of the British gover-nor Sir Andrew Cohen: as Helen Stevenson she had been Thomas's junior at the Dragon School in Oxford. Thomas interviewed members of the Ismaili and African communities and dined with Cohen whom he regarded as much more intelligent than most Governors. Thomas was also gathering information on Ugandan nationalism and history. He met the anthropologist Audrey Richards, political historian D.A. Low and sociologist Peter Gutkind, a graduate of the University of Chicago.

Thomas had found letters from home including one written by Gervase Mathew listing upper class Ethiopians who had been at Oxford and had returned to Addis Ababa in the Imperial service, including Michael Imru, a grandson of Ras Imru. Mathew reported that he was to lecture on African archaeology at the Ashmolean every Michaelmas term. He saw this as the first step towards the establishment of a centre of African studies in Oxford, with an emphasis on history and sociology not linguistics, that would grant a Diploma in African Studies. Mathew was on the unofficial committee drawing up plans, with anthropologists Edward Evans-Pritchard and Godfrey Lienhardt: 'I have already insisted that you should be in on the ground floor of it all.'

Thomas went on to Addis where he was met on arrival on 13 July by a son of Brigadier Daniel Arthur Sandford (the Brigadier and his wife Christine had known Ethiopia since 1920; she had known two of Thomas's maternal aunts at Cambridge). An Ethiopian pilot took him to meet Michael Imru – entirely Oxford (Exeter, PPE) – at the Ministry of Civil Aviation, who in turn led Thomas to other influential people. Thomas went north to Gondar's mediaeval castles and to tea with Ras Asrate Kassa, Governor-General of the Province of Begemder and Semien. He continued to Asmara, in haste since he was tied to lectures in Britain in early August, and on to Khartoum on 24 July, to Rome for a few hours on 28 July and to Paris where Dossie had gone to lecture at the Sorbonne about her work on vitamin B12, whose structure her research team were close to solving.

On return, Thomas wrote up the last stages of his journey for *The Spectator*, but was conscious that he had spent too little time in Sudan to assess current tensions between political factions. The Labour politician Richard Crossman, who had been his senior at Winchester and had been elected to Parliament in 1945, wanted Thomas to speak to a House of Commons sub-committee.

In the New Year of 1955, Thomas continued to accept invitations to speak about Africa. He scaled down his journalism to draft the book that had been in his mind three years earlier as he prepared to leave the delegacy. He had spoken then of a full-length study of West African nationalism. The subsequent travel gave him the confidence to look at the continent more broadly and through the challenges to colonial power from the national movements generated after the Second World War. He had begun when a literature on African politics scarcely existed because African politics was scarcely supposed to exist. Through personal inquiry and from the specialised studies scattered through a variety of journals around the world he tried to account for the political institutions and ideas of African nationalism, in relation to their history. He concluded with recognition that the period of European ascendancy in Africa was drawing to an end and the wish that this end should not inflict avoidable suffering upon Africans, Asians or Europeans.

By the beginning of April Thomas had completed a draft and he carried on in May with supporting material and revisions. By late October he was reading proofs and seeking comment from several colleagues. Early on 4 January 1956, he delivered the corrected proofs to Frederick Muller's in Fleet Street and went on to Victoria just in time for a boat train. Thomas was also completing a note for *West Africa* on French elections and left this with a friendly porter to post.

He had another book project: a long essay on West African political parties, promised for a Penguin West Africa series edited by David Kimble and Helen. Helen suggested he should extend the essay to cover Africa as a whole since Sir Allen Lane at Penguin had agreed to transform the regional series into an Africa-wide series. Thomas was planning a new journey he could make to follow the area of Muslim influence in North Africa and had come to Paris to find specialists on Islam in black Africa (they were sadly few, one specialist told him). The few days in Paris were crammed, including a talk with Leopold Senghor in his French government ministerial office, and a family Sunday lunch on 8 January at the home of the *Présence Africaine* editor Alioune Diop. Thomas found it difficult to tear himself away and just caught an afternoon train to Brussels for a conference on Belgian Africa. He left the Brussels meeting early to be back in time for his Abingdon philosophy class.

Morocco was much in his mind: he secured a Moroccan visa in mid-February and gathered recommendations from Basil Davidson about journalist contacts and from Norman Bentwich about leaders of the Jewish community in Morocco. Thomas, as his nationalism book continued through the production process, began the essay on political parties for Penguin. In addition he was invited to contribute to a series of West African history books supported by the West African Newspapers group and under the general editorship of Gerald Graham, Rhodes Professor of Imperial History at the University of London, with Oxford University Press as joint publisher. Thomas would be expected to provide some 75,000 words of extracts of writings by travellers in Nigeria over the centuries, an introduction and suggestions for illustrations.

When the round of tutorial classes closed at the end of March Thomas was able to go on a three-week family holiday to Greece. In London in early May he collected fresh visas for French West Africa and French Equatorial Africa.

Through Basil Davidson's network he had added the *Daily Herald* to the existing strings of *West Africa, The Spectator* and *Manchester Guardian*. Thomas was far from completing the Penguin book and he secured from the editors an understanding that he could delay delivery until later in the year because his extensive African tour of mid-1956 would allow him to gather more material.

Thomas began his seventh African journey – across Islamic Africa – with two crowded days in Paris in mid-May. He saw Virginia Vernon, Basil Davidson's journalist friends from *France-Observateur* Roger Paret and his wife Eve Dechamp, officials at the French Overseas Ministry and the *Manchester Guardian* correspondent Darsie Gillie. He visited Alioune Diop at the offices of *Présence Africaine* and went on to a lecture on black poetry organised by Diop where he was introduced to Aimé Césaire, the West Indian Communist poet and deputy whose *Discours sur le colonialisme* Thomas had recently been reading.

He sat and talked with Claude Gérard in a café before she saw him off on a night train from the Gare Austerlitz to Bordeaux. She had just spent a fortnight with the Algerian maquis and was going to risk arrest by writing sympathetically about the Algerian anti-colonial struggle. He went by ship from Bordeaux to Casablanca and then by train to Rabat. He chose third class for economy; only to find soft seats and that there was a fourth class with wooden seats where the masses travelled. His third class travelling companions included two soldiers in the new uniforms of the Royal Moroccan Army for a country whose independence from France under Sultan Mohammed ben Youssef had been declared on 2 March.

Thomas felt he had struck lucky when he arrived in Rabat on 22 May; the Hotel Monplaisir, chosen from the lowest and cheapest category of hotel in the guide, was opposite the spectacular tower of a ruined twelfth-century mosque. This French family hotel was close to the British Consulate but not calculated to impress the British Consul-General Harold Freese-Pennefather whom Thomas found uncongenial (though he was a Balliol graduate slightly senior to Thomas and a friend of Gervase Mathew). Thomas had neglected the advice from Mathew not to appear as a doubtful journalist nosing about in current politics, but as a scholarly ex-fellow of Balliol with good connections and archaeological interests engaged in serious research. His presence also aroused interest from a series of French detectives keen to know from hotel staff what telephone numbers he called.

He found the editor whom Claude Gérard had recommended – Zhidi Zhour of *Al Alam* – who gave Thomas further introductions. Thomas, identifying Istiqlal (the independence party) as the most powerful political force in the country, went twice to see the acting general secretary Mehdi Ben Barka who described the local cell structure that allowed the party to survive when it was illegal. On 26 May he continued by train, crowded with French soldiers for the Algerian war, to Fez to an even cheaper entirely Moroccan Hotel Boujlond in the Medina. Thomas was also pursuing an interest in the Islamic sects and brotherhoods – and in the ancient University of Qarawiyin that seemed to him rather like Oxford in the Middle Ages with theology as the queen of sciences. He went on to Mauritania and Senegal with a fifteen-hour lorry ride to Rosso and the subsequent long train journey from Dakar to Bamako: familiar faces in the hotel and encounters with historians Marcel Cardaire and Amadou Hampaté Bâ at the end of June.

Thomas had conceived this journey as an investigation into trans-Saharan communications including the movement of ideas between North and West Africa. He intended as far as possible to travel along the Hajj pilgrim route, in his own case only as far as the Sudan. He left Bamako on 29 June by bus and went south to the Upper Volta city of Bobo-Dioulasso where he thought he would be stuck for days – and was rescued by the chance of a seat on a special pilgrim flight that took him to Niamey (next stop Mecca). From Niamey he chanced upon a lorry bound for Borni-N'Kami on the road to Sokoto. He reached Kano in Nigeria and left through Maiduguri to Fort Lamy (his brief presence again arousing the interest of a French detective). He went on by air to Khartoum, arriving early on 16 July and finding government offices about to close for the four days of the festival of sacrifice marking the end of the pilgrimage.

Khartoum was familiar territory and he called at the university office of academic friends. Sa'ad ad-Din Fawzi, newly appointed as economics professor, had a copy of Thomas's book *Nationalism in Colonial Africa* brought in by air from London by another friend – the first time Thomas had seen his book in print. They found the students' warden Jamal Mohammed Ahmed considering whether to accept the ambassadorship to Ethiopia he had been offered. Sa'ad and Jamal put Thomas up in a university guesthouse and swiftly mobilised for him to spend one out of his two weeks in Sudan on a journey to the south where an army mutiny in August 1955 had troubled the transition to independence on 1 January 1956. The *Manchester Guardian* was particularly keen for something from Thomas about the south. He spent a crammed week of interviews in the south and flew home – to a fresh crop of requests for speaking and lecturing and the first reviews of his book.

Thomas wrote up his recent travels for the newspapers and journals, including a nine-part series on 'Islam and politics in West Africa' that was published in *West Africa* magazine from 15 September. He put on hold his essay on political parties and began to gather elements for the anthology of Nigerian history – from the ninth century on – for the Gerald Graham series. Before plunging into a Wantage philosophy class he had a further brief overseas journey to make.

Alioune Diop sent him the appeal made to black writers and artists to attend the first Congress of Scholars of the Negro World to be held in Paris from 19 to 22 September. The score of signatories included several of the people whom Thomas had met in nearly a decade of close involvement in Africa, amongst them: the Gold Coast painter Kofi Antubam and sociologist Kofi Busia; from Martinique Aimé Césaire; the Nigerian artist Ben Enwonwu (who was introduced to the Hodgkin circle after he travelled to Britain in 1944 to study art), and Leopold Senghor. The US signatories were largely new to him and included the musician Louis Armstrong and novelist Richard Wright.

Thomas crossed the channel on 19 September to attend the Congress. He saw it as dialectic, with the mystical-metaphysical thesis of Senghor, contradicted by the liberal-rationalist antithesis of Wright, generating the Marxist synthesis of Césaire. A compatriot of Césaire, the psychiatrist Frantz Fanon was nominally in the Martinique delegation but since 1953 had been a French government appointee as medical director of the psychiatric hospital at Blida-Joinville in Algeria. His experiences were drawing him closer to the Algerian revolt against French colonialism in late 1954 that soon became a war. Fanon spoke to the conference on 20 September on reciprocal action between racism and culture, with coded references to Algeria (and Thomas's notebook jottings included Fanon's view that the aim of a colonial system is a perpetual agony rather than a total destruction of traditional culture).

Thomas returned to Oxford to his teaching and journalism. The publication of *Nationalism in Colonial Africa* secured his place in history. He had woven together the threads he had gathered on his journeys and was deeply convinced that African political institutions should be studied for their intrinsic interest in the same way as British, French or American institutions were studied. A notice in the *Times Literary Supplement* of 17 August had described him as 'one of the few British students of Africa well versed in non-British African territories' and judged the work as a 'balanced and scholarly book, which regards nationalism as an inevitable growth from the new African society, with common characteristics from Kumasi to Cape Town'. Thomas explored a complex web of social and political institutions from an African perspective drawing on intermittent and highly unconventional travel in Africa that brought him unusually close to his themes. In the *Manchester Guardian* of 31 August he was noted for a scholarly book by a wandering scholar. In the South African liberal journal *The Forum* Julius Lewin characterised the book as a small masterpiece that told more of Africa of the day than a dozen large solid books by men more accustomed to use words to conceal the truth than to reveal it. Other reviewers highlighted that much of the book's information was unobtainable elsewhere and that it provided the best introduction to African nationalism to be found.

Recognition came from the US. David Apter had moved on from fieldwork in the Gold Coast to Evanston, Illinois and was a member of the team teaching African studies at Northwestern University. This African studies programme was formalised by the anthropologist Melville J. Herskovits in 1948 as the first of its kind in the US. Apter believed that Thomas, who spoke French, read Arabic and had a range of knowledge of Africa not common in the US, should be brought to Evanston. Apter was asked to compile a shortlist of people qualified to take temporary teaching posts in the African studies programme and wrote on 28 November with an informal inquiry whether he might put Thomas in as his strongest candidate for the next academic cycle. Apter discussed this invitation with Herskovits, who wanted to meet Thomas. As Herskovits was in London for the last week of December en route to an Africa tour, Herskovits and Thomas were able to meet in Oxford and discuss the matter. They understood that Thomas's past membership of the CP might cause visa difficulties. Herskovits was reassured that the affiliation was indeed in the past. On the last day of 1956 Reynolds wrote from Frederick Muller that the New York University Press would publish a US edition of *Nationalism in Colonial Africa.*

In the New Year of 1957, Thomas and Dossie moved back to North Oxford from Powder Hill in the woodlands of Boar's Hill. They would share a household with Dossie's sister Joan Payne whose marriage had ended and left her responsible for the upbringing of five children. The Hodgkin and Payne families (three adults and eight children) and their helpers took a large Victorian house at 94 Woodstock Road. From this new address Thomas wrote on 31 January accepting an official invitation from Northwestern to spend the fall quarter of 1957-58 teaching a post-graduate course on 'Authority Systems of Africa', previously taught by Apter.

He was already embroiled in preparations for his eighth journey to Africa. After studying communications and links across the Sahara and Muslim Africa, he planned now to look further at trans-Saharan links and influence but along the Tunisia-Tripolitania axis, to see the Fezzan region in Libya and possibly to continue into northern Nigeria.

With the independence of the Gold Coast as Ghana due on 6 March, Thomas was in demand to write on this topic. He provided a guest editorial on 'Ghana in the African setting' for *United Asia.* On the day of independence the publishing house Thomas Nelson published the Prime Minister's *Autobiography of Kwame Nkrumah.* Thomas reviewed the title for the Ruskin College magazine *New Epoch* and commented: 'It would neither worry nor surprise me if Ghana, or any other independent African state, were to evolve a form of democracy quite unlike the forms existing in the West. The prospect of a one-party State does not make my flesh creep.'

Thomas's departure for Africa was drawing close and he had no affirmative response on a US visa application but only a probe into his Communist background. He wrote to Apter of his concerns and Apter mobilised university support. The chairman of the political science department, George Blanksten, acting on the advice of the university's legal department, wrote on 6 May to Margaret McClellan in the visa section of the US Embassy in London: 'Mr Hodgkin is one of the most distinguished and knowledgeable scholars of African studies in the English speaking world.' Thomas, departing for Africa on 18 May, sent his own dossier to Margaret McClellan: he gave as references from Britain three respected figures Archbishop David Mathew, Sir Maurice Powicke late Regius Professor of History in Oxford University, and Professor Asa Briggs in the department of history at Leeds University.

Thomas, with a new typewriter in his luggage, flew from Lympne in Kent to Beauvais in France. He went on to Paris where he renewed contact with friends including Claude Gérard, Virginia Vernon and anthropologist Georges Balandier, and embarked for Tunis with 26 useful names in his notebook. Thomas was allowing himself about a week to build up a picture of the Neo-Destour party, whose founder Habib Bourguiba had taken Tunisia to independence in 1956. He attended a special session of the constituent assembly where Bourguiba spoke about French financial pressures on Tunisia and went on 30 May to visit Bourguiba at his home at Saida. Thomas wrote up their discussion in an article for the *New Statesman* under the title 'The illusion of grandeur' – Bourguiba sensed that the French suffered from the desire to be great to compensate for the humiliation of German occupation in the Second World War. Bourguiba told Thomas that Nkrumah and he shared the idea of African liberation on a basis of friendship with the West: they were planning to hold a conference of independent African states in Accra the following year to ease the transition from colonialism in other African territories – and to keep Africa aligned with the West. Bourguiba saw repressive French policy in Algeria as the great obstacle to such co-operation with the West.

Thomas travelled on by bus through Ben Gardane into Libya on 4 June and to Tripoli where he conducted interviews on the Libyan monarchical and parliamentary political system, but was eager to be away from towns and left on 12 June as a car passenger for a venture into the Sahara, to Sebha, Murzuq and Ghat to probe the historic links of the Fezzan with the Maghrib and Egypt in one direction and the western Sudan in the other. He returned to Sebha at the end of June in the hope of being back with his family by the end of the first week of July.

Thomas's thought of making a swift return to Oxford was forestalled when he met in Sebha someone from the Algerian Front de Libération Nationale (FLN), a political front that emerged in 1954 and directed an armed revolution in the interior of Algeria through an Armée de la Libération Nationale. Thomas's interlocutor urged him to take an opportunity to meet the Army of Liberation in the interior. Thomas was referred to FLN supporters in Tripoli and referred again to the FLN representation in Tunis.

Thomas returned to Tunisia on 4 July and deferred his onward journey to England to mid-July, while remaining cautious about the reasons he gave to his family in a telephone call and letters. At the FLN representation Thomas was vetted by a French Algerian teacher and passed muster to hold a long conversation about the Algerian situation with Frantz Fanon. Since the Paris congress of writers Fanon had resigned from French government service, been barred from Algeria and had made his way to Tunis in January 1957. Fanon continued to work as a psychiatrist but by May his identification with the FLN had become overt. Thomas needed to make or sustain a political rapport with Fanon to be allowed into the interior maquis. He again passed muster and arrangements were made for Thomas to pay a clandestine visit to the Algerian Army of Liberation's 2nd Battalion, Eastern Command. He was offered a visit of several weeks, but could give only several days. Thomas wrote from Tunis on 7 July to his mother saying only that he would be 'spending a few days longer in this neighbourhood' – and to Dossie that he had been offered a lift 'to go over in the direction of the Algerian frontier' and was leaving Tunis next day.

At regimental headquarters he was asked if he would like to see a battle, but declined (the commander of the battalion he was visiting was instructed to avoid attacking the French while Thomas was his guest). Thomas had to don Algerian battledress before going into the hills. He crossed the frontier from Tunisia to Algeria disguised in military gear with further disguise as a Tunisian peasant – the ostensible effect of burnous and kufiya was undermined by his wearing of conspicuously English shoes.

Thomas reached the battalion late at night after a three-hour ride on mountain paths. His principal host was Captain Abdurrahman Bensalem, an Algerian-born former sergeant-major in the French army with service in Tunis, Italy, Germany and Indochina, who had deserted with his unit and their equipment in March the year before. Thomas stayed at battalion headquarters in an oak forest in the mountains: he slept in a brushwood hut on a vast communal bed, and visited individual companies within the battalion and talked to supporters from the villages who came into camp with food and information.

Thomas spent only four days with the fighters but he came away impressed by an organised and efficient uniformed force with strong political consciousness and moved by the character of people engaged in a revolutionary mountain war. He thought their goal was a secular liberal independent Algeria. Thomas returned via Tunis and another long conversation with Fanon, and he left on 15 July on a flight to the Paris Orly airport, fearful of arrest by the French. As a passenger in direct transit, he was not checked by the French control and after the brief transit stop he felt deep relief to be in the air on the next leg to London.

Captain Bensalem had welcomed Thomas as the first English guest of the liberation army and whether this was accurate or not the Algerian expedition was a news story of greater impact than usual for Thomas's journalism. He prepared to spread the story widely, through George Wigg securing an appointment on 17 July to make the Algerian nationalist case to Aneurin Bevan – a Labour MP in opposition, and associated with the newspaper *Tribune* and anti-colonialism – as the British politician of whom the Algerians had seemed to think most highly.

Thomas turned his attention to the newspaper articles he wanted to write on Algeria for the *Manchester Guardian* and for the *Daily Herald*. The *Daily Herald* published Thomas's Algeria article on 31 July as a prominent news feature at the top of an inside page, and for publication underlined one paragraph: 'I heard and saw much of French cruelty. One of the last people I met had been nailed by his hands, heels and back to a board – half crucified in fact. He showed me the wounds, not yet healed.' This was a reference to Shabi Ahmed Ben Rabah, an Algerian refugee in Tunisia.

A *Daily Herald* correspondent in Paris Henry Kahn filed a report published on 7 August under a headline '"Crucifixion" report shocks France' and quoted an unnamed Quai d'Orsay official as sceptical of aspects of what he had read in Thomas's piece. Thomas defended his original report. *The Manchester Guardian Weekly* of 8 August carried a more substantial and detailed report from Thomas on 'Rebel army in Algeria' and this tone was sustained in a broadcast script by Thomas for the BBC on 16 August.

An article Thomas wrote for the June issue of *Current History* on 'Muslims South of the Sahara' appeared with a lead article by Wilfred Cantwell Smith, a Canadian specialist who was now professor of comparative religion and director of the Institute of Islamic Studies at McGill University in Montreal. Cantwell Smith had heard a rumour that Thomas would be spending a term at Northwestern and had written to ask Thomas to Montreal on his way to or from the US to visit the Institute and to give a lecture on African Islam. Thomas's visa application for the US was under consideration by the Attorney General for a temporary waiver of the grounds of inadmissibility. The US Embassy wrote on 16 September to advise Thomas that the Attorney General had authorised his temporary admission into the US for a period of approximately six months. The visa office would issue Thomas's visa whenever it was convenient for him.

Thomas decided to seize the moment and cabled Herskovits that he would proceed as arranged and arrive in Evanston on 30 September.

He was speedily inducted into the Northwestern system. Roland Young, who had written on Tanganyika and whose wife had been a plant pathologist in Kenya, arranged for the university calendar of events to announce two public lectures by Thomas: for 5 November on African Nationalism and European reactions and for 6 December on African Nationalism and the Muslim world.

He faced the first Sunday alone in a flat at seventh floor level at the top of a faculty apartment building. He had to complete a syllabus and reading list for the students and had brought from England several urgent writing chores to complete. The solitary eyrie was in stark contrast with the sprawling household in Oxford of a dozen or so occupants and a stream of friends from many parts of the world. The isolation from that Oxford life made him deeply homesick, but Evanston did not bring him the excitement of his Africa travels. However, Herskovits made sure the way was open for Thomas to meet or renew acquaintance with others in the small and close-knit Africanist community in the US. Thomas warmed to his situation as he came to know colleagues and graduate students better, to learn their particular interests in Africa and to accustom himself to the their propensity for abstract theorising.

Thomas through Apter was in touch with the nearby University of Chicago, where on 16 October he went to lunch with the political scientist Herman Finer – the brother of Samuel Finer, also a political scientist whom Thomas already knew from shared connections to Balliol and Keele. He went on to see the geography professor Edwin (Ned) Munger. Munger was a member of the US stepfamily of AL Smith and had in 1951 visited the Hodgkins in Oxford when a fellow dinner guest was the Nyasaland politician Hastings Banda firmly opposing the Central African Federation.

Thomas had lunch on 21 October with James Coleman, just back from Tanganyika and the Northern Rhodesia copperbelt, and Gray Cowan, just back from Morocco, when they could talk about Africa in a wide-ranging way – Coleman proposed bringing Thomas to Los Angeles and Cowan offered to do the same for Columbia and the East. Herskovits actively supported such contacts and on 26 October sent a round robin memorandum to Gwendolen Carter, Vernon McKay, Gray Cowan and William (Bill) Brown that Thomas would be in the East from 15 to 24 November and could speak on three key topics: 'Nationalism in Contemporary Africa', 'Political Developments in French West Africa' and 'Islam in the African Setting'.

Thomas extended his Chicago explorations on 12 November to Roosevelt University where he met the black sociologist St Clair Drake, who was beginning to interest himself in African matters. The Herskovits memorandum to colleagues on Thomas's availability to give talks drew largely favourable responses and Herskovits was stage-manager for a whistle-stop train tour in late November for Thomas to meet old and new friends in New York, Boston, Northampton and Washington.

In New York Thomas made time to visit Abdel Kader Chanderli, the Algerian FLN envoy to the UN, for an update on that struggle. Bill Brown was Thomas's host at Boston University and brought Thomas together with Carl Rosberg who was doing substantial work on Kenya. Brown took Thomas to the nearby Massachusetts Institute of Technology. He also met scholars including Arthur Porter from Fourah Bay and working on Sierra Leone and Harvard's Rupert Emerson who was writing a great tome on nationalism in Africa and Asia. One of Emerson's doctoral students at Harvard, a black American Martin L. Kilson who had been studying African political developments from secondary sources, wrote to Thomas: 'I feel myself somewhat a disciple of yours, for whenever anyone asks me about African politics I immediately refer them to your writings'.

Thomas went on to Northampton and lectured twice to the young women of Smith College for Gwen Carter. She made telephone calls to Washington and arranged for Thomas to be met by Robert (Bob) Baum responsible for Africa research at the School of Advanced International Studies of Johns Hopkins University. Bob Baum turned out to be a most un-State-Department type, according to Thomas's preconceived notions on the matter. He impressed Thomas with knowledge of Eritrea, Mauritania and particularly the Fezzan where Thomas had travelled recently – and where Baum had been on a UN Commission. Baum led him on to Vernon McKay for a family Sunday then a crowded day of encounters with the African American Institute, Baum's research team at the State Department, a seminar at Howard University and a lecture organised by the African American Institute.

Thomas returned to Evanston in time for his seminar and to be with David and Ellie Apter and their friends for a seven-hour thanksgiving dinner on 28 November. He went on 8 December for an overnight visit to Canada to fulfil a commitment to Cantwell Smith in the Institute at McGill. Thomas was in New York on 12 December for a talk at Columbia University (Gray Cowan following up their October lunch with James Coleman), stayed overnight with Andrew and Helen Cohen (Sir Andrew was now British Representative to the UN Trusteeship Commission) and flew across the US to the University of California in Los Angeles (James Coleman also following up the October lunch).

He was with Philip Curtin at the University of Wisconsin in Madison on 19 December to lecture on the now practised theme of 'Nationalism in Africa' and arguing that the aggressive and expansionist associations of the term nationalism were largely irrelevant to Africa where there was little prospect of counter-colonisation. He returned to England for Christmas at Crab Mill and sent detailed comments on the introductory chapter to the book Herskovits was writing on *The Human Factor in Changing Africa*, and his thanks to Mel and Frances Herskovits for the support and encouragement that had made the US journey possible.

Thomas and Dossie spent the New Year of 1958 at Geldeston in optimistic mood. Cantwell Smith had persuaded Thomas to take a three-year part-time appointment at McGill's Institute of Islamic Studies. This would mean spending a term away from home each year in Canada, but Montreal put Dossie's sister Dilly and her husband Graham Rowley in Ottawa within reach, and Canada did not raise the visa anxieties of the US. Joe Price, lecturer in government at the University College of Ghana, wrote on 13 February to sound Thomas out on a proposal to invite him as a visiting lecturer for the Trinity term to be shared between the economics, divinity and history departments. Kingsley Martin, as editor of the *New Statesman*, wrote warmly on 28 March that he had heard that Thomas was likely to be in Ghana in time for the Conference of Independent African States to be held in April and asking if Thomas would cover the event for him.

The Ghana invitation was confirmed and the University College arranged entry permits for Thomas and for his daughter Liz, then aged 16. They left in the afternoon of 15 April and flew into Accra next morning, going initially to Dennis Austin's house where Liz would stay. Thomas would have a visiting lecturer flat in Commonwealth Hall. The university was built in the grand style and two of the architects, Austen Harrison and Pierce Hubbard, were friends of Thomas's from his Palestine period in the 1930s. Thomas gave his first lecture early on 21 April and went on to the preliminary press conference for the Conference of Independent African States given by an old acquaintance in the Gold Coast and Ghana administration Yaw Adu. He described to Dossie 'a succession of parties – Sudanese, then Tunisian (the former providing squash and the latter, not surprisingly, whisky) – meeting a continual succession of old and new friends. This admirable mixture of Libyans, Moroccans, Tunisians, Sudanese, Ghanaians, etc. whom one kept running into – and talking about totally different subjects to – rather wearing trying to switch one's mind rapidly – and to remember people from the past'.

Accra with Nkrumah's new prestige was the locus for other continental and international events. Thomas met Modibo Keita, leader of the emerging Mali Republic, whom he had previously known in Bamako and Paris. Keita was now leading a Francophone delegation to a conference of the Food and Agricultural Organisation. Thomas invited him to dinner next day.

When the Ghana visiting lectureship ended Thomas and Liz left on 7 June for Nigeria where Thomas could gather material for his historical anthology. He spent a couple of days in Ibadan reading in the library of the University College, with work much interrupted by a succession of scholars seeking him out. The OUP was pressing for delivery of the Nigeria book since they wanted it in the autumn for publication in the run-up to Nigeria's independence. Thomas shared a family summer holiday in Austria as a preliminary to Dossie attending the International Congress of Biochemistry in Vienna. The Gasters were spending the first week of September in a borrowed cottage at Letcombe Bassett near Wantage, and BJ wrote on 26 August to Thomas to see if the Hodgkins could visit the cottage or the Gasters could call on the Hodgkins in Oxford. With the Hodgkins away it was not possible to arrange anything and the Gasters left Letcombe Bassett on 7 September, the day of Thomas's return to Oxford.

Thomas wrote back to BJ and in a postcard of 25 September she accepted Thomas's suggestion that her elder daughter Lucy should call on the Hodgkin household in Oxford if she came to Somerville for an entrance interview. Meanwhile Thomas flew to Montreal on 26 September to take up his McGill part-time post, and took thirteen-year-old Toby with him to spend the term with Dilly's family in Ottawa. The McGill teaching load seemed light in comparison with his Ghana duties and he felt he could make progress on both pending books: Nigerian history and contemporary African political parties.

Word had gone out on the US academic grapevine that Thomas was in Canada and he had received several invitations to universities and Africanist institutions in the US. He went to the American Consulate General where the consul remembered him from his visit of a year earlier and issued a multiple-entry visa for Thomas to take up his lecture invitations. Emerson arranged for him to lecture at Harvard, and Kilson, who was invited to Thomas's lecture and to a faculty club lunch for him, asked if Thomas would be his dinner guest with George Bond (a son of Max Bond and nephew of Horace Mann Bond, prominent educationists) and several others who wanted to meet him: African students and the leftist American economist Paul Sweezy. The Rockefeller Foundation wrote to ask about Thomas's research plans. The Carnegie Endowment for International Peace telephoned to say that they had heard he was going to be in New York and asking if he would come and see them about French Africa. Thomas agreed to visit: Ruth Schachter, a graduate from Barnard College in New York who had recently worked on French Africa in Oxford under Thomas's supervisory eye, was jobless and he thought this might be a means of putting some work in her way.

Thomas embarked on a schedule of five lectures and seminars in the four days from 17 November. In New York he went to talk to Chanderli about de Gaulle's overtures on the Algerian war. Ruth, with whom he was staying, drove him on to an appointment with a publisher Victor Weybright who was familiar with paperback publishing in Britain and, as founder of the New American Library, was key to the development in the US of quality paperback books. Weybright invited Thomas to write a Mentor book on African history for an advance of $3,000: this seemed to Thomas a princely sum in comparison with the £50 advance he received on publication of *Nationalism in Colonial Africa*. He walked on from this meeting to the offices of the Carnegie Endowment, where he met their publications editor-in-chief, Anne Winslow, who wanted some 20,000 words on French Africa for the journal *International Conciliation* – for a fee of $300. Thomas proposed the collaboration of Ruth Schachter (whom he envisaged doing the main work) and that the fee should go to her. Ruth collected him and they went on to dinner and a colloquium at Columbia arranged by Gray Cowan, who had drawn in among others a Princeton anthropologist Paul Bohannan, from Nebraska with a doctorate at Oxford and interest in the Tiv in Nigeria, and a Mozambican Eduardo Mondlane working with the UN Trusteeship Council. Thomas spent an afternoon at the State Department in Washington having informal discussion with Africanists, including several he had previously met in the US, France and Africa, and was able to see the friendly Bob Baum and Vernon McKay over an early dinner.

Thomas was trying in early December to complete the introduction to his Nigerian anthology. He completed the broad draft around midnight on 30 December and – anxious to post it off within the 1958 calendar year – spent the morning of 31 December in Oxford numbering the pages. The trustees of the Rockefeller Foundation in New York approved on 31 December a grant of $7,500 for travel and field expenses in Africa for Thomas's work through the McGill University Institute of Islamic Studies. Thomas's focus on Nigeria meant that he had disappointed Helen and David Kimble over the African political parties paperback that they planned to have in production at the beginning of 1959. David Kimble wrote that Thomas's paperback could be moved down the production schedule but urged him not to slow down. Thomas and Ruth Schachter were collaborating on material for *International Conciliation* about the background and status of French West African territories – for delivery at the beginning of the next year.

Meanwhile Thomas accompanied Dossie, who had science engagements in Leningrad and Moscow in late May, so that he could seek out Africanists and African students in the Soviet Union. He followed suggestions from *Présence Africaine* in Paris and from Dennis Phombeah, the secretary-general of the Committee of African Organisations in London. Phombeah wrote warning Thomas that the number of Africans studying in the Soviet Union was very small. He recommended his friend Professor I.I. Potekhin at the Institute of Ethnography of the Academy of Sciences in Moscow. Thomas already knew of the work of Dmitry Olderogge, as director of the department of African studies at Leningrad University.

Thomas met Gerald Graham in London on 30 July with the intention of handing over a typescript of his historical anthology *Nigerian Perspectives*, albeit not fully revised. He found that with industrial action affecting OUP the book could not be processed until the end of August and Thomas had a reprieve for final changes after circulating the draft for informed comment from colleagues. During September at Crab Mill he worked on the African political parties project and planned his next African journey. He was torn between his interests in Africa and his wish to be with his family in Oxford. He sought to condense the itinerary into as short a time as was consistent with his principal goal of collecting material – documentary and oral – for a study of Islam and its impact upon modern political movements south of the Sahara. His secondary aims were to collect material for the African history book he had promised to Weybright, to bring himself up-to-date on political developments since 1956 in the former French West Africa for the pamphlet with Ruth Schachter promised to the Carnegie Endowment, and to gather historical and contemporary documents for the library of the Institute of Islamic Studies at McGill. Weybright and his wife came to lunch at Crab Mill on 19 September when Thomas could show only a synopsis of the first six of a proposed ten chapters.

Soon the exigencies of his Africa journey took hold. He lunched on 30 October with the North Africa specialist Nevill Barbour (Thomas had contributed to his book *A Survey of North West Africa, the Maghrib*). In Paris on 2 November he collected a Guinea visa and lunched with Philippe Decraene from *Le Monde*. The meeting jogged Thomas's conscience that he had promised Hella Pick at *West Africa* to deliver a review of Decraene's book *Le panafricanisme* by 4 November and he spent much of the afternoon and evening writing the review so that he could post it late that night. He found time also to visit *Présence Africaine* (Alioune Diop had gone to Dakar) and talked about Guinea to the Malagasy poet .of negritude and Madagascar nationalist Jacques Rabemanjara, who was not allowed to leave France.

Thomas flew to Rabat on 3 November. He met André Adam, who was a fellow contributor to Barbour's survey, and then at the university he found an old friend Charles-André Julien of the Sorbonne who said he would send Eve Dechamp of *France Observateur* to talk to Thomas. Thomas initially did not recognise the name but when she appeared within minutes he remembered her as Eve Paret who had taken him round Casablanca during his 1956 visit to Morocco. She again took him in tow – to a press briefing and to the royal palace press office. A palace official al-Alawi, with medical training, recognised the Hodgkin family name ('Maladie de Hodgkin', he said) and instructed Thomas to be ready to start at dawn on the following day for a one and a half day expedition to the Moyen Atlas with the Crown Prince's sister Princess Lalla Aisha (who would be distributing clothes to the needy).

Once back in Rabat he resumed his intended goals and decided for the weekend to revisit Fez as the centre of Tijani pilgrimage and the seat of the University of Qarawiyin. He visited the headquarters of Alal al-Fassi's Istiqlal faction to gather contemporary information: al-Fassi was in Tangier and one of his cousins was willing to arrange a meeting in Rabat. When Thomas met al-Fassi they discussed how the Salafiyya, a traditionalist reforming movement within Islam, first penetrated into Morocco – and who were the people and what were the ideas that had most influence on al-Fassi. Thomas met representatives of other political parties (with the Kimble book in mind) including the Moroccan CP, whose ban by the monarchy had been ruled unconstitutional in the courts. He spent his last day in Morocco pursuing these political contacts in Casablanca until it was time for a flight to Dakar. There he met old friends including the Islam scholar Vincent Monteil who had arrived to take up a professorial post at IFAN. Monteil (whom Thomas had known in Morocco in 1956) was much out of favour with the French authorities for active opposition to the war in Algeria. Thomas also met the veteran administrator and politician Gabriel D'Arboussier, who had been born in Djenne and who provided introductions to heads of Tijani marabout families in whom Thomas was interested. Thomas's travel continued with the almost habitual train ride to Bamako and then slowly by pirogue to Djenne and the historically important Hamdallahi (capital of the nineteenth-century Fulani Empire of Massina).

Thomas intended going on to Guinea and was anxious to return home, but Kimble wanted him in Ghana to participate in a weekend school and the Attorney General Geoffrey Bing wanted to discuss in confidence a committee on university education in Ghana. After a few days in Conakry, Thomas took a hedge-hopping flight on 10 December to Accra, where Bing explained the reasons for an urgent meeting. The Ghana Government hoped by 1961 to set up a University of Ghana from various existing and proposed educational institutions, and wanted to assemble an international committee of sufficient strength and ability to review the whole of university education. The committee should visit Ghana in April and December of 1960 and two secretaries would work more or less full time through the year. Thomas was being asked to be one of the secretaries. The other would be the Ghanaian Nana Kobina Nketsia IV, who as Omanhene of British Sekondi was a paramount chief and with Nkrumah and others had been imprisoned in 1950 for defiance of emergency regulations.

(Nana subsequently took a doctorate in anthropology with a thesis on the impact of Christian missionaries on Akan social institutions). Thomas advised Bing that he could be available from the following February provided that he had one short break to deliver a course of lectures already pledged.

New prospects were opening for Thomas's family. In the early days of January 1960, Sir William Bragg wrote to the chairman of the Nobel Committee for Physics with a cluster of names including Dorothy Crowfoot Hodgkin for prize consideration for work on the X-ray crystallography of proteins. Liz, who had declined the offer of an exhibition at Somerville and accepted an offer from Newnham in Cambridge, went away to Sudan to spend several weeks with the Bedri family at Ahfad School in Omdurman. When Thomas again set off for Africa to take up the Ghana task he went first to Omdurman in Sudan on 23 April to spend a weekend with the Bedri household and to collect Liz to accompany him to Accra. They were met on arrival by Dennis Austin and installed in a university house, with modern equipment and supplied with a cook – and were visited by Nana to discuss the joint secretaryship. Thomas and Nana saw Nkrumah who explained that the sort of a university he wanted would differ from the existing pattern – with good provision for part-time evening students and plenty of African studies and Arabic.

Dossie, in London to hear papers read at the Royal Society on 5 May, was tipped off by the president Sir Cyril Hinshelwood that the council had just decided to offer her the first Wolfson professorship – this was a new kind of personal science professorship funded by the businessman and philanthropist Isaac Wolfson to encourage research. Dossie wanted to hold the professorship at Oxford and Thomas's own plans for the future, while fluid, did not rule out the possibility of working in Ghana on African studies once the committee's work was done.

Thomas, after five weeks' work almost entirely on the committee preparations, felt he had done as much as he could on the ground and could write keynote documents in Oxford. He reported on 3 June to the committee chairman, the politician and Nkrumah confidant Kojo Botsio, that he would be involved in research and teaching at McGill from mid-September until mid-December, and again from mid-January until April of 1961. Thomas returned to Oxford. Nkrumah took office as president of a republican Ghana on 1 July.

Thomas's *Nigerian Perspectives* was ready in time for Nigeria's independence on 1 October and provided a history of the various civilisations that were the ancestors of the modern state, with an emphasis on the continent's own geographers and chroniclers from legendary origins of the eleventh century to the 1900s. He pointed out that no outsider could possibly have described the Fulani educational system as it existed in the late eighteenth century in the way in which Abdullahi dan Fodio described his own education. Thomas saw the book as an anthology of insights into history, but in the absence of any collection of documents relating to Nigerian history in any European language he saw that it would also provide a sourcebook for students and scholars to follow.

Thomas drafted proposals for the new Ghana university structure for presentation at working sessions in Ghana over the Christmas holiday period. Thomas and Dossie had decided to follow up a proposition by Botsio and to go together, taking Toby with them. They travelled out on 16 December for a swearing-in of members of what had been elevated from a committee to a commission. The commission included the Soviet Union's nominee – the chemical engineer Nikolai Torocheshnikov – and Thomas's suggestion of Desmond Bernal as a distinguished physicist and the most distinguished British Marxist. The commission initialled a draft report in January 1961 for Botsio to submit the findings to Nkrumah. The situation became confused when Nkrumah said he wanted two independent universities, one at Legon and one at Kumasi, while the commission had assumed there would he just one. A process of revision by correspondence began and the administrative secretary, an expatriate civil servant David Carmichael, undertook a round of overseas visits to discuss the further report and reconcile divergences with individual members.

When Thomas was again in Montreal for his McGill seminars, Dossie in Oxford was pursuing the notion of an Oxford academic base for Thomas. Their friend Sally Chilver, as director of the Institute of Commonwealth Studies, had hinted at the possibility of a part-time research fellowship. She told Dossie there could be a choice between a basement and attic room in the Institute's Keble Road building and likewise space for Thomas when the Institute moved to Queen Elizabeth House. Nkrumah wrote to Thomas on 24 February thanking him and Dossie for their contribution to the commission deliberations. He was supportive of Thomas's perspective on African studies: 'I have taken note of the points you have raised in your letter regarding, in particular, the establishment of the Institute of African Studies which, as you know, is regarded as one of the most important developments which the Universities of Ghana should undertake. Without it, they will not have the personality which African-based universities must have if they are to make any contribution at all to human knowledge and experience.'

Thomas's stay in Montreal was not all work. He lodged in a rooming house in Pine Avenue and this brought him into contact with Canadians beyond the immediate McGill circle. Some of the younger residents decided to hold a Roman feast on 11 March, where guests should come in Roman dress – they drew on costumes that had been made for a production of a Paul Toupin play 'Brutus'. The kitchen and rooms were decorated with torches and fasces. Thomas, who arrived late and had to make do with a makeshift costume of bed cover and gold necklace, spent most of the evening with a supply schoolteacher of English and French literature Madeleine Poulin. Thomas was captivated for several hours of French conversation about her life and literary work until she was borne away by an escort.

Later in March Thomas turned down an offer from Cantwell Smith of an associate professorship with the Institute. He gave a series of five lectures in early April on Islam in Africa for Boston University's African studies programme and returned to an unstructured summer in Oxford that would allow time for writing. His apparent poor health was arousing the family's concern. He was coughing a great deal and Joan Payne thought this was due to his smoking. Sally Chilver wrote on 29 June confirming progress on making a niche in Oxford for Thomas and that the accommodation was secure. He was working on a paper on the idea of freedom in African national movements for an international anthropology conference in Austria to be held early in August at Gloggnitz. Since Dossie had tasks she wanted to do in Germany, she and Thomas decided to combine the Austria conference with a family holiday, with Liz and Toby. All four went on to Greece and Cairo, and then Thomas and Liz carried on to Sudan for another visit to Ahfad and travel in Ethiopia.

Carmichael had sent Thomas a letter that had followed him to Sudan asking him to come to Ghana. After Thomas had seen Liz safely off for return to Cambridge in October he went round to the Ghana Embassy and found a telegram asking him to come to Accra at Ghana Government expense and to advise on an Institute of African Studies. He spent a couple of hours with Embassy officials gathering background on forced resignations that included Botsio and detentions that included Danquah – which he felt sure was a mistake that Nkrumah might be persuaded to reverse. With much misgiving, Thomas prepared to leave on 8 October for an exploratory few days in Ghana. He was taken for a private interview with Nkrumah who asked what Thomas thought of a British candidate for the new university and Thomas replied that he favoured a Ghanaian solution. Nkrumah seemed to be taking for granted that Thomas would come and run the Institute of African Studies. Thomas consulted widely about whether he should take a post in Ghana and was encouraged to do so by several friends including James Coleman and Basil Davidson. By early December he felt that he was being propelled towards Ghana almost despite his own views. He made up his mind to take up the Ghana task in the New Year with an absence in February to keep existing lecture engagements in the US and Canada.

He had a new lecture theme on the political parties that had emerged in Africa in the post-war phase of decolonisation, with theoretical analysis enriched by his personal knowledge of many of the key figures. His Penguin book *African Political Parties*, completed with Liz's help on an appendix deciphering a welter of acronyms, appeared as an intricate account of political movements and personalities including origins and typologies, organisation and objectives. Thomas drew a broad distinction between radical ideologies, whether reformist or revolutionary, and conservative or traditionalist ideologies: mass parties tended to be radical and élite parties to be conservative. Ideological oppositions within a mass party might be as significant as the oppositions existing between parties. The book was enthusiastically received by his peers. An anonymous reviewer in *The Times Literary Supplement* of 29 December commented on Thomas's great quality as a writer on African affairs that the questions he asked were always interesting ones and noted his characterisation of Nkrumah as an arbiter and reconciler within his Ghana party. Thomas presented the work as an introductory guide, in a context where material was hard to come by and there had previously been little attempt to look at the evidence in a connected or systematic way. It was a third groundbreaking work for others to follow.

Thomas planned to fly to Ghana on 15 January 1962, but had to postpone departure when he was admitted instead to the Tropical Diseases Hospital in London with a suspected amoeba. The doctors found him well, except for lungs that were damaged by childhood ailments and by smoking in adult life: he was again advised to give up smoking. He arrived in Accra on 26 January and was issued with a two year residence permit – Dossie accompanied Thomas for the first week and helped him settle into a university house at 33 Little Legon. Thomas was soon on the move again to Swarthmore in Pennsylvania for a promised lecture on self-government for developing nations. He went on to Los Angeles for more seminars and lectures and then eastward again to Boston and Harvard where Ruth Schachter and Martin Kilson both wanted Thomas to look through their respective book drafts. He spoke on several campuses and travelled back to Accra on 6 March. Nkrumah's eventual choice for vice-chancellor was the Irish diplomat Conor Cruise O'Brien who, with his new second wife Maire MacEntee, was invited to visit Accra to consider the appointment.

Liz, studying at Cambridge, dined in hall in Newnham on 18 May where a fellow student Jan Penney had brought as guest a London visitor Polly Gaster – Jack and BJ's younger daughter. Liz, who had accepted an invitation to use part of her Cambridge vacation for some weeks of tutoring on a course at Tsito, arrived in Accra on 17 June. Thomas was leaving Accra for a five-day expedition to Yendi and Kete Krachi in the north of Ghana to seek out Arabic or Hausa manuscripts as sources of history – accompanying the Ghana historian Adu Boahen, another colleague Ivor Wilks and al-Hajj Osmanu Boyo, a devout elderly man from Kintampo who would help with contacts and translations.

Thomas returned to England and, with Dossie and their houseguest Madeleine Poulin from Montreal, attended the wedding party on 14 July at the Gasters' home in Hampstead for Lucy Gaster's marriage to an Oxford contemporary John Syson. While Dossie and Thomas spent a summer holiday at San Remo in Italy, the situation in Ghana worsened after Nkrumah, on a road journey on 1 August from a presidential meeting in Upper Volta, came under a hand grenade attack at the Ghana border village of Kulungugu. Thomas returned to Legon on 25 September and found an evening and night curfew in effect, police searches in the streets and a delay in parliamentary approval of the Institute grant for the academic year from 1 October. Thomas was favourably drawn to O'Brien as vice-chancellor and found him supportive in the scramble to prepare the Institute premises for the first intake of MA students on 11 October. Thomas confessed to Nkrumah that he had been wrong in pressing for a Ghanaian vice-chancellor.

Thomas was making yet another rapid Africa tour to lecture in Kampala and to recruit an Arabist in Khartoum for the Institute in Ghana. The chosen candidate was Salah Ahmed Ibrahim, who had lost favour with the Khartoum establishment by writing militant poetry on African politics. Dossie joined Thomas in Ghana for the latter part of the term when Thomas had many friends arriving for the International Congress of Africanists. The participants considered establishing a centre of Arabic documentation that would record how for centuries some peoples in sub-Saharan Africa wrote in the Arabic language or in African languages in Arabic script. During the congress, Thomas and Dossie celebrated their silver wedding anniversary and then returned to England for a family Christmas.

Thomas returned to Legon on 16 January 1963. His teaching and administration work load continued to increase, and each week he was lecturing to students twice at Legon and twice at Kumasi and holding a tutorial group on French-speaking West Africa. Salah, on arrival from Sudan, was staying temporarily in Thomas's house at 33 Little Legon – where there was a stream of visitors. Al-Hajj Osmanu and his young son arrived at the house with luggage, but at Maire O'Brien's suggestion were decanted to guest rooms at the vice-chancellor's house.

The Institute's groundwork of the previous year was paying off and was attracting to Legon a signal congregation of leading African scholars and thinkers on Africa. Gervase Mathew had now moved into Thomas's spare room. Other Legon guests included anthropologist Audrey Richards, philosopher Ernest Gellner, African historian Joseph Ki-Zerbo, and Maghrib historian Jamil Abun-Nasr. Thomas was asked to join a political committee to prepare the Ghana delegation position for a forthcoming Addis Ababa conference on African unity and began a series of meetings at Flagstaff House with Nkrumah's close advisers.

Thomas through his participation in the first year African studies lectures was by late June working almost through the nights to mark batches of more than two hundred examination scripts. He interrupted his stint on 24 June to go out to dinner with a neighbour Alan Nunn May and the law professor William Burnett Harvey. Nunn May, who had been imprisoned in Britain for sharing atom secrets with the Soviet Union, had some years later been invited to Ghana by Nkrumah on an Osagyefo professorship and was now university professor of physics. His Austrian-born wife Hilde had been a medical officer for the city of Cambridge and continued medical work as a children's doctor at Ghana's Korle Bu Hospital.

Thomas, attending a State House party given by Nkrumah for a journalists' conference in mid-November, was glad to meet the veteran trade unionist from Sierra Leone, I.T.A. Wallace-Johnson, who had been active in the 1930s with Jomo Kenyatta and the political mentors C.L.R. James and George Padmore. He met Wallace-Johnson again at a conference ball at the Star Hotel in Accra where Thomas had mainly gone to sit out and talk over a beer with Nana. Wallace-Johnson reminisced about the West African Secretariat in London in the mid-1940s, run on a shoestring and with Wallace fund-raising by playing his clarinet outside London cinemas.

Thomas had been feeling unwell for several days at a time of intense work pressure. By the evening of 19 November and in preference to waiting to be seen in the university clinic he called on Hilde with what looked like malaria symptoms. She treated him and sent him to bed, but next day Thomas developed a rash and was suspected to have dengue fever. Maire O'Brien (who had herself suffered from dengue fever) moved Thomas to the vice-chancellor's lodge and installed him in the best spare bedroom.

When Thomas was in England on Christmas leave he attended an appointment at the Tropical Diseases Hospital in London. The hospital wanted him to return for admission for further tests. He came back on 16 December when the initial physical examinations detected no tropical disease. He was reminded to keep off cigarettes, but told that pipe smoking was relatively harmless. Thomas was mulling over a problem for his Nunn May neighbours in Ghana with their son Johnny who had learning and behavioural difficulties that had led to his withdrawal from schools in Britain. The Nunn Mays wanted someone to help so that Johnny could live full-time with them in Ghana while the parents continued their demanding jobs. Liz knew from her Cambridge friend Jan Penney that the Gasters' daughter Polly was at a loose end and suggested her for the job.

BJ and Polly came to see Thomas in hospital to discuss the possibility. Polly was willing to go to Ghana: BJ was willing to let her go with the Hodgkin household only two doors away – for some of the time at least. Thomas wrote to Hilde Nunn May to tell her about Polly. He was allowed out of hospital since the staff was reasonably sure he was free of tropical disease but his general condition raised the concerns of a year earlier. In a chilly Oxford on 22 December, Thomas strolled with Liz along the High Street and had acute symptoms of shortness of breath.

Thomas returned to Africa on 2 January 1964, pausing en route to Accra for the fifth International African Seminar at Ahmadu Bello University at Zaria. Thomas knew many of the participants but thought that for the theme of Islam in tropical Africa there were too few serious Islamists, too few Africans, and too many anthropologists. Thomas's contribution gave details of the Islamic literary tradition in Ghana that was being recovered from the manuscripts in Arabic script gathered by the Institute of African Studies.

In discussion between Thomas and the Nunn Mays it was agreed that Polly Gaster should come to help with Johnny. Thomas was approaching a point of exhaustion over crisis in the university and was taken into hospital with severe bronchitis. He telephoned to tell Dossie who booked the next available flight and on arrival in the evening of 1 February was taken to the hospital where Thomas was under treatment with antibiotics and sedatives. The university crisis had taken a further downward turn two days earlier when Conor was informed that four foreign members of the university staff were engaged in subversion. It emerged over the next day or so that they faced deportation. Two of the four were well known US lawyers – the law professor Harvey and a senior lecturer Bob Seidman who acted as head of the law school in Harvey's absence – and Conor was at pains to defend them, in writing to Nkrumah. Thomas from hospital wrote to Nkrumah that Harvey and Seidman were people he knew and respected – Seidman had the kind of progressive record it took a great deal of integrity and courage to acquire in the US.

Basil Davidson, who was on a visit, and the Hodgkins added their voices to the various pleas to Nkrumah and were particularly concerned for Seidman, whose wife the economist Ann Seidman would be remaining at Legon with five school-age children. They talked to Nkrumah on the morning of 4 February, although Thomas in fits of coughing could scarcely speak. Nkrumah – noncommittal on the deportation issue – was concerned for Thomas's health and told Thomas that his own doctors prescribed him large doses of Vitamin A. A police car came to the campus in the afternoon and the driver delivered to Thomas a bottle of Vitamin A tablets and a hand-written note from Nkrumah 'Dear Prof. Hodgkin Here's a bottle of the Vitamin A I spoke to you about. I hope it will do you some good. K.N. 4/2/64'. Thomas and Dossie went for a further talk with Nkrumah on 18 March about a project for a people's history of Africa and about Thomas's own plans. Thomas proposed retiring from the Institute directorship at the end of the academic year (autumn of 1964) while retaining an association as a visiting professor and consultant if this was wanted – Nkrumah was sympathetic.

Thomas on his Easter break in England contacted BJ to give her news of Polly and her teaching progress with Johnny. He presented what BJ termed a rather wild scheme for her to visit Polly in Ghana. She was disposed to raise the possibility of a visit with Alan Hill at Heinemann – Nkrumah's publisher – where she worked, but was anxious not to impinge on Polly's independence. Thomas, leaving London for an Institute staff meeting, was with BJ and they drove to London airport – she was buying strawberries to send to Polly. They talked about their respective children. BJ was moved by Thomas's kindness to Polly and felt that she was forgiven for what she now regarded as her horrible treatment of Thomas at San Vigilio in August 1933 – their holiday meeting in Italy when Thomas returned to England from his spell of archaeology in Palestine.

In the summer the Nunn Mays sailed away from Ghana for a vacation and Conor's secretary Ilsa Yardley and her architect husband Maurice Yardley took Polly to stay in August in Accra. Thomas had a Little Acropolis lunch on the pavement in Charlotte Street with BJ when they resumed the theme of mutual forgiveness. Ilsa wrote to Thomas suggesting that Polly's mother stay with the Yardleys for a week before the Nunn Mays came back. BJ went in early September to meet the Nunn Mays and Johnny and they worked out dates for her Ghana visit. Alan Nunn May was returning in early October and Hilde following a few days later via Vienna. BJ would travel on 27 September and was accepting Ilsa's invitation to stay for the first days, since builders were due in the Nunn May house – and Hilde was worrying that covers would not be on the cushions.

Dossie and Thomas went on their holiday on 22 September – to Austen Harrison's house at Limni in Euboea – with Thomas en route to Ghana and Dossie returning to England for the university term. Meanwhile BJ arrived in Accra and was ensconced with Polly under the care of Ilsa. Thomas returned to Legon – met by BJ and Polly among others – to find a telegram urging him to go to Ibadan on 7 October to examine a doctoral thesis by Murray Last on nineteenth-century Sokoto. He had to defer the examination to allow himself time to read the thesis, and because BJ had moved into 33 Little Legon on 6 October and Thomas did not want to abandon her as soon as she had arrived. He gave her the main bedroom and took the study. They spent much time in somewhat sentimental talk about times past, or reading favourite literature (Shakespeare,

George Eliot's novel *Middlemarch* and Yeats) from a rapid stock bought at the campus bookshop.

Thomas found it strange and beautiful to be going around with BJ. They went early on the morning of 13 October for bird watching in the Botanical Gardens with field glasses borrowed for BJ, and an enthusiast – a physicist sent by Nunn May – to guide them. Thomas gave a supper party for BJ in the evening with visitors including Martin and Marion Kilson who now had two small children. Nana and his wife Cecile took BJ and Thomas to visit Koforidua where Nana was organising the building of a national theatre with communal labour. They were entertained to lunch by the regional commissioner and had drinks with the chief. Dossie was due to come to Legon the following Tuesday and Thomas sent on to her an urgent request from his Institute colleague Stephen Andoh for 60 sets of cutlery for a canteen the Institute wanted to open.

Thomas and BJ made an early start on 15 October since they were being taken on another bird watching expedition – on salt flats this time. A general election was taking place in Britain that day: Sir Alec Douglas-Home, who had become Conservative Prime Minister on the resignation of Harold Macmillan in October 1963, was challenged by Harold Wilson, who had become Labour Party leader in February 1963 after the death of Hugh Gaitskell. Thomas and BJ went out to listen to results as they were being announced from mid-evening and within an hour or so the trend pointed toward a Labour government.

Thomas and BJ walked back towards the house and Thomas took BJ in his arms. She, more hesitant than he, wanted time to decide. Thomas expressed his belief that being happily married was not incompatible with making love to others and that BJ was for him essentially the same person he had loved in their youthful engagement. BJ was convinced that if – as she had done memorably in the past – she said 'No' the situation would still be undecided. She accepted Thomas, not knowing where it might lead in the future and knowing that there were only three days before Dossie arrived. Thomas and BJ lived these days in the past and the present, with Thomas affected by a suspected recurrence of malaria, and given medical advice by Hilde, who sent Polly to add to the company over the weekend.

Dossie arrived in Accra on the evening of 20 October and was met by Thomas, BJ and Polly and by Stephen Andoh who dealt with formalities as Dossie talked to the others – she had brought the cutlery Andoh had requested. The Hodgkins and Gasters shared the next few days. BJ had come to Ghana to see Polly and to further Heinemann's publishing interest in Africa. Thomas secured a meeting for them all with Nkrumah on the morning of 23 October – for BJ to ask Nkrumah about his next book and for Thomas to talk of his Ghana plans.

BJ was shy and tearful on 26 October when she left (fearing it might be a final farewell) and Thomas was anxious to comfort and reassure her with a letter and a poem he wrote. BJ left laden with gifts for all her close family and on the flight had an empty seat beside her to spread her belongings. She sat writing to Thomas with tears dripping off her chin: 'But the chief thing that I want to say you know already: that I love you and have had twenty days of unbeliev-able happiness.' On the envelope she added that she would soon write a proper 'Collins' thank you letter (named for the young clergyman William Collins in Jane Austen's *Pride and Prejudice* writing fulsomely to Mr Bennet).

BJ was about to write her 'Collins' on 29 October when history intervened. The Nobel Prize Committee in Stockholm announced that Dorothy Crowfoot Hodgkin was the sole winner of the chemistry prize for 1964. Jack Gaster tel-ephoned BJ with the news so she sent first their immense congratulations. The Stockholm news broke on wire services in time for the afternoon papers and BJ gathered the London cuttings to send.

When the news broke in the newsroom of the *Oxford Mail* reporters quickly found that Dossie was in Ghana with Thomas. In Accra Thomas was the first to hear the news when he was telephoned in the afternoon by an Associated Press correspondent who had been asked to file 300 words on Dossie. Thomas, fol-lowed by reporters, came to the chemistry department library to find Dossie with a Nigerian research student Samuel Adeoyi. Dossie and Thomas took Samuel to 33 Little Legon and telephoned to invite friends for an impromptu celebration: Conor and Maire, Polly, Hilde and Alan Nunn May and Stephen Andoh. The journalist Walter Schwarz came from Lagos to interview Dossie and Thomas; Christian Gbagbo took photographs of them for *The Observer* magazine. After the first impromptu party, Ghana saluted Dossie's award with a presidential command performance on 11 November of Ghanaian dances by music and drama students at the Institute – attended by Nkrumah, who saw Dossie and Thomas again on 27 November on the eve of Dossie's departure for England. Thomas, wanting to give his Monday seminar, followed on 3 December and was met by BJ on arrival. She and he met in London again on 7 December and they went on corresponding while Thomas and Dossie were in Sweden.

When the prize was announced the Hodgkin family was widely scattered. Luke and his wife Anna Davin, the eldest of three daughters of a New Zealand writer Dan Davin, publisher of the Clarendon Press in Oxford, were with their three children in Algiers where Luke was teaching mathematics at the university. Liz was teaching at the girls' secondary school at Kasama in the north of newly independent Zambia. Toby – between school and university – was travelling in India. Liz and Toby and Payne and Crowfoot relatives gathered in Stockholm. Dossie spoke at the Nobel Banquet on 10 December and to a gathering of university students. Thomas's mother had turned down an invitation to Stockholm but watched the television news avidly and was impressed to see Dossie curtseying elegantly to the Swedish royal family.

BJ in Hampstead was likewise impressed by the television pictures. Dossie gave her Nobel lecture next day. Thomas too was elegant but uncomfortable as for a royal dinner party he donned full dress clothes – something he could not recall doing since he was a Balliol undergraduate. BJ saw *The Observer* magazine of 13 December with its picture story on 'The amazing Mrs Hodgkin' and was moved to tears on seeing a photograph of Thomas leaning against a familiar tree at Legon and looking much younger than his years. Then Thomas telephoned her with what she deemed beautiful, extravagant talk.

Chapter 5
Alma mater, chapter and verse: 1965-1982

By 1965, the lives of Thomas and BJ had taken on a diverse but shared duality. Thomas was transparent to Dossie and his immediate family about the renewed relationship. BJ hid it from Jack whom she thought unprepared to condone her renewal of interest in Thomas. Thomas and BJ talked by telephone on New Year's day about Thomas's car – damaged in a minor accident and to be retrieved by BJ – and about Thomas's return to Ghana due later in the month. Dossie and Thomas, who were returning by train on 3 January from Dossie's family in Geldeston, had supper that evening with BJ and Jack at the Gaster home in Hampstead before taking the damaged car back to Oxford. BJ and Thomas walked together in St James's Park on a chill afternoon and on a further meeting BJ was tearful as she drove home with the thought of Thomas's departure.

Thomas flew to Ghana on 10 January and Polly Gaster came round next day to collect BJ's gifts. BJ writing to Thomas in secrecy tried a successful experiment of writing a letter in her bath. Thomas and Polly went on 18 January to a Monday afternoon seminar organised by a Cuban ethnologist Angelier Leon, where Cuba's Minister of Industries, Ernesto 'Che' Guevara, who had arrived from Algeria on an African tour, unexpectedly turned up. Guevara, accompanied by Cuba's Ambassador to Algeria Jorge Serguera, sat through the seminar and spoke at the end (in Spanish – with impromptu interpretation by a Cuban) on the necessity for political liberation to be reinforced by economic liberation. Thomas, with Polly again, went to a party next day given by the Cubans for Guevara and after the official event Guevara and members of the Cuban party and others came round to Thomas's for drinks.

Thomas was writing frequently to BJ and she raised a note of alarm on 19 January in a letter to Thomas reporting that Jack had said rather grimly: 'There's a letter from Polly and another from your soul-mate'. She suggested that Thomas ration himself to one letter a week unless he could discover which posts produced afternoon deliveries in Hampstead.

Dossie joined Thomas in Legon on 24 January bringing the pleasing news that Thomas's Balliol contemporary and long-standing friend Christopher Hill was to become Master of Balliol. Thomas took to his bed from 3 February with an illness that was construed as a mixture of influenza and malaria leading to bronchitis. When Dossie left on 11 March she was met from her flight by her sister Joan Payne and niece Sue Payne with a very large envelope from the Queen offering her the Order of Merit (OM) – Dossie and Thomas had already agreed that this if offered would be acceptable. BJ wrote on 22 March that she would come to London airport to meet Thomas's arrival on 29 March and would joyfully dine with him and take him to a train home.

Thomas spent the day and night of 1 April in London then he, Teddy and his daughter Joanna met Dossie off a morning train from Oxford for a stroll in St James's Park before Dossie went to Buckingham Palace to receive her OM from the Queen. By convention, Dossie went in alone without relatives and the police tried to move Thomas and Joanna on until they explained why they were hanging about. Thomas and Dossie were flying from London airport on 10 April to Algiers to visit Luke and Anna and their children. At the same time, BJ and Jack were at the airport to welcome Polly from Ghana. Jack went to the observation roof to see Polly's aircraft arrive. BJ stifled a wish to go to another part of the terminal in the hope of catching a glimpse of Thomas.

Thomas reluctantly set off again for Ghana on 13 May. He saw these Ghana days as offering a very quiet life, but with too many immediate tasks to allow him to settle down to long-term writing projects such as the Africa history book long promised to Victor Weybright or the Nkrumahist project for a collective people's history of Africa edited by Basil Davidson. He was resisting an invitation from David Kimble to go to Dar-es-Salaam in the summer to do a fortnight's lecturing to East African diplomats. Oxford University unexpectedly entered the lists on 31 May when the vice-chancellor Kenneth Wheare telephoned Dossie to say that an electing committee had just met to consider an appointment to a newly created lectureship in the government of African States and had decided unanimously to offer the job to Thomas. Thomas was intrigued by the Oxford proposal but unsure whether he should let himself be deflected, and whether it was a deflection. The University Registrar wrote that the appointment to a post entitled Lectureship in the Government of New States would be for five years in the first instance – at the end of which Thomas at 60 would be eligible for re-appointment until retirement age at 67. The duties would be: to engage in advanced study or research; and to give, under the direction of the Committee for Commonwealth Studies, no fewer than 36 lectures or classes in each academic year, spread over no fewer than 12 weeks of two terms of the year.

Thomas had arranged to be met again by BJ for a late night reunion on 9 June, despite the likely disapproval of Jack compounded by concern that Polly was at home in London where she had just been offered a job at Penguin Books. Dossie would be making a brief visit to Munich and would be flying back to London on 10 June when Thomas would meet her. BJ wrote that she was sure her airport meeting would be all right and that she was determined to do it since the ostensible purpose of Thomas's timing was to enable him to travel to Oxford with Dossie. In the event BJ was in the kitchen at home at 1 Antrim Road, Hampstead, brewing tea for the late arrival when Jack, who had been asleep, came down to look for BJ and was displeased. BJ was for days too worried to write to Thomas but resumed on 14 June with an admission of wanting to be with Thomas even more.

Thomas and Dossie went back to Ghana to clear up their home and Thomas accepted the Oxford lectureship. Just as Thomas was settling back into an Oxford life, Dossie, under her aura as a Nobel laureate, was becoming even more of a world traveller. In mid-September she went on a British Council sponsored visit to Japan coupled with a journey to China at her own wish to see scientific progress there. Thomas continued his regular visits to BJ in London. He met her from her work at Heinemann on 21 September and stayed over in London – this time at a Hammersmith riverside house on loan to Alexander Cockburn, a recent Oxford graduate who had been a neighbour and friend of Luke and Anna in their Oxford home.

With Thomas back in Oxford harness in the new lectureship from 1 October, he and BJ were together again in London a week later when BJ heard what she described in her letter to Thomas next day as the 'unmanageable cough'. She went with some nervousness to Oxford on 22 October and stayed at the Hodgkin house at 94 Woodstock Road, meeting Dossie's sister Joan and some of her children. Next morning Thomas and BJ snatched a fleeting walk at Cumnor – where they had walked together in the autumn of 1930. They were now meeting almost every week. When time and season allowed they had begun driving on their Thursday outings to the Surrey village of Abinger Hammer near Dorking, where they could have a drink and lunch at the Abinger Arms or take a picnic and walk up the steep lane to Lord Farrer's Abinger Hall estate and enjoy bluebells or rhododendrons and the birdlife. When time was more limited, they walked among the birches on Hampstead Heath or ate biscuits by the Serpentine in Hyde Park.

Christopher Hill wrote to Thomas that the Balliol College meeting on 10 November had elected Thomas to a senior research fellowship – no emoluments, but a right to free dinners and lunches. To the formal notification he had added in ink 'Whoopee'. Thomas returned to Ghana in mid-November, held seminars for post-graduate students at the Institute of African Studies and even did some writing. As usual he gave help to other scholars, this time to Ann Seidman in revision of her book on African economics, and to a promising young researcher from Bahia in Brazil, Paulo de Moraes Farias, who needed sources on conquests of the Muslim Almoravids.

By the New Year of 1966 BJ's dissembling to Jack about her frequent meetings with Thomas had worn very thin. In a letter to Thomas on 30 January, she recounted several pointed comments by Jack during a single weekend. When Douglas Jay telephoned twice to BJ to go for a walk and BJ said she was driving Jack into town, Jack said later: 'I don't want to prevent you from seeing your old loves – except one, who has become too obtrusive lately.' In a subsequent conversation, when BJ said she enjoyed talking over the past with Thomas, Jack said: 'As long as he doesn't make you unhappy, either by making you regret the past that you've missed or by trying to relive the past, which never works.'

In February Nkrumah was absent from Ghana on a peacemaking mission in Vietnam and his administration was overthrown on 24 February by a military coup. Thomas late next day read a hostile leader in *The Times* that seemed to him simply a statement of the opposition's case against Nkrumah, alleging that he had abolished political opposition, free speech and the judiciary, and dismissed, expelled or hamstrung ministers. Over the ensuing days he wrote a rejoinder letter for publication with a conclusion: 'Ghana during the past fifteen years became a society in which rapid and exciting advances were made in education and other fields; in which there was a real effort to canalise people's energies to achieve social change; and in which it was possible (as in few other countries) to have rational intercourse between people of widely differing political standpoints.' Thomas also appeared on the BBC television current affairs programme 'Twenty-four Hours' on 1 and 2 March when he sought to keep Nkrumah's role in perspective and point to the benefits to the Ghanaian people in their town and villages against a critical view by Dr Kobina Taylor representing the opposition United Party.

In Ghana, many academics rushed to dissociate themselves from the Nkrumah past in which they had shared and rising figures signed a collective letter of 14 March for *The Times* to counter Thomas's letter sympathetic to Nkrumah. The letter reached the newspaper too late to be included in the correspondence. The lead signatory of the unpublished letter was an associate professor K.A.B. (Soas) Jones-Quartey designated as the chairman of a Legon Committee on National Reconstruction, and the second was the Institute of African Studies secretary Stephen Andoh signing as chairman of the Political Sub-Committee.

Jones-Quartey wrote privately to Thomas on 16 March that before Thomas's letter appeared 'some of us Legonites' had begun to organise into 'an instrument of reform and reconstruction for our country, or at least into a source of advice and assistance to the Interim Government'. They had seen Thomas's letter as one of the first challenges to their self-respect and sense of duty. Thomas was disheartened and, after seeing a copy of the collective letter, he wrote to Stephen Andoh saying that he did not wish to continue as external examiner for the Legon MA in African studies or in political science, and would not be coming to Ghana for that. (He did offer to read, though not examine, Paulo Farias's thesis.)

The Hodgkin household was joined on 3 April (Thomas's fifty-sixth birthday) by a young political refugee from Rhodesia, Wilson Katiyo, who had been staying in Zambia with Liz at Kasama – where the wardrobe he had accumulated after escaping with almost nothing from police harassment in Rhodesia had been stolen in a break-in in March. Wilson was helped by Liz and her friends to travel to Britain to resume his education and came from Oxford to London on 9 May with a large sum of money from Dossie to replace his twice-depleted wardrobe. At a Davin family request, he was shown round by Michael Wolfers (on the staff of *The Times*). Wolfers visited Wilson at the Woodstock Road house the following weekend and met Thomas and Dossie for the first time.

In early July, Dossie went to Moscow where she was attending a crystallography congress and Thomas – delayed by a fever – joined her for the latter part of a journey to Samarkand, Bokhara, Sochi and Yalta and a sailing to Istanbul. Jack and BJ were to spend a holiday cruising on the Black Sea with members of the British Peace Committee. BJ, finding that Jack believed the coincidence was planned rather than fortuitous, wrote to Thomas that if they should chance to meet in Odessa ('I can't force myself to wish that we don't meet') they should avoid doing so in Istanbul.

In the event there was a fleeting and awkward meeting in Odessa where the two couples were on adjacent boats. BJ saw Thomas up on deck, hung back to wave and when challenged said she was waving to a peace supporter on the dock. BJ thought she and her travelling companions would be away looking at Odessa before the other boat's passengers had completed landing formalities and disembarked. Suddenly Thomas appeared; BJ passed a quick warning message and avoided a substantive meeting. Jack later scolded BJ in their cabin since he was convinced that the encounter was planned (and that Thomas planned to share BJ's holiday). BJ argued that these were the last circumstances in which she and Thomas would plan to meet and she told Jack that she would hide in their cabin until Thomas's boat had gone. BJ did not dare tell Jack that there was a further overlap in Istanbul on 14 August and there she wore a bright pink dress so that if Thomas saw her in the distance he could turn tail.

Thomas returned to Oxford teaching and supervision and an accumulation of requests for help. A South African exile Ronnie Kasrils wanted to study African history. The Nigerian Vincent Bakpetu Thompson wanted to show Thomas a manuscript on Pan-Africanism. The Congolese Thomas Kanza wanted as-

sistance in entering St Antony's College or London University. Martin Kilson
wanted Thomas to look at the book he was writing on local political change in
Ghana. Philip Mason of the Institute of Race Relations wanted Thomas to join
a group of people trying to frame proposals on trends and possible research
concerned with future race relations in Britain. He agreed to give seminars in
London, Keele, Sussex and Bradford and at the request of his friend from undergraduate days Alec Peterson he sent to the journal *Comparative Education* an
article on African universities and the state.

The professor of history at Ibadan, Jacob Ajayi, had invited Thomas as a visiting Nuffield professor and Thomas and Dossie travelled on 12 January 1967
– to Nigeria and India respectively. Ibadan seemed much as usual to Thomas
despite the ethnic upheavals in Nigeria – an Ibo driver at the airport, a familiar
Ibo steward at the Nuffield Lodge – but some Ibo dons and students had left
for the east. He had a recurrence of a troublesome cough and began a remedial
course of the antibiotic drug Penbritin. He prepared four lectures on his chosen
subject 'Islam and the radical tradition in Africa' and two Saturday seminars on
related Islamic themes. In his first lecture, he defined the radical tradition as one
that took a levelling egalitarian attitude to differences of rank, status, wealth,
lineage, sex etc., and the privileges based upon these; and one that had the idea
of men and women belonging to an international community, whose claims
transcended those of a particular state, region or ethnic or linguistic group.

Ann Seidman wrote from Madison, Wisconsin that Penguin Books were interested in publishing the manuscript on the economics of African unity she
had written with Reg Green, economic adviser to the Treasury in Tanzania.
Penguin would ask Thomas to write a foreword. Thomas returned to Oxford
for a summer of students and seminars. A South African anti-apartheid cam-
paigner, Ruth First, now exiled in London, wrote to him about her project for
writing on armies and coups in selected African states. When she had begun
people had told her she must mean Latin America rather than Africa: 'Now
look what's happening, coups thick and fast in so many states the subject is
unmanageable...'

Thomas's mother decided to move from Crab Mill to the smaller Grey House
along Grump Street in Ilmington so that Thomas and Dossie could take full pos-
session of Crab Mill, keeping 94 Woodstock Road as an Oxford home. When
the Oxford term resumed in October, Thomas sought to establish a routine of
spending the week in Oxford and travelling for the weekend in Ilmington from
a Friday seminar he had at Queen Elizabeth House at five in the afternoon.
He went to East Berlin from 22 to 26 October for a conference marking the
Oriental Institute's twentieth anniversary and met BJ before departure and on
return. In November he was writing up the material he had used for his Ibadan

lectures, agreeing to requests from Cambridge and from SOAS to give seminars, but beginning to weary of the academic round. He wrote on 2 November to Ivor Wilks now at Northwestern University: 'I am coming more and more to the conclusion that Oxford is a waste of time and am planning to retire again shortly'.

Thomas had a hankering for more writing and was pleased when Alexander Cockburn wrote on 14 November for the *New Statesman* offering him three books on imperialism to review and suggesting that these with other books he had sent Thomas would provide matter for a 'Books in General' piece about the foundation of imperialism. Thomas accepted. He had a jolting reminder from the New American Library about the long promised but neglected Africa history book, when the NAL secretary Michael Cohn wrote that there had been no communication for about four years and asked for some word on progress. Thomas wrote back on 10 January 1968 that the matter was on his conscience but his interests had changed since his discussions with Weybright. He was working on a plan for a book on 'The Radical Tradition in African Politics' based partly on the lectures he had given at the University of Ibadan and would be giving in Oxford. He thought too many general books on African history had been written in recent years and offered the new subject for consideration by NAL as an alternative.

Thomas had another house move in mid-January 1968 – in Oxford from 94 Woodstock Road to the top flat at 20 Bradmore Road, the house that Thomas's parents had leased after the First World War and where after conversion into flats Dossie with Luke had lived during the Second World War. Thomas now found the flat small though agreeably warm and nearer to work places for himself and Dossie – the Woodstock Road house was to be sold when Joan Payne had found herself an alternative home. He travelled to Khartoum in February for an international conference on the place of Sudan in Africa organised by the University of Khartoum's Sudan Research Unit . He was surrounded by friends and spent the first half of the week with Norman Daniel of the British Council and the second half with Yusuf Bedri in Omdurman at Ahfad University College for Women, as it had now become. Mohamed Omer Beshir told him the University of Khartoum was offering Liz a teaching post in the history department on a three-year contract. Back in Oxford, Thomas renewed acquaintance with Eduardo Mondlane, who was the principal speaker on 9 March at a national student conference on the theme of revolution in southern Africa.

Sally Chilver, as principal of Bedford College in the University of London, wrote in April asking if Thomas would give the annual Fawcett Lecture endowed in memory of the suffragist Dame Millicent Fawcett and intended to address changes in the position of women since 1830. BJ was staying with Diana

Hopkinson in Cornwall at the Hubback family's Trethias Cottage on Treyarnon Bay and Thomas joined them for a few days (Dossie was on a visit to Australia), though, as BJ had not fully confided in Diana, BJ was in an upstairs bedroom and Thomas in a downstairs room.

Thomas wrote on 8 May to Michael Cohn at NAL accepting that the Mentor contract should be cancelled since they were not taking up the subject of the radical tradition in African politics: 'This seems likely to be the only book on African history that I shall ever write'. He was ever being urged to write. Yusuf Fadl Hasan wanted Thomas to revise and expand a paper on 'Mahdism, Messianism and Marxism in an African setting' for publication in a book. On 19 July Thomas was a lunch guest of James Bell and Richard Brain of OUP to discuss a second edition of *Nigerian Perspectives* with a new introduction and material for delivery by the end of the year.

Thomas was now reading widely in preparation for his Fawcett lecture examining whether revolutionaries had revolutionary ideas about love – and drawing on his friends and students for inspiration about Marx's household and Marxist champions. Thomas was exploring the ideas of European revolutionaries of the nineteenth and twentieth centuries – grouped in the circles of Shelley and Godwin, Marx and Engels, William Morris and Eleanor Marx Aveling, Rosa Luxemburg and Lenin – and the crux was to explain a revolutionary attitude to love. Privately Thomas and BJ saw this exploration in the light of their shared relationship. BJ attended the Bedford College presentation on 26 November and noted several literary references to romantic texts they shared as favourites.

Thomas in his Oxford teaching on African political thinkers was taking a more detached view of Nkrumah pointing out that significant writings in his name had been ghosted – 'Consciencism', a hotchpotch philosophical text of 1964, was owed to Dorothy Padmore – but Nkrumah's strength lay in his grasp of African history and keen sense of African politics. However, Nkrumah's turn to repressive legislation to secure his position made his administration less secure and led to the 1966 coup.

A Balliol College meeting held on 3 January 1969 re-elected Thomas to his senior research fellowship to 30 September 1972. BJ was helping to entertain Janet Mondlane on a visit to London and took her to London airport on 2 February for her return to Tanzania – only to learn next day that Eduardo Mondlane was killed by a parcel bomb. Thomas lost another friend in the death from a heart attack on 19 February of Stephen Swingler, Minister of State for Social Services in the Labour Government. Thomas was in London for Swingler's funeral and carried on to Cambridge where he made a brief oration in honour of Mondlane at memorial ceremonies organised by Ivor Wilks and his fellow historian Phyllis Ferguson.

Thomas reported to the university in early March on his work as university lecturer from October 1965 that he had conducted lectures and seminars and supervised at various times between three and six research students, tutored two or three students taking the 'Politics of New States (Africa)' paper in their B. Phil. and supervised thesis preparation. The University Registry advised that Thomas's five-year appointment had been renewed until he reached retiring age. Thomas's work with students left him insufficient time for work on a revised edition of *Nigerian Perspectives* even with a delivery date delayed to the spring. He advised OUP that he did not expect to do much further work until the summer long vacation. OUP's John Bell wrote that he was considering a reprint of a small quantity of the existing edition to fill the gap until the new edition.

Thomas – after family holidays and visits in the summer – was distracted by work on a paper on African theories of imperialism he had agreed to contribute to a seminar planned for the next academic year by Roger Owen and Bob Sutcliffe. Thomas, with the persistent feeling that academic duties took too much time from his writing, was contemplating early retirement by 1970 when he would be 60. He wrote in September to Christopher Hill as Master of Balliol: 'I really do want to spend my declining years (if any) writing all sorts of non-academic things rather than going on pretending to be an academic.' Thomas's students, under a notional veil of secrecy from Thomas, were already deep in planning for his sixtieth birthday. R.W. (Bill) Johnson at Magdalen wrote to Christopher Hill in December about a plan with Chris Allen at Nuffield for a festschrift book already more than a year in the making. Manuscripts had been sent to press at the beginning of that month and the editors proposed holding a party for Thomas on 3 April to which contributors or would-be contributors would be invited.

In the New Year of 1970, Thomas confirmed his wish to retire. He wrote to the vice-chancellor Alan Bullock with his decision to leave the university lectureship and to Christopher Hill that he would also resign the college fellowship that had accompanied the university appointment. The secret of special birthday celebrations for Thomas in April was wearing thin as rumours leaked through to him. Bill Johnson wrote to Thomas in February confirming that he and Chris Allen had been attempting surreptitiously to arrange: a small and informal afternoon party in the Magdalen senior common room for guests who had worked with and under Thomas. Dossie was thinking of giving a buffet supper in Somerville to follow on from the Magdalen event and to include a broader selection of Thomas's friends and admirers. On 21 February BJ received her invitation to the buffet but was thinking that she should not turn up 'a half stranger from the past, a ghost grieving on the periphery', though her daughter Polly would come.

The Times diary on 3 April carried an item about Thomas's impending retirement in September because he wanted to write historical novels, possibly for children, on themes from Asian and African history. At the Magdalen gathering he was presented with several fat volumes of typescripts of essays from Africanist and Islamist scholars from around the world, with a select bibliography of Thomas's own works to date. Many of the authors were in Oxford for the Magdalen gathering and at the Somerville supper party Thomas, in a bashful speech, likened himself to A.A. Milne's Winnie-the-Pooh in whose honour Christopher Robin gave a party ('A party for Me?' thought Pooh to himself. 'How grand!')

In the last week of April, Dossie was lecturing in the US and Thomas went away to Trethias Cottage on Treyarnon Bay to be with BJ. The Hopkinson presence this time was only a fiction that BJ presented to her own household. She dissembled Thomas's presence even from her daughter Polly, who was to visit Crab Mill in the second week of May. The Oxford trinity term was ending on 20 June and Thomas took his last formal seminar and his 'last cigarette'. Then he and his daughter Liz left Oxford for a holiday and drove across England and France through the great Burgundy and Alsace vineyards.

Thomas was trying to reshape his life for retirement. He wrote from Crab Mill on 23 August to Teddy: 'I personally feel very content to spend any declining years I have writing as many as possible of the things I have failed to write over the past forty – my main worries being simply my own slowness and the constant distractions and one's own terrible distractibility.' He added the rider that the house was full of visitors including grandchildren 'so almost nothing gets done'.

Thomas had already taken the first steps to a principal new distraction: his perceived new role as novelist rather than academic. He experimented with a work of fiction that had nothing to do with Asian and African history and was in no way intended for a child readership. His subject was a transparent transposition of his early love for BJ and the rekindling of their relationship that had blazed in Ghana six years earlier. A tentative synopsis had a protagonist university professor Pierre waiting at a Muscobiya airport for a novelist Natasha to arrive from Tashkent where she had been attending a writers' conference. The Russian names were quickly modified and new protagonists Pericles and Thaiza were drawn from the classical world by way of Shakespeare. The heroine Thaiza was also Theta by loose analogy with Maire's 'BJ' nickname.

Thomas's 'distractibility' continued to be fuelled in other ways. After he had resigned his Balliol fellowship, he was elected as a supernumerary emeritus fellow. He was in Poland in November for a British Council lecture visit and faced an exhausting schedule of seminars, lectures and official contacts, albeit on recurrent themes of his recent teaching and writing on Islam and Africa. In Cracow he met Professor Tadeusz Lewicki to learn about his work in Islamic and African history. The Cambridge University Press was sending out advance copies of the festschrift for Thomas entitled *African Perspectives* for publication on 10 December. Allen and Johnson were joint editors of 17 papers selected from the essays presented to Thomas on 3 April. Johnson, in an introductory biographical note on Thomas, commented that the Oxford lectureship he held for five years from 1965 was 'a post he accepted to the probable detriment of the work he wished to do, but to the enormous benefit of the numerous students he has taught since then...'

Thomas was embroiled in writing his novel along a trajectory that was more recollection than invention, with strong encouragement from BJ who in professional life was an experienced publisher's reader and editor. Thomas in this narrative recalled how two young people in the 1930s followed the code defined by their families and upbringing to defer sex until marriage and to defer marriage until the completion of education – with the outcome that they had lost each other on the way and then made a rediscovery after 33 years.

Thomas was returning in his new role as writer to another concern he had articulated some five years earlier in discussion with his daughter Liz. He was influenced partly by his experience in Ghana and the wider African context in which he deemed that agents of the United States Central Intelligence Agency (and some American political scientists in the CIA orbit) were intervening in African politics for reactionary purposes and to foment military coups. When he and Dossie visited Liz in Zambia in 1965, he had already sketched out ideas for a story whose hero would be 'Qwert Yuiop' and whose villains would be CIA collaborators. (He had managed to leave behind the folder with material for the story at Kitwe airport, at the Zambia Airways office in Lusaka and at Salisbury airport in Rhodesia.) Liz was now a university teacher in Sudan and wrote to her parents from Khartoum on 21 February 1971 about the internal weakening of the Sudanese CP and a split within that party over a possible merger into a broad front supporting the government.

Thomas had missed a reprieve 15 March deadline for the new edition of *Nigerian Perspectives* but on 8 June he delivered the manuscript of the revised edition to the OUP office in London, to the surprised pleasure of his commissioning editor Richard Brain. Thomas next day contemplated other literary projects and prospects he had before him – he identified seven. He had a first draft of part of the 'Thaiza' novel. He had an idea for a 'Jihad' novel – aimed at a teenage readership in Africa – and set in the Sokoto Caliphate and Bornu in the early nineteenth century. The protagonists would be a group of students, and the historically important people would appear as subsidiary characters. He had a chapter-by-chapter outline for the 'Qwert' novel close to completion. He had a possibility of rewriting his 'Love and the Revolutionaries' lecture as a book. He had some work on colonial studies. He might expand to book length his writings on Islam and the radical tradition. He might write a book drawing on Hodgkin family papers that were held at Crab Mill – and frequently consulted by other researchers.

Thomas chose the 'Qwert' project and carried it with him through the summer months, with BJ visiting him at Crab Mill in early July, and a holiday with Dossie at the French village La Croix in Valmer where they had spent their honeymoon. The 'Qwert' novel was developing as a complex account of a week in the life of a polymath academic Qwert Yuiop being invited by the ambassador of the imaginary country Fasolia to go to his country to counter a coup in the making. Qwert has an Uzbek father and Cornish mother and has been educated in Samarkand, Prague and Kerala before coming up to Balliol to read Oriental Languages and History. A Tuareg airhostess of great beauty, the Tamasheq-speaking Rahmata Tamakkaka, rescues the hero Qwert from an assassination attempt. They are embroiled with scores of lesser figures such as a trio of CIA agents Galba Schatzkammer, Lully Lavender and Barny Basilio, and an anti-hero repentant CIA man Ozymandias Scunthorpe who in the end weds Rahmata. The president is ousted but within days Qwert and his friends with the Fasolian Workers Party and popular intervention restore the president to his rightful office.

As Thomas returned from France to Crab Mill with his Fasolia scenario refined, events in Sudan seemed to mirror such a tale, albeit with a leftist movement thwarted by rightist forces. Sudan's president Major-General Jaafar al-Nimeiry was put under house arrest in a coup on 19 July led by Major Hashem al-Atta in Sudan and by two fellow officers Lieutenant-Colonel Babiker al-Nur and Major Farouk Osman Hamadallah, who were in London at the time. Al-Nur and Hamadallah were returning by air to Sudan when Libyan fighters forced their aircraft down in Libya. The coup was reversed on 22 July with some military action and external intervention. On returning to power Nimeiry initiated a purge of Communists and sympathisers, including al-Nur and Hamadallah who were flown from Libya to Khartoum under military detention. The military leaders were executed along with leading civilian politicians the secretary-general of the Sudanese Communist Party Abd al-Khalig Mahjub, the trade unionist al-Shafie Ahmed al-Sheikh and the Minister of Southern Affairs Joseph Garang.

Thomas was appalled at the bloodshed. He spoke at a House of Commons meeting on 28 July, signed a letter of protest, and wrote obituaries in *The Times* for key victims of the repression. He told the Commons audience that while his meeting with al-Nur and Hamadallah was recent he had recollections going back to 1956 of Garang as a brilliant revolutionary student – the first Southern Sudanese Marxist he had met. Thomas had come to know Abd al-Khalig Mahjub over the previous three years and to respect him tremendously for his political understanding – and they had last met in March 1970 when Thomas had been lecturing in Khartoum.

Thomas contemplated going back to Sudan to plead with the president, but, with the Nimeiry vengeance coming swiftly and without proper trials, Liz persuaded Thomas he could do nothing. He gave support to a solidarity committee with the Sudanese people formed in August with an Egyptian clinical psychologist Fawzeya Makhlouf-Norris and a publisher Nick Jacobs as joint secretaries, under the aegis of Liberation, the new incarnation of the Movement for Colonial Freedom. Dossie and Thomas left in September for a visit to Hanoi arranged through Lai Van Ngoc, the chargé d'affaires in London of the Democratic Republic of Viet Nam (North Vietnam), during which they would lecture in their respective fields of crystallography and Africa. At the Institute of History on 23 September Thomas recycled his Khartoum lecture of March 1970 on revolution and counter-revolution in Africa, adding the fresh evidence of the events in Sudan.

Thomas was soon back in Crab Mill trying to go on with 'Qwert' – he was encouraged by BJ's enthusiasm as they read portions of the draft together – but his energy was diminished by the recurrence of a troublesome cough. Thomas had a sentimental project to celebrate BJ's forthcoming sixtieth birthday. He began in late January 1972 to send letters of invitation to a birthday lunch at Balliol on the year's leap day. This would bring together old friends – particularly those shared by BJ, Sigle and Thomas in their school and university days – and spouses where work did not prevent them attending a mid-weekday event in Oxford. Thomas secured a score or so acceptances including Sigle; his brother Teddy; Dossie; Sir Evelyn Shuckburgh (retired as a Foreign Office mandarin and making clavichords); Diana Hubback and her educationist husband David Hopkinson; J.B. Priestley and his archaeologist wife Jacquetta Hawkes; classical scholar Tony Andrewes; Sir Isaiah Berlin (now head of the Oxford house Wolfson); and Christopher Hill, head of the Oxford house Balliol, and his wife Bridget. Sir Christopher Cox wrote on black-bordered mourning writing paper on the day after the birthday lunch that he had become confused over the leap year date and unintentionally missed it ('the loss is quite crippling and deservedly mine'). Teddy remarked how unfussy and unpompous everyone seemed though forty years on and in most cases successful: 'This must be due to some innate good quality in all them, combined with the mellowing effect of duck, crème brulée and booze.'

Thomas returned to 'Qwert' and by the second week of March had finished the fifth chapter, with seven to come according to his plan. His academic work on Africa continued to resonate. Peter Waterman wrote from the School of Arabic Studies at Ahmadu Bello University that he and Peter Gutkind of McGill would like to include Thomas's '3M piece' – the essay on 'Mahdism, Messianism and Marxism in the African setting' in a radical African reader.

Thomas spent the third week of April in Cornwall with BJ. Then back with Dossie they heard on 27 April of the death of Kwame Nkrumah in a Rumanian hospital where he had gone for medical treatment from his exile in Guinea. A long, hostile obituary in *The Times* with references to 'detested dictator' and 'diabolic force' exacerbated Thomas's sadness. He sat up late at night to write his own note and telephoned it to *The Times* where Teddy as an assistant editor was on duty. *The Times* eventually published on 10 May Thomas's tribute depicting Nkrumah as 'the most unstuffy head of government that I have met – the most intellectually alive, the most serious, the most responsive to new ideas'. He concluded that Nkrumah's contributions to philosophy and politics were 'likely to outlive those of his severest critics'.

Thomas had been expecting the second edition of *Nigerian Perspectives* to appear in 1972, but OUP advised that with considerable stocks of the 1969 reprint of the first edition they would delay the second edition as an Oxford paperback to autumn 1973 or the beginning of 1974. Thomas continued his preoccupation with 'Qwert' but for *Presence Africaine* wrote an article on Nkrumah's radicalism. In December he agreed that despite his earlier decision to end such expeditions to he would go next year to northern Nigeria as external examiner of a thesis by Muhammad al-Hajj.

In the New Year of 1973, Thomas continued to give priority to the writing of 'Qwert' and to share each instalment with BJ. By late February, they were putting final changes to a complete text. Thomas signed off on a typescript of 500 pages to be shown on a friendly basis to Ilsa Yardley – with her professional knowledge of publishing and of literary agency – before submission to Heinemann. Ilsa did not share BJ's enthusiasm and BJ relayed her response – 'It really was a sad surprise to find Ilsa disagreeing with me so much about Qwert … thinking that its leisurely pace makes it old-fashioned, whereas it's lovely to have something different from the slick novels that keep coming in. But she did enjoy the funny bits about the CIA. And of course she's right, as we both know about it being too long.' Thomas continued with revisions and cuts to 'Qwert' and he felt ready again to take up other tasks such as book reviewing. On 19

September the *TLS* sent him for review the Tony Hopkins *Economic History of West Africa* and other books.

BJ was now suffering problems with her pancreas. She was admitted in mid-October for surgery that left her a scar with thirteen stitches – 'like a wadi in the Sahara seen from the air', she wrote to Thomas. A delicate matter of convalescence arose. BJ was going away initially to Diana Hopkinson, where Jack wanted her to spend as long as possible, and then to Thomas where BJ wanted to be. She told Jack that Dossie had suggested her convalescing with the Hodgkins, and Jack hoped this meant staying with Thomas's mother in Ilmington and not in Oxford. BJ went to Diana for a tactful couple of days and then moved on 1 November to Crab Mill for a fortnight with Thomas.

Two students who had carried out substantial research on Africa for their doctoral theses supervised by Thomas were ready to submit: Richard Joseph on radical nationalism in Cameroon and Sholto Cross on the Watch Tower movement in South Central Africa. The examiners seeing Cross on 14 November noted a thesis lucidly written and thoroughly documented, parts of which were publishable with only minor amendments. Cross wrote to Thomas '... your leadership – both in the intellectual and the wider sense – has been the most important thing for me which I gained from Oxford...' The examiners, including Thomas's former pupil Bill Johnson, saw Richard Joseph on 27 December for a longish viva in which they found that the candidate performed 'capably and powerfully'. They felt in retrospect that his scholarship brought him close to rendering the viva purely formal.

In the New Year of 1974, Thomas followed his daughter Liz in exchanging Africa for Asia where the American war in Vietnam was being fought. He arrived in Hanoi to spend three months in the Democratic Republic of Vietnam as a guest of the Institute of History. He wanted to write a book but was not sure what kind – in content an emphasis on history or the contemporary situation; in form a learned work, or popular guide or travel history. He wanted to explore how the Vietnamese revolution was possible and how the society or nation made the leap from colonial rule to socialism. He wanted to visit historically important sites and those connected to Ho Chi Minh and the liberated areas. He had much to learn about the workings of Vietnamese society. He could not expect to learn the Vietnamese language in the time, but hoped to learn enough to be able to pronounce properly, particularly names and places. He would work through interpreters and with materials translated into English or French.

On his first Sunday morning – 20 January – he went to the market with its rich array of food, flowers and fruit for the lunar new year festival of Tet, in the company of Phan Gia Ben, who was to be constant guide and companion through the process of discovery. He was then plunged into a great lunch party given by the Committee of Science and Technology and found old friends from his previous visit to Hanoi in 1971. He began the main task with a discussion next day at the Institute of History on the convergence of the Vietnamese nation and the relationship of Marxism to the Vietnamese revolutionary situation. He went later to the National Committee for Social Science to go deeper into the question of the Vietnamese nation with the committee president Nguyen Khanh Toan. Thomas was exposed to a perception of a history of Vietnamese nationhood measured in thousands of years rather than centuries and in no way a product of capitalism.

After three weeks of a dozen meetings with Vietnamese scholars and some work in the Institute of History library with guidance from the librarian Nguyen Khac Dam, Thomas could see a book taking shape that would address four thousand years of Vietnamese history and the political context of the August 1945 Revolution, the abdication of the last Nguyen king Bao Dai, and Ho Chi Minh's declaration of independence. The working method was morning and afternoon sessions of several hours with Vietnamese historians – 'drinking innumerable cups of tepid tea in a fairly cold and draughty room in the Institute of History – or elsewhere…', as Thomas informed his mother in a letter of 10 February.

'Qwert' was not forgotten: BJ was having the revised pages retyped (by her son Nicolas's wife Cathy Lloyd) and was copy-editing the text in which the original long chapters had been broken into shorter sections. She put final touches to the manuscript on 4 March and finished her reader's report to Heinemann. In a favourable recommendation, she noted: 'Peripatetic novels are known to be favourites with readers, and the author here moves his characters rapidly from place to place.' She included a modest declaration of interest: 'The book is beautifully written, and I have helped the author to cut and tighten the story considerably. It now moves at a very good pace…' She submitted the book the next day for the consideration of colleagues at Heinemann who knew that she attached personal importance to this submission.

The weeks passed as the book went to several other readers and BJ could garner no sense of their reaction. By the end of March, she dropped a hint that another publisher William Collins might be interested. BJ walked along Piccadilly on 7 May cursing and feeling like crying after learning that Heinemann were rejecting 'Qwert'. She was trying to fathom the reasons for the refusal. It seemed that Thomas had not made up his mind what sort of novel it was going to be; not quite enough happened; it was rather long, although thought to be clever and full of fascinating stuff and lovely conversation. BJ suggested that the Marxism had frightened Heinemann, though colleagues denied this.

Dossie was admitted in June as an honorary fellow of the Royal College of Physicians and her guide through the ceremony was Charles Fletcher, a pulmonary expert, so she mentioned Thomas's chest trouble. He turned out to be the Charles Fletcher who had been a neighbouring best friend to Thomas in 1917 when they had attended the Norland Place School in Holland Park Avenue and Thomas would borrow books from the Fletcher family. Thomas's GP wrote to Fletcher about Thomas's case and Fletcher wrote on 16 September from the medical school at Hammersmith Hospital that he would be glad to hear from Thomas to arrange an appointment and delighted to see him again after so many years.

The Centre of African Studies at Edinburgh University held a two-day seminar in November convened by Christopher Fyfe, the Reader in African History, to consider the changes that had taken place in African studies since the end of the Second World War and to honour Basil Davidson's sixtieth birthday on 9 November. Fyfe asked Thomas if he could be prevailed upon to write a paper to be included in the proceedings to be published by Longman. Basil was eager for Thomas to do so. He was expecting that many contributors to the seminar would be friends who scarcely shared his own and Thomas's views on the analysis of politics. He hoped that Thomas would be in the mood to write something that bore on the shift from 'orthodox studies' to 'Marxist' or at any rate 'unorthodox' studies in the political field.

'Qwert' was tried and failed at Collins, Chatto & Windus, and Barrie & Jenkins: it was literary and full of interest, but thought unlikely to find a very large audience. Thomas and BJ pondered what to do next with 'Qwert' and whether Thomas should write an alternative happy ending, as one publisher suggested. Thomas was engaged with his Vietnam material. The Institute of Race Relations had been radicalised under the influence of the Sri Lankan writer Ambalavaner Sivanandan (Siva), who had invited Thomas to go on the editorial working committee for the institute journal and to write something from his stay in Vietnam. Thomas responded with an article for *Race and Class* on 'The Vietnamese Revolution and Some Lessons' and dedicated this to Basil Davidson on his sixtieth birthday. With increasing concern over Thomas's health, BJ accompanied him when he went on 19 December for his consultation at Hammersmith Hospital with Charles Fletcher and Bill Cleland who had developed new techniques in surgery, notably cardiopulmonary bypass. The two specialists told Thomas that he had a shadow on his lung and that he needed to take daily walks.

In the New Year of 1975, Thomas and BJ decided to try 'Qwert' with Livia Gollancz who might appreciate its leftish tinge. Thomas then gathered his Vietnam notebooks and notes and went off to Bamburgh to stay alone in a cottage to work on the new book on the Vietnamese revolution – with his neighbour aunt Barbara (widow of the neurosurgeon Sir Hugh Cairns) checking that he had proper meals. He already had a preliminary draft of an introductory chapter and had sent this to the historians in Hanoi for their comments. He was working on the early history of Vietnam to the fourteenth century. After three and a half weeks in Bamburgh he had drafted the equivalent of a couple more chapters and was ready to return to Crab Mill. He had done less than he wanted but felt he was out of a rut and would try to keep up his output in more usual surroundings.

In late February, Livia Gollancz turned down 'Qwert' with what BJ described as dotty but wounding comments. Anna's father the novelist and publisher Dan Davin offered his help over the hapless 'Qwert'. He read the novel with a highly professional eye and wrote on 1 April a thoughtful appraisal that began with the gentle judgment that he considered it 'certainly publishable'. He tempered this with cogent reasons why Thomas was having difficulty finding a publisher: 'What you seem to have intended and, if so, carried out successfully, is a romantic thriller, laced with comedy, which inverts one of the usual premises of the thriller: that the left are the wicked and the right the goodies. I've got nothing against that idea, think it a refreshing change, in fact; but it's going to give you trouble finding a publisher unless you find one who is prepared to take a chance on selling in the US a book that has the CIA for villains at the time when the Americans are coming round to that view themselves.'

In May, Thomas returned to the Hammersmith Hospital for chest X-rays after increased problems of breathlessness, even sometimes when walking the long corridors at Crab Mill. OUP advised on May 20 that the first copies of the cloth edition of *Nigerian Perspectives* had arrived for publication on 3 July. Thomas was regretful that not expecting years of delay in publication he had missed an opportunity to arrange new translations of some of the Arabic texts.

He now met again Sydney 'Joe' Josephs who had been a brilliant student in Thomas's Oxford philosophy class of the mid-1950s. Joe had become publishing director of Macmillan's higher and further education division. Thomas told him of his various unpublished typescripts and invited him to bring his wife and four children on a visit to Crab Mill after which Joe offered to look at typescripts to see if he could find homes for them. Joe Josephs with his wife Debbie and three of their children came to a Sunday lunch at Crab Mill on 28 September. He took away all the material already typed of Thomas's Vietnam book, to see if Macmillan might be interested.

Thomas went to Birmingham on 12 March 1976 as a speaker alongside Basil Davidson and Polly Gaster at a conference on 'Angola: The wider implications' organised by LaRay Denzer, his student in Ghana days, and sociologist Robin

Cohen. Thomas addressed the wider implications of the almost complete liberation of Angola as the last of the former Portuguese-dominated African countries. He could draw on his Vietnam study and partial resemblances he saw between nineteenth-century European liberation movements and twentieth-century African liberation movements.

Thomas was host at Crab Mill on the weekend of 23 to 25 April to a gathering of more than a dozen of the staff and core contributors to *Race and Class*, including Malcolm Caldwell and Sivanandan. Proud radicals were concerned that the influx might be too much for the household and were reassured by Thomas that he would have help with the cooking. Guests new to Ilmington were astonished to see the cooking help provided by 79-year-old Annie Humphries, who as Annie Bull had begun service as a kitchen maid in the King's Mound home of Thomas's maternal grandparents.

Thomas had frequently taken on book reviews, though acutely conscious that such tasks slowed down his own Vietnam writing – slowed further by a continuing problem of bronchitis. Liz, now back from Vietnam but unemployed, had helped on the Vietnam book. However, she was now offered a job at an immigrant reception centre in Birmingham and was being interviewed for a half-time post to teach African and world history at Birmingham's Westhill College. Guests continued to throng to Crab Mill. The historian Muhammad al-Hajj from Kano came to visit in mid-August and wrote later in a letter of thanks that he had heard how guests from different parts of the world frequented the house but he could not really imagine the frequency until he saw it himself. He commented: 'An early Arab poet said about people like you: "Their visitors are so numerous that their dogs no longer bark at strangers."' Thomas's breathlessness had by now been formally diagnosed as emphysema and the condition affected his daily activities, whether in writing or in simple mobility. He had dining rights in Balliol on Wednesdays and found it difficult when the college back gate was closed in the evening to make his way to the common room by the front gate and lodge. He wrote on 6 October to Christopher Hill as Master asking if he might have the use of a back gate key: Christopher naturally gave immediate consent.

Thomas went into the men's chest ward at the Radcliffe Infirmary in mid-November for a week of observation and tests that stretched into two. The Longman volume for Basil Davidson was published as *African Studies Since 1945* with Thomas setting the tone for the book in an essay looking back about a quarter of century to when he and Basil started writing about African questions. Thomas could not attend the launch on 29 November, but Basil took an opportunity to write: 'Your contribution to the volume absolutely made it for me.'

Thomas came out of hospital and by early January 1977 was contemplating leaving the English winter for a warmer climate, possibly in Egypt. Yusuf Bedri, hearing of this via Liz and his own niece Sulafa Khalid Musa, wrote on 27 January urging Thomas to book his ticket to Khartoum since he had a second home with the Bedris at Ahfad College. Thomas stayed on in England as he had been recommended to have intensive physiotherapy. Christopher Hill invited Thomas and Dossie to stay for the first fortnight of February in the Master's Lodging at Balliol for Thomas to be on hand for the treatment.

Thomas returned to Crab Mill, Dossie went to California, BJ came to spend a few days at Crab Mill. Thomas was being seen by the local GP Dr D.E. Olliff, who was also attending Thomas's mother Dorothy, and by an Oxford specialist Dr David Warrell. Thomas's condition worsened and in late March he was taken back into the Radcliffe Infirmary. Physical tests showed no new problems and the medical team decided that he had been taken too quickly off the cortisone that had been used to treat his asthmatic condition. With an adjustment in his medication, he was writing to friends in mid-April that he was 'able to eat and drink and work and enjoy nature and people again'. The illness, though intermittent, had affected his work and on 2 March Joe Josephs agreed a new deadline of the end of the summer for Macmillan to see the Vietnam book.

Thomas was methodically making provision for his eventual death. He had discussed with Balliol's domestic bursar Brigadier D.W. (Jacko) Jackson arrangements for his wake and on 4 March wrote to confirm what they had agreed. He asked Jacko to order ten dozen bottles of a 1975 claret, and lay them down in the cellar labelled 'T.H.'s Wake' – and for which Thomas would pay now. Thomas, with his keen sense of food, wine and music, wanted the wine to be in good condition and added the rider: 'In the unhappy, but not improbable, event of my dying before the 1975 claret becomes entirely fit to drink you would generously substitute an equal quantity of some reasonable 1970 claret from the college stocks and take over my 1975 claret in exchange.'

Thomas sent a copy of these instructions to Christopher Hill with a further note on his wake. He hoped for no religious ceremony, a few words by Christopher as Master or emeritus Master, and a reading by Liz's school and university friend the actress Miriam Margolyes (he had in mind lines from Robert Browning's 'The Bishop orders his tomb at Saint Praxed's Church'). Thomas assured Christopher that he did not intend to die just yet. The Balliol bursar duly ordered ten dozen Château Abiet 1975 that lay in the cellars in Bordeaux and would be shipped to Britain.

Thomas and Dossie took a ten-day package holiday in Crete. On return they were greeted with a further sign of mortality when Teddy sent an obituary of another of Thomas's Oxford friends, the playwright Lionel Hale who had died on 14 May. Thomas and BJ were together in Cornwall for a few days he had booked at the Trethias Cottage and again at Crab Mill in August. Thomas found circumstances changed when his mother, because of frailty, moved back along Grump Street from the Grey House to Crab Mill – and this meant among other distractions from work heavier meals in the middle of the day rather than at night. Thomas found a new distraction and began a verse autobiography in the style and metre of Byron's 'Don Juan'. Now chapter and verse were in competition through the autumn as he moved to the close of the first canto of an intended twelve cantos and the last chapter on Vietnam that he hoped to complete by the end of the year.

BJ was suffering from high blood pressure, a small thrombosis in her leg and thyroid problems and on 15 November she was admitted to the Middlesex Hospital for X-rays and scanning. Thomas visited her on 17 November. Jack Gaster came and found him at his wife's hospital bedside. Courtesy from both men covered the awkwardness: BJ felt a slight blush, but after Thomas had gone, Jack told her he would have come later if he had known she had another visitor. Thomas was also concerned about his mother's condition that now required full-time professional nursing care at Crab Mill. Thomas had made a provisional plan to go to India with Dossie early in the coming year and possibly move on for another short visit to Vietnam. He now felt it would not be possible to leave his mother for so long a period and wanted to finish the Vietnam book. Dossie was in China in December and Thomas remained at Ilmington working on the introductory canto of his Byronic poem about the family forebears under a provisional title of 'Don Tomaso'.

In the New Year of 1978, Dossie flew to Bombay for Madras, and Thomas tackled book reviews for *Events* and *Times Educational Supplement*. It was the end of January before he gave serious attention to the Vietnam book. For the first time in several months he gave sections for typing to his Ilmington neighbour Irene Sabin: Her relative Gwen Sabin was taking dictation for his correspondence. In that correspondence an unexpected invitation came from the US with a letter of 9 February from the history department of Dartmouth College, Hanover, New Hampshire. An associate professor Leo Spitzer recalled meeting Thomas at Philip Curtin's house many years earlier when Thomas was giving a public lecture. More recently, Thomas had given helpful advice on an article Spitzer and LaRay Denzer had written jointly on Wallace-Johnson and the West African Youth League. Spitzer's department could invite a visiting professor specialising on any aspect of Third World history for the ten week fall term of 1978 and Spitzer was delegated to ask if Thomas would give a seminar course to selected senior students and a lecture course open to undergraduates.

Thomas drafted a cautious response to the Dartmouth proposal. He found the invitation pleasing and attractive and in principle would love to come – 'what a wonderful idea in a sometimes bleak world'. He envisaged an undergraduate course breaking newish ground on 'The Theory and Practice of National Liberation'. This would consider the ideas of revolutionary Third-World theorists and practitioners during the period 1880-1970, and cover such personalities as Muhammad Ahmad (the Sudanese Mahdi), Jamal al-Din al-Afghani, Phan Boi Chau, Sultan Galiev, Lamine Senghor and Garan Kouyaté, Abd al-Krim, Alal al-Fassi, Wallace-Johnson, Ho Chi Minh, Kwame Nkrumah, Joseph Garang and Frantz Fanon. The seminar could be related to the lectures or separately on 'Vietnam, the historical background to the August 1945 Revolution', about which he had almost finished writing a book.

Liz had joined a local CP branch in Birmingham and her branch secretary, on a visit in 1976 to Thomas to hear about the Vietnam experience, had presented him with a CP membership card. In retirement he had thus rejoined – almost casually – but he did not want to hush it up. He told Spitzer that in the past he had needed the Attorney-General's waiver to visit the US. Dartmouth made a formal appointment offer on 3 April – Thomas's sixty-eighth birthday – and this reached Thomas as he was leaving for a Trethias Cottage holiday with BJ. They went for walks – now very short – and Thomas in two sessions read BJ the entire first canto of his autobiographical poem with its 222 stanzas.

Thomas led a discussion at a meeting of the Oxford University Africa Society on 16 May on the theme of 'The National Question in Contemporary Africa'. He contrasted the complexity of the contemporary African situation with that of 1956 when he published his *Nationalism in Colonial Africa*. He referred to controversial figures such as Idi Amin, Mobutu, Hastings Banda and Emperor Bokassa, and to issues affecting Eritrea, Ethiopia, Somalia and Chad. He raised questions on the prospects for African national cultures and languages. In the discussion, a St Antony's doctoral student from South Africa Renfrew Christie drew a comparison between liberated Africa and occupied Namibia and argued that even neo-colonialism would be an improvement on the colonialism represented by Namibia's continuing captivity. Thomas spoke to Christie at the end of the session to encourage him to be in touch, but Christie felt shy and unwilling to impose himself.

During the summer, Thomas worked on his Vietnam writing while friends in the US were lining up speaking engagements on other campuses – an early bid came on 3 July from Thomas's former student Charles Stewart, now acting director of the African studies programme at the University of Illinois Urbana-Champaign campus. Stewart wanted to set up a three lecture series based on Thomas's 'theories of national liberation' course at Dartmouth. In the latter part of August, Thomas joined Dossie in Bulgaria including six days in the Rhodope Mountains before a conference of Dossie's in Varna. He was reading Nikki Keddie's biography of Jamal al-Din al-Afghani and reflecting on the Dartmouth course.

Thomas left for the US on 24 September and was driven from Boston airport to settle in what he thought an elegant and splendid apartment at Choate House, an old two-storey white clapboard house within two blocks of the history department's office and classroom building. Thomas's lecture course harked back to theories of imperialism he had been developing since October 1969 in the seminar organised by Roger Owen and Bob Sutcliffe. He also drew on research he had supervised such as the American scholar Jim Spiegler's work on nationalist thought among French-speaking West Africans. For Dartmouth, he enriched the subject from his travel and research in India and Vietnam and prepared ten new lectures, dropping the Sudanese Mahdi from his projected list. He pointed out to his students that the short list of theorists was in no sense representative of the full range and diversity of the Third World and he apologised that all the theorists were male. The seminar was centred on the historical explanation of the August 1945 Revolution in Vietnam, but was less burdensome in preparation as he drew on the latter chapters of the book on which he had been working since 1974. By late October he had begun to use odd moments to write the first few stanzas of the second canto of his autobiographical poem.

He returned to England and in January 1979 he travelled to India with Dossie, to escape the remainder of an English winter that was forecast to be severe. She was visiting professor at the Indian Academy of Sciences under the auspices of Sivaraj (Siv) Ramaseshan, who had spent a year in her Oxford laboratory. They went to Bangalore to the Raman Research Institute, named for Siv's uncle the scientist C.V. Raman, from where they would travel to other parts of India. They went to Kerala and Trivandrum in the far south where Thomas met E.M.S. Namboodiripad to ask about his political history, the background to his leadership of the Communist election victory in Kerala in 1957 and his identification with the Communist Party of India (Marxist) – created in a split from the CPI in 1964. Thomas met other Communists including the Kerala party secretary who argued the crucial role of the peasantry in the Indian revolutionary movement.

On return to Bangalore, Thomas caught a cold and suffered a severe onset of breathlessness. He was moved to a specially air-conditioned room to shield him from pollen and was given oxygen under the care of day and night nurses. Thomas made a good recovery in Bangalore. As a precaution, his Oxford specialist Dr Warrell telexed his medical history since 1958 and a full account of the therapy being used to treat his combination of obstructive bronchitis with emphysema, allergic bronchial asthma and chronic narcolepsy. During a five-day visit to Hyderabad in February, Thomas pursued his interest in the philosopher Jamal al-Din al-Afghani, and on 17 February he visited Osman Yar Khan to collect recollections of his grandfather's relations with al-Afghani, who had lived and taught in Hyderabad for a while a century earlier.

Thomas had left the draft of his Vietnam book with Liz, who had made slight amendments and delivered the typescript to Macmillan in Basingstoke. While Thomas was in Hyderabad, he had a letter from Liz saying that Macmillan was prepared to go ahead with the Vietnam book and wanted it complete as soon as possible. Thomas, with this encouragement, was eager on return to Crab Mill to prepare the book for publication with footnotes and revisions. The publisher expected the task to be done by the end of March – Thomas was desperately working on it in the first days of April. He and BJ had a few days in Trethias Cottage – from 8 to 12 April – though they realised that the poor health of each might make this the last time. By the end of April the Vietnam text was in the hands of the Macmillan in-house editor.

Thomas's mother, Dorothy Forster Hodgkin, died on 16 June and was buried beside her husband's grave in the churchyard of the village church, St Mary's Ilmington. Thomas had been planning to return to India in late October (when Dossie would be going for a further stint as Raman Professor). He was now locked into a Macmillan production schedule for delivery by 20 October of corrections and glossary and other supporting material of a complex text. Erica Powell, formerly Nkrumah's private secretary, had been seeking advice from Thomas on finding a publisher for her book on her experiences. Thomas, over-running on the Vietnam tasks, invited her help on the final stages of his book. She came for the last two weeks of October when Dossie was fulfilling a schedule in India and Bangladesh. Thomas, with the secretarial and domestic support from Erica Powell among others, was able on 7 November to deliver to Macmillan's office in London a final typescript, though it had blemishes he would have liked more time to remove.

Thomas and BJ had a feast to mark the finishing of the book and her imminent departure with Jack on a three-week visit to Polly who had been working in Mozambique since January. LaRay Denzer was at Crab Mill for much of December with her work on Wallace-Johnson, and St Clair Drake wrote from Stanford that he had feelers out in several directions to bring Thomas to campuses in California.

Early in 1980, Thomas published in *Race and Class* an article on 'The revolutionary tradition in Islam' that spanned Africa, Asia and the Arab world. *History Workshop*, a journal of Socialist historians, sought and gained permission to reprint the article in their own forthcoming November issue. Eve Hostettler wrote on 25 March: 'We feel your article is a model of its kind – clear, accessible and instructive about a delicate and complex subject.'

Thomas celebrated his seventieth birthday on 3 April and with a multiple entry visa for the US was admitted on 8 April for a round of university visits. In a tour from Northwestern University via Minneapolis to the University of California in Los Angeles Thomas explored his current interest in the radical tradition in various permutations of Islam and of Muslim West Africa. He was also developing another theme of the anti-colonial tradition in British politics. He considered a very broad range of writers and thinkers in Britain and relationships between them and the resistance and liberation movements in the Third World colonial countries. He looked at the movements against slavery and against racism and at radical, revolutionary streams of political ideas and practice. LaRay Denzer and Charles Stewart planned a collection of essays on radicalism in West Africa for an American Sage Publications series and on 27 May they wrote confirming a request for Thomas to develop a particular thread within his study of the revolutionary tradition in Islam. This would be on the legacy of Kharijism – the Khawarij were Muslims who separated from the rest of the community in protest against an arbitration agreed by the fourth Caliph in AD 657.

Thomas drew up a bibliography on the anti-colonial tradition in British politics for a seminar held in October at the University of Birmingham's Centre of West African Studies, where he was an honorary fellow. Though this was so far only one lecture Thomas saw it as the germ of another book – one that Nick Jacobs, planning to start his own imprint, was interested in publishing. He began the third canto of his autobiographical poem covering his undergraduate memories of Balliol. Roger Owen, as director of the St Antony's College Middle East Centre, wrote in December inviting Thomas to deliver the George Antonius memorial lecture towards the end of Oxford's next Trinity Term.

In the New Year of 1981, Thomas distributed among close family and friends the first two cantos of his autobiographical epic, now entitled 'Don Tomás', in an edition of 20 photocopies made by Liz. He sent a copy to the publisher John Murray for that house's historic links with Byron, and a copy to Anthony Kenny who from Michaelmas Term 1978 had succeeded Christopher Hill as Master of Balliol. John Murray soon replied commending the bravery of the 'Don Tomás' project but warning of the monotony of Byron's verse form. Murray could not envisage a sufficiently wide and attentive audience to allow them to publish the poem.

Meanwhile Thomas and Dossie had visited Katy Antonius in Cairo to gather biographical material about George, not staying with her in Maadi since she had health problems of her own but with the Egyptian scholar and linguist Magdi

Wahba and his wife Josephine in Zamalek. They went on to Sudan to stay in Omdurman with Yusuf Bedri who conducted his guests on small expeditions to other parts of Sudan, including places in the north that Thomas had not visited during his previous stays in the country.

On return to England, he went back to the third canto of his poem and in March with Teddy's help he gathered up his correspondence from Palestine of the mid-1930s for his Antonius reminiscences and began research on Antonius and official papers to add to his own perceptions. He was working hard on the lecture but took a genuine holiday in Greece with Dossie in April and May at Tolon, near Nauplia, on the Aegean shores of the Pelopponese. This, rather like Bamburgh, was a fishing village that had become a holiday resort. They stayed at the Hotel Minoa run by the friendly Georgidakis family from Crete, and enjoyed the view over inlets, islands, and small boats on the sea.

In a further health scare, Thomas was admitted to Oxford's Churchill Hospital on 30 May. He was allowed home on 10 June physically frail but in sufficient spirits to write a doggerel sonnet in praise of a male staff nurse John O'Brien who had overseen his care. Teddy helped with the preparation of a final typescript for the Antonius memorial lecture at St Antony's on 17 June. Thomas was present huddled in a chair, but unable to read his lecture, and Teddy read it on his behalf. Many of the audience were thrilled at the brilliance of the talk but alarmed for Thomas's health.

Thomas went back to hospital at the beginning of July for a further week of treatment, leaving on 10 July with a high elbow frame to assist mobility. Despite the physical difficulties, he pressed on with his intellectual interests. Rather than writing, he was dictating his thoughts to a tape recorder, with help and encouragement from Liz. Thomas – with BJ and with suggestions from other members of his circle – had been working on an anthology of writings on various aspects of love, under a working title of 'Love and Revolution'. In mid-July he dictated on tape an introduction to the collection as a kind of successor to the Robert Bridges anthology made in 1915, *The Spirit of Man*, carried in first-world-war soldiers' knapsacks to France and enjoyed by the young in successive decades (Thomas recalled being taken as a child by his uncle Lionel Smith to visit Bridges who was married to their relative Monica Waterhouse).

Thomas's book *Vietnam: the Revolutionary Path* was published on 23 July and promoted by Macmillan as an account of the first time a revolutionary movement under Communist leadership succeeded in overthrowing a colonial state. Thomas's Vietnamese friends had envisaged the history as a weapon in the conflict with the US that might discourage US bombing of the north. Thomas's slow rate of writing meant that his book appeared after the US withdrawal from

Saigon and the unification of Vietnam and it had been left to others to furnish agit-prop.

In early August, when Thomas had graduated to walking with a stick rather than a frame, he was hatching the literary conceit of a birthday book for BJ's seventieth birthday due the following March when friends of their youthful days would write tributes in verse or prose. Teddy, who had been an amateur printer in his young days, was giving advice and Thomas agreed with a suggestion that contributors should eventually be sent sheets of hand made paper on which to write their pieces and these sheets would then be bound together as a book.

In another literary project, LaRay Denzer was putting together a selection of Thomas's essays and papers over the years that could be published in book form. Thomas at Crab Mill on the afternoon of 17 August began dictating to the tape recorder an introduction pointing to the way political decolonisation implied the decolonisation of history and the rediscovery of the African past: 'It was necessary that the peoples of Africa, deprived of their independence by the European colonial powers by a combination of force and fraud during the epoch of imperialism (roughly the last quarter of the nineteenth century), should regain control of their own destinies, whatever the price to be paid.'

Thomas was planning to escape the English winter for an earlier and longer stay in the Sudan than the year before. He had the advice of his Smith cousin Oliver Wrong, professor of medicine at University College Hospital, who had invoked the interest of pupils and colleagues in the Sudan medical profession on Thomas's behalf. The head of the University of Khartoum's department of medicine Professor Abdurrahman Mohamed Musa wrote on 18 August recommending a chest physician Samir L. Damian who had had considerable experience in Glasgow before returning to the Sudan. Thomas, staying quietly at Crab Mill, was receiving treatment from a physiotherapist and on 27 August was with help able to climb a few steps into the rose garden. Dossie was away at a Pugwash meeting in Banff, Canada, and BJ came to stay with Thomas for the first few days of September.

During October Thomas canvassed for contributions to her birthday book – it was being kept secret from her – among people from the Oxford where he recalled she was the centre of a circle of exciting friends and admirers. Since Thomas would be abroad, he was entrusting the responses and further organisation to BJ's elder daughter Lucy Syson. BJ wrote on 11 October: 'How sad it is that the pattern of our lives has changed so much ... Instead of your once-a-week and then once-a-fortnight trip to London, now it seems to be a once-a-month dash to Crab for me, with long blanks in between.'

Thomas had in mind a further literary project to write prose portrait sketches of various precious friends, each associated with a particular phase of his life.

The list included his school friend Randall Swingler, university contemporary Derek Kahn, from the Palestine years Prudence Pelham (and George Antonius), from adult education in the Potteries Gladys Malbon, from the West African experience the Nigerian Muslim intellectual and diplomat Isa Wali, from working and teaching in Oxford Gervase Mathew, from early and late visits to Sudan Joseph Garang and Abd al-Khalig Mahjub, and the Vietnamese historian Tran Van Giau.

Thomas, Dossie and Liz had sent a birthday card for the thirty-second birthday on 11 September of a South African political prisoner and former St Antony's student Renfrew Christie. Christie had been arrested in October 1979 and sentenced in June 1980 to a long term of imprisonment under the Terrorism Act on charges of conspiring with the African National Congress of South Africa to supply information on coal, electricity and nuclear activity in South Africa, including work on nuclear explosives research. The message on the birthday card was too long to be counted as a greeting and had to be censored as a letter while the outside correspondent was vetted. Christie received the message on 23 October with permission to correspond with Thomas and on 1 November he asked Thomas for a letter of strictly no more than five hundred words without any mention of South African politics that must be posted in the first week of January in the New Year.

Oliver Wrong provided an advisory note to airlines for Thomas's travel to escape the main period of chest infections in Britain: 'Mr Hodgkin is still very weak. He can walk with assistance, but should have a wheel chair for any but the shortest walk.' BJ drove on 3 November to Crab Mill for a farewell lunch before Thomas and Dossie left on their winter journey abroad. They flew on a British Airways TriStar and on the dinner menu Thomas wrote for BJ's forthcoming birthday book a conscious pastiche of the Shakespeare sonnet 104 in 'To me, BJ, you never can be old'.

They arrived on 6 November to a warm Bedri welcome. The plan was for the long Sudan stay to begin in Khartoum North with Sulafa Khalid Musa and her husband Ahmed Bedri at their Shambat house near the Food Research Station where Sulafa worked. Sulafa and Yusuf's son Gasim were at the foot of the aeroplane steps with a chair and the quests were taken in two cars to Ahmed and Sulafa's home. They quickly felt established with their hosts and their two daughters in a setting of flowery garden, palm trees, water lilies, butterflies and innumerable small birds.

Thomas wrote to Michael Wolfers in London about this 'Garden of Eden' of the first days and of the serpent appearing in the guise of accident proneness so that in one week he had two tumbles and one nasty cut in the leg. Thomas was wondering if Wolfers might like to come out to join them: 'You could write some articles. Help me to work on Abd al-Khalig and Joseph Garang…' Thomas envisaged more journeys round the Sudan and suggested January as the time. On 7 December Thomas copied his two poems for BJ's birthday as neatly as he could onto the sheet of good paper that Lucy had sent him: the pastiche written on the flight to Sudan and a poem composed for her in 1968 when an ardent Communist Ron Bellamy speaking at Thomas's Oxford seminar raised the question 'How Socialist was Ghana under the CPP?'

Michael Wolfers, who coincidentally had been invited for the first graduation at the University of Juba where he had been visiting lecturer, arrived in Khartoum on the morning of 12 December and went to Shambat, with letters and deliveries from Liz. He brought a full-page notice in the *London Review of Books* of 3-16 December by Victor Kiernan on Thomas's Vietnam book. Kiernan wrote: 'It was a happy inspiration for a writer who has spent many years studying Africa to transport himself to the other end of the world and look at the evolution of a totally different society, though one equally in the end herded by Western guns into a new era … The result is a fine achievement …' Thomas, keeping score, wrote to Liz on 15 December of four rave reviews.

Lucy Syson, encouraged by Thomas, had disclosed the secret plan for the BJ birthday book to her father. Jack's jocular reaction was that as long as Thomas was safely in the Sudan he thought it a thoroughly good idea and he would like a party at Antrim Road for all the contributors. Thomas, much recovered during his stay at Shambat, sent back the typescript of his now overdue Khawarij chapter on 20 December for Liz to forward to LaRay Denzer and Charles Stewart.

Thomas began writing to Teddy on New Year's eve that he thought he could hardly have survived the English winter: the claret laid down for the wake in Balliol could go on maturing a little longer. Then he was helped into his respectable dark suit and went to a party he hugely enjoyed in the courtyard of Ahfad College attended by many members of the Bedri family and by Ahfad graduates. Guests danced in Sudanese style to a singer and Thomas danced a while in a gentle fashion.

In the New Year of 1982, Thomas wrote to Liz that Dossie wanted to accept an invitation from the Queen for an OM get-together lunch at Windsor Castle on 1 April and he had not the heart to discourage her: 'Indeed I have said and I am prepared to sink my principles on this occasion and go too, seeing that she has been sacrificing the whole of the winter to me, looking after me so wonderfully all this time.' This new plan meant arriving in England on 30 March and they would go to Tolon for a holiday Thomas had booked for the last fortnight of March.

Sulafa was preoccupied with a grand dinner party she was giving on 7 January for a Sudanese diplomat and government minister Abdurrahman Abdalla and the Hungarian Ambassador Karoly Hackler. Wolfers came to the dinner and collected the Hodgkin letters as he was leaving next day for Britain. Thomas stressed the urgency of the letter he was sending to Renfrew Christie in the Pretoria Maximum Security Gaol and Dossie that of the letter she was sending to Sir Edward Ford informing the Queen that Thomas would attend her OM lunch (on a recent royal occasion the Queen had regretted Thomas's absence abroad – a pretext when he was actually at home).

Thomas and Dossie began a sentimental journey on 11 January with Yusuf Bedri to Rufa'a on the Blue Nile in central Sudan where Sheikh Babikr Bedri in his hometown had established the first school for girls and to Wad Medani where they had been the previous year. They moved on 1 February to Yusuf's rooms at Ahfad College in Omdurman – Thomas given an iron bedstead with two mattresses to aid mobility.

At the end of February, BJ's children showed her the birthday collection that Thomas had inspired. She was delighted and genuinely surprised at seeing Thomas's poems and the moving contributions from other friends.

Thomas and Dossie with Yusuf flew on 3 March to Port Sudan where Yusuf was fundraising for Ahfad. They travelled on to Erkoweit on 7 March (where Thomas found the slightly greater altitude made his breathing more difficult than in Port Sudan) and briefly to Suakin with a mosque and ruined palace that Thomas had long wanted to see. When they were stopped and questioned by soldiers about their purpose they found that a visit was imminent by the Duke of Edinburgh and there were security concerns – Thomas fled rapidly back to Port Sudan. They returned to Omdurman for a final few days before the start of the homeward journey on 14 March via Athens where they were joined by Liz and her partner Peter Carter, and the four went on to Tolon. Thomas telephoned BJ in London to arrange to meet in the week after his return to England. He was making new friends among fellow hotel guests including a German honeymoon couple Andreas Käde and his wife Karin.

Andreas took Thomas in his car on a drive over tracks through olive groves and hills to see a frescoed chapel in a beautiful valley through which Liz and Peter had walked the day before and to which the others were returning on foot. On 22 March Thomas joined a British archaeological tour party, organised by the Oxford Town and Gown travel agency and mainly from Oxford, on a chara-banc journey to Mistra and Sparta. The sunshine of the first week had turned to clouds and rain. Thomas was affected by travel sickness as the bus was swinging round mountain bends. On a meal break, he had more or less to be carried up steps to a taverna in Mistra, but had no appetite.

Thomas rested in the hotel on 23 and 24 March and on the second evening attended an archaeology lecture. At dinner after the lecture, he complained of feeling unwell. He was helped up to bed and the family made an appointment with a doctor to see him next morning. In the morning, he seemed better and he asked Liz to help him prepare for the doctor's visit. In the washroom adjoining the bedroom, he fell forward on the washbasin. They carried Thomas to his bed; Liz called Andreas in to help. They tried resuscitation and when the doctor Andrianos Anyfantis- with a colleague – arrived, he too attempted resuscitation while indicating that it could be of no avail. The doctor explained that Thomas's heart had given out and that his death had been immediate at 7.45 that morning – on 25 March 1982. It was Greece's national day marking the anniversary of the outbreak in 1821 of a seven-year revolutionary war of independence against the Ottoman Empire.

Epilogue

Shortly after nine in the evening the Georgidakis family and hotel guests joined Dossie and Liz in a small gathering with wine in Thomas's memory. The local registrar Ioannos Giannakos early on 26 March recorded the death and Dimitrios Bikakis dug a grave in the Tolon cemetery. Permission was given to delay the funeral until 27 March to allow time for Teddy and Luke to fly out from England. Thomas was buried covered with flowers, as was the Tolon custom, in the hillside cemetery overlooking the Aegean Sea and islands.

Dossie came home on 30 March, in time for the Queen and the Duke of Edinburgh's lunch party on 1 April at Windsor Castle for members of the OM. Liz wrote to BJ to tell her of the funeral. BJ replied on 10 April that she was finding life very strange because all her thoughts had for years taken the form of letters to Thomas; now she did not know what to do with them and she came up against a terrible blank every time. BJ was going away with Jack to Devon from 10 to 23 May. She wanted to come to Thomas's wake – and Dossie and Liz encouraged her to do so. When the date was set for mid-May, she could not tell Jack that she wished to cut the holiday short and why – so she stayed away.

Thomas's memorial service in Balliol College Chapel at 4.30 p.m. on 15 May was much as he had envisaged in his note to Christopher Hill five years before. Miriam Margolyes read not from Browning, but from another favourite, William Wordsworth's sonnet to Toussaint L'Ouverture. Christopher Hill as former Master delivered his few words – echoing a comment once made by Thomas – that Balliol and the Communist Party were the only two institutions Thomas had ever loved. Diplomats and scholars from around the world thronged to celebrate Thomas and he was saluted by the heads of several Oxford houses.

The Chateau Abiet that Thomas had laid down for the wake was ready for drinking. Of the ten dozen bottles from the Balliol cellar, 102 were opened for nearly three hundred family and friends. The domestic bursar Peter Roberts (successor to 'Jacko' Jackson who had bought the wine) informed the Viceregent Maurice Keen on 17 May that the balance would be held in the cellar pending instructions. Keen in turn spoke to Dossie who said she would like it to be drunk by the fellows of Balliol after the Master had returned.

Thomas before leaving for Sudan in the winter of 1981 had given Polly Hill written authority to act for the unpublished novel 'Qwert' and after his death she tried unsuccessfully to place it. Teddy arranged for private printing in 1983 of the three cantos of Thomas's autobiographical epic *Don Tomás* in an edition designed by Humphrey Stone and subscribed by relatives and friends. Thomas's wife outlived him until 1994 and Maire until 1990.

When Thomas died at the age of 71 his obituary in *The Times* said that he did more than anyone to establish the serious study of African history in Britain. *The Guardian* tribute under the headline 'Spokesman for revolutionary nationalism' described him as someone who grasped the nettle of the revolutionary fervour of the twentieth century, while never relinquishing the old-fashioned grace of his upbringing in a network of Quaker families whose members distinguished themselves in the science, medicine and the arts.

Half a century ago Thomas Lionel Hodgkin published a seminal work on Africa *Nationalism in Colonial Africa* (1956) that went into numerous impressions. He was shortly afterwards to publish a rich anthology of historical source material in *Nigerian Perspectives* (1960) and an intricate account of political movements and personalities in *African Political Parties* (1961). Late in life he published a much revised edition of *Nigerian Perspectives* (1975) and from close contact with Vietnamese scholars a study of four thousand years of Vietnamese history in *Vietnam: The Revolutionary Path* (1981). He contributed to a dozen more books and to numerous journals, gave countless lectures and seminars: a partial bibliography is given in a festschrift published after his sixtieth birthday *African Perspectives* (1970). Key texts are included in political science readers and on current university course reading lists.

A publications' list understates his influence on scholarship over generations. Thomas had a sometimes peripatetic career – in colonial cadetship, adult education and academia – and remained the wandering scholar. He gave much to colleagues and to those he taught. He was a man of immense personal charm, beloved by creative collaborators but the bane of bureaucrats. His productivity was limited by the sleep disorder of narcolepsy and he wrote slowly, although he could sometimes sustain all-night sessions to meet deadlines that had already been stretched to their limit. In his last years of failing health, he devoted much time to projects of private or limited interest – the early parts of a verse autobiography, a politically motivated but arcane novel never published.

Thomas witnessed the start of the Palestine Arab revolt of 1936 against the British mandate. He had visited political prisoners and was impressed that Muslims, Christians and Jews were working together within the Palestine Communist Party. On return to Britain he joined the Communist Party. He was, like many of his generation, sympathetic to the agitation for the Spanish government against the rebellion led by General Franco. He remained on the fringe of the Communist Party, gave occasional talks to student or other groups, and in 1946 was briefly involved in drafting a paper on Marxist education and the working-class movement for the party's education sub-committee. He was not under party discipline and in 1949 he resigned with a sense that he was not doing anything effective and – with the advent of the Cold War – that membership could be an embarrassment to his work in adult education and to his plans for more extensive travel in Africa. In retirement he did rejoin the Communist Party in 1976, but almost casually.

However, he remained a Marxist from the mid-1930s. He learned in Palestine that the survival of colonial systems depended on inter-communal conflicts and that these could be overcome through a revolutionary movement based on a supra-nationalist Marxist-Leninist ideology. When Thomas later travelled in Africa he had a characteristic preference for the means of transport used by the local people: lorries, buses and trains, preferring third or fourth class when available to first or second. This was a habit he acquired in youthful wanderings through Greece and nearby countries. The friendships with African radicals that he formed on his travels meant that he knew the leaders of post-colonial Africa in their formative years and this intimacy informed and enlivened his writing and teaching.

Thomas did not make the decolonisation process – that was the work of others. He was one of those who opened the way to the decolonisation of history, especially African history. This first generation of new Africanist historians – including Thomas Hodgkin and Basil Davidson – asserted that Africans had a significant, intrinsically interesting, rich, constantly changing past and that contrary myths of the colonial period were merely ideological weapons of colonial rulers.

Index